CONSTRUCTING EDUC

FO   )EV

York St John

for   ation Services

Reference Books in International Education
Edward R. Beauchamp, *Series Editor*

CONSTRUCTING EDUCATION FOR DEVELOPMENT
INTERNATIONAL ORGANIZATIONS AND EDUCATION FOR ALL

COLETTE CHABBOTT

Routledge
Taylor & Francis Group
NEW YORK AND LONDON

Published in 2003 by
Routledge
270 Madison Ave,
New York NY 10016
www.routledge-ny.com

Published in Great Britain by
Routledge
2 Park Square, Milton Park,
Abingdon, Oxon, OX14 4RN
www.routledge.com

Routledge is an imprint of the Taylor & Francis Group.

Transferred to Digital Printing 2009

Library of Congress Cataloging-in-Publication Data

Chabbott, Colette.
    Constructing education for development : international organizations and
    education for all / Colette Chabbott.
       p. cm.—(Reference books in international education)
    Includes bibliographical references and index.
    ISBN 0-8153-3829-5
    1. Educational assistance—Developing countries 2. Education—Inter-
    national cooperation. 3. World Confernece on Education for All (1990 :
    Bangkok, Thailand). 4. Fundamental education—Congresses. 5. Basic
    education—Congresses. 6. Literacy—Congresses. 7. Education—Social
    aspects—Congresses. I. Title. II. Series

LC2607 .C39 2002
379.1'.29172'4—dc21   2002017897

ISBN10: 0-8153-3829-5 (hbk)
ISBN10: 0-415-87499-8 (pbk)

ISBN13: 978-0-8153-3829-1 (hbk)
ISBN13: 978-0-415-87499-1 (pbk)

Publisher's Note
The publisher has gone to great lengths to ensure the quality of this reprint
but points out that some imperfections in the original may be apparent.

Contents

List of Figures

List of Tables

List of Graphs

List of Acronyms

ACCIS	Advisory Committee for the Coordination of Information Systems
AID	Agency for International Development
ASFEC	Regional Center for Functional Literacy in Rural Areas for the Arab States (previously Arab States Fundamental Education Center)
ASI	Antislavery International
BCIES	British Comparative and International Education Society
BHN	Basic Human Needs
BRAC	Bangladesh Rural Advancement Committee
CAME	Conferences of the Allied Ministers of Education
CARE	Cooperative (for American) Relief Everywhere
CCEA	Commonwealth Council of Educational Administration
CES	Comparative Education Society
CGIAR	Consultative Group on International Agricultural Research
CIDA	Canadian International Development Agency
CIES	Comparative and International Education Society
CREFAL	Latin American Regional Center for Fundamental Education
CSI	Child Survival Initiative
DAC	Development Assistance Committee
DAE	Donors to African Education
ECLA	Economic Commission for Latin America
EDI	Economic Development Institute
EFA	Education for All
ERNESA	Educational Research Network for Eastern and Southern Africa
EWLP	Experimental World Literacy Program
FAO	Food and Agriculture Organization
FAR	Federal Acquisitions Regulations
GEB	General Education Board
GNP	Gross National Product

HDI	Human Development Index
IAC	Interagency Commission
IAEA	International Association for Educational Assessment
IBE	International Bureau for Education
IBRD	International Bank for Reconstruction and Development
ICCDA	Interregional Coordination Committee of Development Associations
ICDDR/B	International Center for Diarrheal Disease Research/Bangladesh
ICE	International Conference on Education
ICED	International Council for Educational Development
ICRC	International Committee of the Red Cross
ICVA	International Council of Voluntary Agencies
IDA	International Development Association
IDC	International Development Conference
IDIN	International Development Information Network
IDRC	International Development Research Center
IDS	Institute for Development Studies
IEA	International Association for the Evaluation of Educational Achievement
IEB	International Education Board
IGO	International Governmental Organization
IIE	Institute for International Education
IIEP	International Institute for Educational Planning
IIIC	International Institute of Intellectual Cooperation
IIP	International Intervisitation Program on Educational Administration
ILO	International Labor Organization
IMF	International Monetary Fund
INGO	International Nongovernmental Organization
IWGE	International Working Group on Education
JICA	Japanese International Cooperation Agency
LNGO	Local Nongovernmental Organization (based in one part of one country)
LSMS	Living Standards Measurement Surveys
NASEDEC	Nordic Association for the Study of Education in Developing Countries
NGO	Nongovernmental Organization
NIEO	New International Economic Order
NNGO	National Nongovernmental Organization
NORRAG	The Northern Research Review and Advisory Group
NPA	National Plan of Action

OAU	Organization of African Unity
ODA	Overseas Development Agency
ODC	Overseas Development Council
ODI	Overseas Development Institute
OECD	Organization for Economic Cooperation and Development
PQLI	Physical Quality of Life Indicator
RECSAM	Regional Centers for Education in Science and Math
RNGO	Regional NonGovernmental Organization
RRAG	Research Review and Advisory Group
SDA	Social Dimensions of Adjustment
SEAMEO	Southeast Asian Ministers of Education Organization
SEARRAG	South East Asian Research Review and Advisory Group
SID	Society for International Development
SIDA	Swedish International Development Agency
SIDEC	Stanford International Development Education Center/Committee
UNCTAD	United Nations Conference on Trade and Development
UNDP	The United Nations Development Program
UNESCO	United Nations Educational, Scientific, and Cultural Organization
UNICEF	United Nations Children's Fund
UNIDO	United Nations Industrial Development Organization
UNRRA	United Nations Relief and Rehabilitation Agency
UPE	Universal Primary Education
UPEL	Universalization of Primary Education and Literacy
WCC	World Council of Churches
WCCES	World Council of Comparative Education Societies
WCEFA	World Conference on Education for All
WEF	World Education Forum
WHO	World Health Organization

Series Preface

This series of scholarly works in comparative and international education has grown well beyond the initial conception of a collection of reference books. Although retaining its original purpose of providing a resource to scholars, students, and other professionals who need to understand the role played by education in various societies or world regions, it also strives to provide accurate, relevant, and up-to-date information on a wide variety of selected educational issues, problems, and experiments within an international context.

Contributors to this series are well-known scholars who have devoted their professional lives to the study of their specializations. Without exception these men and women possess an intimate understanding of the subject of their research and writing. They have studied their subject not only in dusty archives, but have lived and traveled widely in their quest for knowledge. In short, they are experts in the best sense of that often overused word.

In our increasingly interdependent world, it is a matter of military, economic, and environmental survival that we better understand not only what makes other societies tick, but also how others, be they Japanese, Hungarian, South African, or Chilean, attempt to solve the same kinds of educational problems that we face in North America. As the late George Z. F. Bereday wrote more than three decades ago: "[E]ducation is a mirror held against the face of a people. Nations may put on blustering shows of strength to conceal public weakness, erect grand facades to conceal shabby backyards, and profess peace while secretly arming for conquest, but how they take care of their children tells unerringly who they are" (1964, p. 5).

Perhaps equally important, however, is the valuable perspective that studying another education system (or its problems) provides us in understanding our own system (or its problems). When we step beyond our own limited experience and commonly held assumptions about schools and learning in order to look at our system in contrast to another, we see it in a very different light. To learn, for example, how China or Belgium handles the education of a multilingual society, how the French provide for the funding of public education, or how the Japanese control access to their universities enables us to better understand that there are reasonable alternatives to our own familiar ways of doing things. Not that we can borrow directly from other societies—indeed, educational arrangements are inevitably a reflection of deeply embedded political, economic, and cultural factors that are unique to a particular society—but a recognition that there are other ways of doing things can open our minds and provoke our imaginations, resulting in new experiments or approaches that we may not have otherwise considered.

Since this series is intended to be a useful research tool, the editor and contributors welcome suggestions for future volumes, as well as ways in which this series can be improved.

Edward R. Beauchamp
University of Hawaii

Preface

Doing research on a topic of current interest can be like doing surgery on a patient who won't stay anaesthetized and keeps sliding off the operating table. Trying to stabilize the subject, while at the same time finishing the operation and reaching satisfactory closure is messy.

The original purpose of this study was to explore the effects of the organizational field of international development on the construction of the idea of educational development, using the World Conference on Education for All (WCEFA) held in Jomtien, Thailand, in March 1990 as a case study. The temptation to keep updating the case study has been extreme. I was working on this manuscript in the last half of the first decade of Education for All and polishing it off in June 2000 as the World Education Forum met in Dakar, Senegal, to assess that decade. Similarly, the study of international organizations was revolutionized in the 1990s by the advent of web pages for all sorts of international development organizations, each with tantalizing links to "Other Organizations." At the same time, the number of scholarly and popular books and papers on the role of nongovernmental organizations (NGO) at all levels of world society expanded greatly.

In the interest of finishing this book, I have retained the original, now somewhat historical purpose, focusing on the evolution of international development discourse, organizations, professionals, and conferences up to and just beyond the 1990 World Conference on Education for All. As such, I focus on the origins rather than implementation of WCEFA, or the 2000 World Education Forum.

The picture of the international development field presented in this book is biased to the extent it draws mainly on literature published in English and on contacts I have established over the last 18 years through my work in UN- and U.S.-based international development organizations. I suspect this is a larger limiting factor with respect to scholarly literature than with the documents I gathered from international development organizations, many of whom use English as one of their working languages.

Figure 1.1 and Table 3.1 first appeared in a chapter on "Development and Education" in *The Handbook of the Sociology of Education*, edited by M. Hallinan. Table 4.1 and Graph 4.2 first appeared in a chapter on "Development INGOs" in *Constructing World Culture: International Nongovernmental Organizations since 1875*, edited by J Boli and G. M. Thomas. Table 6.1 is based on a table originally published in *The International Journal of Educational Development*, in my article, "Constructing Educational Consensus," 1989 with permission from Elsevier Science.

Acknowledgments

My thanks go first to Francisco O. Ramirez and John Meyer, who have encouraged me and so many others in their comparative systems workshop to think in terms of big concepts. Their patience and steady stream of constructive advice bolstered my courage as this project stretched over more years than I expected. I am indebted to Margaret Sutton, my first and one of the most generous informants on the World Conference process; she opened doors to a dozen other informants. John Boli deserves thanks for the many rounds of comments he offered on the original international development NGO analysis that first appeared in a 1999 volume he and George Thomas edited. Karen Mundy kindly introduced me to the international relations literature on international organizations and epistemic communities. Nancy Kendall rescued Chapter 1 when I was ready to give up on it. Thanks also go to an anonymous reviewer. Many librarians and program officers in international development organizations generously opened their archives and shared their thoughts with me, particularly at the Institute of International Education and the Education Division of the Swedish International Development Agency in Stockholm, the International Institute for Educational Planning, the UNESCO Education Documentation Centre, and the OECD's Development Centre library in Paris. This work also benefited from an invitation to participate in the 1995 Conference of the Nordic Association for the Study of Education in Developing Countries. Parts of this research were also funded by the National Science Foundation, as part of a broader study of the ties between society, education, and development (RED9254958).

Finally, to my long-suffering husband, Ted Thomas, who has read so many versions of this story in the last seven years that he deserves a medal, many thanks and a promise I will try to write about something different for a while.

1
Introduction

In the last half of the twentieth century, much of the world embraced two new fundamental human rights: the right to development and the right to education. Since they were first asserted in the Universal Declaration of Human Rights in 1945, transforming these rights from principles into facts has become imperative for most governments. Subsequently, despite radical differences in financial and administrative means, history, culture, and climate, governments the world over have rationalized this imperative into fairly standardized national development goals, development plans, and frameworks for using education to accelerate socioeconomic development and help distribute its benefits equitably.

The 1990 World Conference on Education for All (WCEFA) was both a product of and a further catalyst for this standardization process. On the last day of the WCEFA, 1500 men and women representing 155 governments, 33 intergovernmental organizations, and 125 nongovernmental organizations rose, some with tears in their eyes, to accept by acclamation the World Declaration on Education for All, a nonbinding statement that asserted every human being has a right to a quality basic education. By this each delegate agreed to adapt a common Framework for Action into a National Plan of Action to ensure that within the foreseeable future all citizens would receive a quality basic education.

In several respects, this conference is typical of a number of world conferences convened in the 1990s. First, it provided a stage for enacting some of the world's highest ideals. Second, it attempted to marshal the resources and influence of both governments and nongovernmental organizations. Third, the conference declaration and framework for action were adopted knowing they required funds far in excess of what governments had been able or willing to commit to date.

As such, the WCEFA was clearly not a case of national governments taking rational, measured steps to address the specific needs and unique interests of their particular nation-states in the context of their resources. Rather, it was, in large part, the product of the global environment and a world culture that gave rise to the nation-states themselves and to the international organizations that organize events like the WCEFA. This world culture is not a democratic amalgam of many cultures, rather it is a distillation of Western Enlightenment ideas about progress and justice and the unique role that science plays in promoting them. These ideas have given legitimacy to a host of new human rights, such as the right to development and the right to education. At the same time, these ideas also have given rise to a whole new set of government responsibilities. Among these responsibilities, the development imperative looms large. This imperative demands both governments and international organizations promote *progress* in social and economic conditions in less industrialized countries and *justice* in the equitable distribution of the rewards of this progress.

This book explores the rise of a development-oriented world of nation-states and international organizations, a rise that accelerated and intensified throughout the post-World War II era. Throughout this era, espoused beliefs about appropriate development goals, appropriate means to translate these goals into policy and practice, and appropriate ways to target recipients for the benefits from development activities were increasingly rationalized and standardized. This standardization is, in large part, the work of both international development organizations and international development professionals who articulate and carry packages of "correct" principles, "appropriate" policies, and "best" practices to national governments and local nongovernmental organizations alike. By the last decade of the twentieth century, these organizations, professionals, and principles had taken on a life of their own: setting agendas, establishing priorities, and mandating action somewhat independently of both the nation-states that funded them and their stated beneficiaries. The current world culture that drives this process is itself so institutionalized it is practically invisible to most Westerners. Comparing the state of international cooperation and human rights in 1940 with those in 1990, however, throws world culture into sharp relief.

In contrast with the 155 governments represented at WCEFA, fewer than 54 independent countries comprised the world in 1940; scores of colonies and protectorates would not become independent nation-states for another 20 or more years and were not vested with the power to represent their own interests in international forums. In 1940 there were only a handful of international governmental organizations and the predecessor of the United Nations—the League of Nations founded in 1920—lay in ruins. In contrast with the view so central to the WCEFA—that all countries might advance simultaneously and cooperatively—in 1940 several of the world's largest industrialized countries were acting on a different assumption: that progress in their own countries could come only at the expense of others.

Hundreds of women participated in the WCEFA, but in 1940, women in many countries had no civil rights independent of their families and very few women were appointed as delegates to international conferences. In contrast to the individualistic and universalistic assumptions at the core of WCEFA, the inhabitants of colonies and protectorates in the first half of the twentieth century enjoyed few, if any, de facto civil or political rights.

By 1940, compulsory primary education laws had been enacted in over 80 percent of the independent countries in the Americas and Europe (Ramirez & Ventresca, 1991), but few colonial powers felt obliged to extend publicly funded mass education to their colonies in Africa, Asia, or the Caribbean. However, some colonial powers, such as Britain in India and France in Algeria, did educate a small group of colonials to serve as colonial administrators. These colonials were sometimes members of a local elite, but in many cases they were chosen because, to European eyes, they appeared more intelligent than the rest of their race, or at least more docile, and ready to adapt to the colonial order. By comparison, independent, critical thinking and intellectual autonomy were hallmarks of the quality mass education endorsed at the WCEFA.

The unequal distribution of human rights in 1940 was in no small way related to the widespread acceptance of eugenics, the study of physical and mental differences between ethnic groups. Prior to World War II, many respected researchers pursued the goal of improving the human race by planned genetic selection and population control. The genetic superiority of some races and the inferiority of others were central tenets of Axis ideology in the 1930s and 1940s. Moreover, these assumptions were shared by many in Allied countries, including the United States. In 1940 the notion that all human beings are in some way equal, that each is endowed with a similar potential for learning, and that nation-states should foster the potential of each citizen through a universal, common education system, would have appeared patently misguided to many political and intellectual leaders.

The WCEFA, of course, is neither the cause nor the culmination of the radical reorganization of the world that took place in the 50 years between 1940 and 1990. However, WCEFA's origins and evolution illustrate the process by which new ways of thinking came to be institutionalized at the global and national level. These new ideas included a radical expansion of who qualifies as a full human being and what his or her potential might be; what constitutes a nation-state and what its responsibilities might be with respect to promoting human potential; and what role education might play in mediating this process. The purpose of this book is to unpack the process by which these new ways of thinking became embodied and taken for granted in new international organizations, in new nation-states, and in recent international education agreements and national education policies.

Moreover, the widespread acceptance of certain ideas about the nature of human beings has not necessarily lead to their actualization. For decades prior to WCEFA, many less-industrialized low-income countries had proclaimed similarly ambitious education goals, and they reiterated them on a regular basis in international conferences. This began in the 1940s and 1950s, when few development planners in newly independent countries suspected how costly universal primary education and adult literacy might be. By the time the high cost became more widely understood, public commitments had been made and would not be retracted. From the 1960s to the present, few governments in less industrialized countries nor donors in industrialized countries have proved willing or able to provide funding commensurate with public pronouncements on the right to education. This pattern persisted into the 1990s; despite the efforts of several powerful participants, the WCEFA documents do not directly address funding. Few, therefore, were surprised when the World Education Forum held in Dakar, Senegal, in April 2000 documented disappointing progress in achieving education for all in most less-industrialized countries and deteriorating conditions in others. What should surprise us is that the Dakar conference nonetheless produced another ambitious declaration and framework for action, including, this time, specific target dates for achieving universal primary education and literacy.

Some might say the WCEFA and the more recent Dakar Declaration and Framework are best understood as one of an ongoing series of efforts on the part of the less industrialized countries to establish a claim for more development aid from industrialized countries. Others might argue that the WCEFA and the Dakar conference are simply more instances of the industrialized countries, through their aid policies, dictating development and education priorities to the less industrialized countries. More idealistic observers, on the other hand, might counter that only by setting high goals do people—or governments—discover what they are capable of, and that the pressure created by high goals has, on occasion, called forth the means to achieve them.

This book does not attempt to adjudicate these arguments, nor does it focus on the specific conditions that led one nation-state or another to endorse the WCEFA agreements, though such studies might be useful. Instead this book highlights aspects of the global environment that made the outcomes at the WCEFA practically a foregone conclusion and it draws attention to a previously neglected influence in this process: the global environment in which these agreements and nation-states emerged.

This global environment has three important features. First, it is permeated by an ever expanding development imperative. Since World War II, the scope and targets of this imperative have expanded to cover both more economic and social activities—from agriculture and large-scale infrastructure development to family planning and education—and more subgroups of the population—women, the disabled, minorities. As a result, over time, more activities and subgroups of society become linked to development and thus become potential targets for international development activities.

Second, isomorphism is the rule; over time, principles, policies, and practices everywhere tend to adopt the same form and language. As noted earlier, despite great variations in history, social structure, and economic resources from country to country, and within countries from one locality to another, standardized blueprints or models of how to "do" development tend to emerge and prevail. This does not mean that all development activities end up looking exactly the same everywhere. Instead, idiosyncracies persist from one place to another, at the same time basic ingredients prevail in all settings, with local variations. Over time, the realm of potential development principles, policies, and practices is increasingly scripted, and deviation from that script becomes less likely. This tendency towards isomorphism comes into conflict with Enlightenment ideas about the uniqueness of individuals and, by extension, their collectivities. This conflict creates much of the generative tension in development discourse.

Finally, in this global environment, loose coupling between values espoused and action taken is endemic. This decoupling is easy to interpret as dysfunctional, as an attempt by dominant national or local groups to derail more equitable development outcomes. Nonetheless, this loose coupling may reflect a healthy resistance to isomorphism, the assertion of local values and practices over world culture, skewed though it may be towards local elites.

Much of the development studies literature recognizes these three features of the global environment and explains them in terms of an imbalance of power between nation-states, an imbalance of power between elites and less advantaged groups at various levels, or as indicative of poor planning and management. In contrast, this book emphasizes the important role that organizational relationships and bureaucratic culture play in establishing and maintaining a global environment in which isomorphism and loose coupling are natural outcomes, particularly in sectors with difficult to measure output, such as education. The next two subsections of this chapter introduce world-culture theory and institutional analysis, the logic and the analytical approach, respectively, that undergird this argument. The fourth subsection introduces some terminology conventions intended to make reading about agency, organization, and institution, at once both subjects and theories, somewhat less confusing.

World Culture and Organizations

Traditional scholars of international relations often analyze changes at the global level in terms of competition for resources between actors, primarily nation-states, who are constrained mainly by their self-interest and their power with respect to other actors. In contrast, world society scholars, among others, argue that nation-states are just one among several actors at the global level, including international organizations. Moreover, these scholars emphasize that the repertoire of action or role for each of these erstwhile actors is severely constrained and heavily scripted by an overarching cultural framework (Mead, 1934; Goffman, 1959) or world culture (Thomas, Meyer et al., 1987). Though this world culture places much value on purposive action flowing from rational alternatives and individual choice, it also defines what constitutes "rational" alternatives and choices in a relatively narrow way for any given actor, thereby limiting the scope of his or her legitimate purposive action. Rather than focus on differences in interest and power between actors as an engine for change, world society scholars are principally interested in where these roles and scripts come from and how they become institutionalized.

Identifying World Culture

The historical fault line underlying the shifts in the way the world conceptualizes human rights and education—as described above in the contrasts between conditions in 1940 and 1990—lies in the eighteenth century Western Enlightenment. In broad terms, the Enlightenment triggered a series of rationalist critiques of previously accepted social doctrines and institutions, a process that continues to challenge older social arrangements up to the present day (Marshall, 1994). In the nineteenth century, Enlightenment ideas and values favoring the scientific method were associated with a "rational" approach to social problems. These ideas spread as Western technology and bureaucracy expanded into more and more areas of modern life in Western countries and their colonies (Berger, Berger, et al., 1973). At the same time, Enlightenment ideas delegitimated premodern traditional collectivities—family, race, clan, kingdom—and established individuals with free will as the central unit of society.

This culture of rationality materialized in two critical ways. First, scientific explanations increased both in scope—covering more areas of social life—and in authority. In the modern Westernized world, traditional religious belief, that looked for salvation outside humanity, was replaced by faith in the intrinsic power of rational human beings to bring about universal material and social progress in all domains (Wuthnow, 1980; Keohane, 1982; Aronowitz, 1988; Ramirez & Lee, 1995). Second, rational purposive action, or organization, to promote progress through science became obligatory. Those in positions of authority were responsible for rendering, based on scientific evidence, rational decisions that would be implemented by rational means, such as formal organizations.

World society scholars do not assert that the present world culture is the only possible one, nor that it necessarily represents the culmination of humanity's best efforts to date. Rather they argue that this particular culture, based in the Western Enlightenment, is simply the de facto operative world culture and that it faces no credible rivals at this time. In the eyes of these scholars, the present world culture is, quite simply, the dominant empirically measurable one.

Studies of World Culture

World society scholars measure the global origins and spread of Western Enlightenment ideas over time by the appearance of those ideas in the statements of international organizations, the ratification of international agreements, the convening of international conferences, and other collective action institutionalized at the international and national level. The subjects of their studies range from laws regulating homosexuality (Frank & McEneany, 1999), to the establishment of Ministries of Science (Jang, 2000), the promulgation of population growth policies (Barrett, 1995), and the dramatic increase in the number of governmental and nongovernmental organizations around world cultural norms, such as the environment and women's rights (Boli & Thomas, 1999).

All of these authors approach their subjects with a long-range perspective. This is because institutions, once established, take on a life of their own and become taken for granted; they often outlive their original purposes and the individuals or groups benefiting from them at one point in time are often not those who established them at some earlier point. Therefore explanatory approaches that rely mainly on the current interests and purposive actions (agency) of various individuals or groups to explain the status quo often miss the mark. Historical analysis is often necessary to understand the forces that put institutions in place and to begin to identify the many taken-for-granted aspects of society that hold them there.

World culture and education

Education is an area of particular interest for world society scholars (Ramirez, 1997). The way progress and justice are conceptualized in the current world culture brings them frequently into conflict. On the one hand, the use of science and purposive action to increase the material well-being of society undergird twentieth-century ideas about technical/economic development. For example, Western Enlightenment concerns about justice as equality lead to an emphasis on individual human rights and twentieth-century notions of social development. Historically, however, rapid technical/economic development has often resulted in greater disparities in income and welfare.

Berger, Berger, and Kellner (1973) identified education as a secondary carrier for modernization and, by extension, Western Enlightenment–based world culture. They see education, simultaneously human capital and a human right, is constructed as a means to fulfill both visions of development. Quality education fosters the critical thinking necessary to participate in the rationalizing world culture and produces scientifically minded individuals. Such individuals are equipped to participate in and contribute to modern progress. At the same time, quality education is a prerequisite for the actualization of individual potential and the full exercise of individual human rights, ensuring more equitable distribution of development benefits.

Education has been closely associated with development, in part because of an ecological fallacy, that is, a confusion of units of analysis, leading to the conclusion that individual education causes individual development and individual development necessarily aggregates into national development. In fact, individual education may be put to uses that produce no public benefits, as when individuals find no employment commensurate with the public investment in their education. More importantly, education has also been identified as central to nation-state building, in its capacity to create citizens, indoctrinating individuals into a national consciousness and building in them an attachment to the state and its chosen development strategy (Boli, 1989). At the same time, education is also a source of much generative tension as the nation-state attempts to address simultaneously demands for both economic development—calling for workers with specific technical training and higher education—and for social development—demanding mass education.

Finally, world society scholars note that the rate at which education systems adopt common forms—curriculum, universal primary education—tends to be faster than other forms of integration into the world economy and society (Meyer & Ramirez, 2000). The establishment of education institutions often precedes any material conditions—such as industrialization or democracy—that might call for universal literacy or numeracy. In the 1990s, world society scholars have turned their attention to the role of international governmental and nongovernmental organizations as carriers or vehicles for world culture and as mediators of the tension in world society between progress and justice (Boli & Thomas, 1999). This book explores the role of international organizations in the spread of standards about education and in the managing of the tension between progress and justice in education.

Mechanisms for Carrying Models of Development and Education

Figure 1.1 shows a mechanism for carrying models of development from the world societal level through discourse, organizations, professionals, confer-

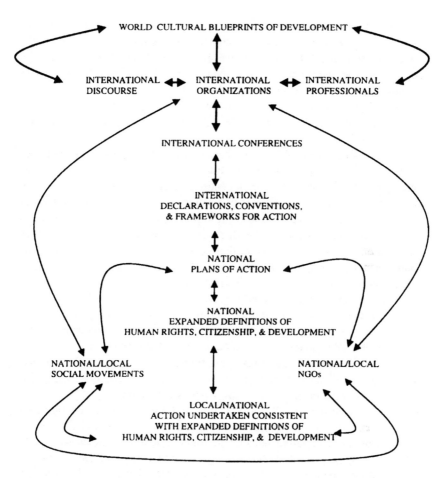

Figure 1.1. Mechanisms for Constructing and Disseminating World Cultural Blueprints of Development.

ences, national frameworks for action, and local governmental and non-governmental action. Note that although the motion initially described is top-down, there is much that is recursive: professionals reformulate discourse, conferences grow into permanent organizations, and so forth. In addition, in recent years, efforts based on world societal values such as equity have resulted in the creation of bottom-up linkages. For reasons discussed later in the book, however, these bottom-up linkages remain weaker than the top-down ones.

At the world societal level, Western notions of progress and justice provide the material for *discourse* about development, and later for more specific discourse about education and development. This rationalizing discourse promotes both networks of development *professionals* and international development *organizations*. These professionals and organizations, in turn, sharpen and standardize the discourse by sponsoring activities such as international *conferences*. Each of these conferences brings together not just national delegations, but also hundreds of international governmental and nongovernmental development organizations.

These conferences regularly produce nonbinding *declarations* and *frameworks for action*. These declarations and frameworks typically invoke the highest ideals of progress and justice, thereby making endorsement by national delegations practically mandatory. In order to be consistent with the high ideals in both the declarations and frameworks for action, the *national plans* developed subsequent to the conference often incorporate *expanded definitions of human rights, citizenship, and development*.

For most of the post–World War II period, the conference-declaration-framework-national plan cycle described above contributed to a significant amount of loose coupling because national education policies were produced in response to international standards rather than to local conditions and resources (Nagel & Snyder, 1989; Meyer, Nagel et al., 1993). In recent years, however, the international governmental development organizations have increasingly recruited and supported the participation of *regional, national, and local nongovernmental organizations (NGOs)* in international conferences. In this way, NGOs sometimes serve as proxies for the intended beneficiaries of development: the historically disadvantaged and the poor (Riddell, 1995). The international governmental development organizations have also supported NGO efforts to monitor the implementation of declarations and national plans of action at the national and local levels.

In the 1990s, the advent of new, inexpensive information and communication technologies, such as the Internet, made it easier for local NGOs and *social movements* to tap into international support and information networks. This technology created new feedback loops in the mechanism described in

Figure 1.1, enabling NGOs to publicize expanded definitions of human rights, citizenship, and development, and to attract international attention when national governments failed to take action consistent with those definitions (Social Watch, 1998).

The incorporation of these last two components of the mechanism—NGOs and social movements based in less industrialized countries—have not necessarily produced results consistent with international declarations and national frameworks. This is not necessarily due to lack of effort or will on the part of NGOs, rather it is because their role in this global mechanism has important ritualistic value, apart from whether NGOs ever receive the financial and other support necessary to carry forward programs at the grassroots level. At times the NGOs serve as stand-ins for the poor in the development planning and implementation process; their presence in international fora and activities enable international organizations to claim that the concerns of the poor are represented.

The Structure of the Book

This book analyzes the mechanism described above by showcasing carriers of world culture—discourse, organizations, professionals, and conferences—and by using WCEFA to highlight these carriers in action. The next chapter examines the historical context of twentieth-century notions of development and identifies some of the sources of the education for development discourse in the post–World War II period. Chapters 3 through 6 each explore the evolution of one carrier—discourse, organizations, professionals, conferences—during the post–World War II period; each uses a different aspect of WCEFA to illustrate how these carriers operate. Two of these chapters—organizations and professionals—also include institutional analysis sections that locate international development in the broader context of organization theory. Because the WCEFA is being used as a case, the time period covered by many analyses in this book stop around the mid-1990s. The World Education Forum in Dakar is not systematically addressed.

Chapter 2, "Setting the Stage," begins with an overview of the factors that helped to build international support for modern notions of development and education prior to World War II. The chapter concludes with the first installment of the WCEFA story, focusing on the role of the leaders of the four organizations that sponsored the conference. Much of the background for this section, as for EFA sections in other chapters, draws upon over 50 semistructured interviews conducted from 1994 to 1996 with a broad range of professionals engaged in WCEFA or in earlier education conferences.

Chapter 3, "Discourse," focuses on the rise, the shifts in themes, and the increase in complexity in the discourse about development and education as it was articulated in the Universal Declaration of Human Rights and in the rationales for foreign aid following World War II. The largest section of the chapter analyzes the discourse about development at the international level from the 1950s through the 1990s, before turning to the narrower topic of education in development discourse during the same period. The data for the development discourse section are drawn from the development practitioner literature of the time and from analyses of trends identified in the development studies literature. The data for the educational development discourse section are drawn from studies of the education policies of UNESCO and the World Bank conducted by Phillip W. Jones in 1990 and 1992, respectively.

Chapter 4 provides a framework for conceptualizing educational development as an organizational field, outlining its components, describing its activities, and exploring how the structure of this field encourages interdependence among various types of international development organizations. This book uses data from the Union of International Associations' *Yearbook of International Associations* and from the Organization for Economic Cooperation and Development's database of nongovernmental development and human rights organizations. I analyze the increase in the number of these organizations in the late 1970s and early 1980s, and relate that increase to shifts in the international development discourse described in Chapter 3. The chapter also describes how governance, belief systems, and hierarchies within the international development field help to mediate conflicts and competition among member organizations. The final section analyzes the role of the international organizations involved in the WCEFA, focusing particularly on the ability of the sponsoring organizations to articulate education policies somewhat independently from the nation-states that fund those organizations.

Chapter 5 introduces several concepts from the study of international relations and the sociological study of professionals, before analyzing the historic conditions, terms of service, and nature of the activities that have produced a generation of development professionals. A second section describes the rise of international and comparative education as a discipline, and a third outlines rocky attempts to establish educational development as a specific area of expertise within the international development field. The data for this section come from interviews with development professionals, directories of education and research institutes, biographies and autobiographies of development professionals, and other secondary literature sources. The final section explores the role of educational development professionals in EFA.

Chapter 6 looks for precedents and predecessors of WCEFA in the increase in global education and international development conferences in the post–World War II era. The data for this chapter derive from conference materials and publications, as well as other secondary literature sources. A section on WCEFA illustrates how professionals drew on a well-established recipe for presenting and following up global conferences to ensure that WCEFA goals reached the level of national policies and local action.

Chapter 7 summarizes the conclusions from earlier chapters and explores their implications for world culture, the international development field, and education around the world.

Development Studies and Terminology

Like most institutional analyses, this book focuses on how things become and stay the same, on enduring institutions and persistent isomorphism, on a process, on describing what is, rather than what should or could be. As a result, it does not engage the central question common to both the practitioner-oriented and the scholarly development literature studies—how to bring about positive change. For example, many practitioners, though acutely sensitive to differences in culture from one place to another and determined to tailor development models to local conditions, nonetheless, proceed in their work as though, at some level, development can be a scientific, apolitical, acultural undertaking. When the desired change fails to occur, practitioners tend to attribute that failure to bad data, bad models, bad management, inadequate funding, or individual inadequacies, including corruption. Their central concern is finding a better way to "do" development activities; they tend not to question the underlying positivist assumptions of development. In this they are like professionals and practitioners in many organizational fields, that, to a greater or lesser extent, recognize the inconsistencies and absurdities in their work, but remain convinced of its underlying worth, committed to their colleagues, and/or unwilling or unable to find another line of work.

In contrast, many scholars of development are more critical, emphasizing that development activities, intentionally or otherwise, tend to advance the interests of national elites or hegemonic states at the expense of less powerful groups and states (Escobar, 1995, p. 232). To these scholars, the failure over time of many development activities is evidence of the flawed political and cultural assumptions underpinning the entire development enterprise. However, implicit in their critique is the notion that development is a less equitable, less broadly productive enterprise than it might be.

The focus on process in this study neither negates nor confirms either the practitioner rationalizations or the scholarly critiques of development. Rather than analyze individual activities, individual organizations, or the world system as a whole, this study is located at an intermediary level: *the organizational field*. The field of international development organizations encompasses all organizations engaged in development activities, including:

- development banks and funds;
- UN organizations;
- other multilateral development organizations;
- bilateral donor organizations;
- research, training, and professional organizations;
- for-profit firms with government contracts;
- nonprofit international nongovernmental organizations based in high-income countries; and, to a lesser extent,
- nonprofit groups based in low-income regions.

This book argues that generative tension in their tasks and resources bind these organizations closely together and promote isomorphism, resulting in a great deal of loose coupling between development aims, means, and results.

All studies of development grapple with the relationship between modernization, Westernization, progress, and development. This book follows conventions suggested by Berger, Berger, and Kellner (1973). They propose that modernization occurs as individuals and society as a whole attempt to adapt to technological production and bureaucracy, the two chief carriers of modernization. Since current manifestations of both of these phenomena are products of Western culture, modernization has been synonymous with Westernization throughout the post–World War II period. For Berger, Berger, and Kellner, by definition, modernization even in the Western cultures from which it arose, fosters alienation (homelessness) between, on the one hand, modernized individuals and organizations strongly influenced by Western standards of rationality and universality and, on the other hand, non-Western or nonrational aspects of society. In these terms, neither modernization nor Westernization nor industrialization represents an unadulterated good.

For the purposes of this book, "development" is interpreted as any efforts to bring about a Western Enlightenment idea of "progress," that is, (1) increased understanding about the world and (2) increased control over the world that generate (3) an increase in moral virtue and (4) an increase in happiness (Keohane, 1982). In the Western Enlightenment context, economic development and social justice are both means to this end. For most of the postwar period, development activities have generally focused on the first two material aspects of progress, but support for development activities by the general public has been driven by all four aspects.

After more than 50 years of talk about development, almost all terms designed to distinguish between countries at different levels of modernization or Westernization either come with ideological baggage or serve to disguise a continuous variable as a dichotomous one. Modern/traditional, developing/developed, Third World/First World, South/North, less industrialized/more industrialized, low income/high income, core/periphery, and poor/rich all are problematic. For the sake of argument, where such a designation is called for, this book distinguishes between *less industrialized* and *industrialized countries*, assuming no necessary association between industrialization and *development*, as described above.

In other contexts the terms international education, development education, and educational development are sometimes used interchangeably but are distinguished from each other here. *International education* involves the exchange of scholars and students between countries, and the promotion of global understanding and peace through education. As such, *development education* is the subset of international education activities that aims to raise awareness of international development issues and of less industrialized countries among the public in industrialized countries, often with the goal of increasing support for international development activities. In contrast, *educational development* refers to systematic efforts to improve education systems in order to support more general socio-economic development in less industrialized countries. International education may be part of an educational development program and development education may be used to raise awareness of and funds for educational development.

What to call the funds, equipment, and personnel flowing from industrialized to less industrialized countries for the stated purpose of development also remains problematic. Given that these flows often do not achieve their stated benevolent purposes, the terms development "aid," "help," or "assistance" are somewhat euphemistic. This is particularly the case for "aid" provided in the form of loans. Theoretically, these loans were to be invested in activities that would lead to an increase in GNP, enabling the recipient country to repay the loan with interest. Since these investments were, more often than not, less productive than anticipated, and interest rates have tended to increase, this "aid" became, in later years, a debt burden. Similarly, the term development "cooperation," used in early United Nations documents and preferred by the Organization for Economic Cooperation and Development, also becomes euphemistic as the scripted nature of the cooperative venture becomes more apparent. In the interest of brevity, the preferred terminology in this book is "development aid." Development aid is just one component of the broader term "foreign aid," defined here as the flow of resources from one country to another for any supposedly nonremunerative purpose, including development aid, military aid, or disaster relief.

Chapter 4 provides a more nuanced definition of organizations, but for now, "*Organizations* are social units (or human groupings) deliberately constructed and reconstructed to seek specific goals" (Etzioni, 1964, p. 3). Both "agency" and "institution" will be used throughout this book to make sociological arguments. In order to avoid confusion, these terms will not be used as synonyms for organization, even when an organization incorporates the word "agency" into its formal name, as in the case of the U.S. Agency for International Development. In the institutional analysis of organizations, the words industry, sector, and organizational field are sometimes used interchangeably. The word "industry," however, sometimes carries pejorative connotations in a field engaged mainly in nonprofit activities. The word "sector" may also be confusing, since it is commonly used in the development field to refer to areas of activity, such as health, education, and agriculture. For this reason, international development will be referred to mainly as an organizational field, rarely as an industry, and never as a sector. Finally, the term "network" will be avoided, since the analytical approach used here is very different from the more mathematically oriented network analysis often associated with organizational studies.

Nongovernmental organizations (NGOs) play an important role in the international development field and many terms exist to describe them. This book distinguishes between NGOs operating at the international, national, and local level with the acronyms INGOs, NNGOs, and LNGOs, respectively. The term NGO is used when the level at which the NGO operates is irrelevant.

Summary

This book is organized around the four principal carriers of world cultural blueprints of education and development from the industrialized to the less industrialized world: discourse, organizations, professionals, and conferences.

This book is not about the right or wrong of international development projects or educational development policies as such, but rather about the process by which a limited range of policies was selected, packaged, and carried to the remotest parts of the world in the decades since the end of World War II. It is about why the range of legitimate development and education policies narrowed on a set that neither satisfies most educators nor serves the interests of elites or more powerful nation-states. It is about the surprising degree to which the organizations and professionals most directly involved in carrying these policies, mainly from industrialized to less industrialized countries, are operating neither as agents of dominant nation-states nor on their own behalf. They are, instead propelled by universalized development concepts, by somewhat autonomous organizational operating procedures, and by ritualized rationality and professional standards and activities, all closely linked to what the world society scholars call "world culture." In many less industrialized countries, much of the gap between the education policies articulated at the international and national level and practice at the subnational and classroom level can be explained by the culturally proscribed and institutionalized actions of these organizations and professionals.

2
Setting the Stage

In 1957, Gunnar Myrdal, later to win the Nobel Prize for his work in development economics, claimed:

> ... the emergence in underdeveloped countries of this common urge to economic development as a major political purpose, and the definition of economic development as a rise in the levels of living of the common people, the agreement that economic development is a task for government ... all this amounts to something entirely new in history. (as cited in Arndt, 1987, p. 9)

Standing at the beginning of the twenty-first century, it is easy to forget the relatively recent provenance of international development. Throughout history states have taken measures to improve the economies that serve as their revenue base. In modern history, systematic government planning along these lines was well established by the sixteenth and seventeenth centuries in the form of mercantilist trade policies designed to maximize the flow of gold into the royal treasuries. Later in the nineteenth and twentieth centuries, colonial powers promulgated plans for the economic development of colonies, again, with an eye to maximizing revenue for the colonizers. Both old and new nation-states found in nationalism a powerful incentive to appear rich and strong in the community of nations, but felt less obliged to look responsive to the needs of the general population. Education was one tool in the state's efforts to compete with other states. In the eighteenth and nineteenth centuries, the state used education to produce the bureaucrats and soldiers needed to seize and maintain empires. Later in the nineteenth and early twentieth centuries, the welfare state began to emerge in Europe and North America (Lumsdaine, 1993) but until World War I, economic development was more often synonymous with the amassing of national or imperial wealth (Arndt, 1987). The idea that everyone was entitled to development and to an education was not expressed clearly until after World War II. The idea of international development, or bringing international resources to bear to promote national development, is mainly a product of the post–World War II period, but its roots lie in the sixteenth and seventeenth centuries.

Historical Antecedents

The idea that one has obligations outside the traditional boundaries of family, kin, religion, and nation, and that foreigners and their needs might exercise some claim on distant individuals was not common throughout most of human history. Many scholars consider this idea a product of the Western Enlightenment, and the Enlightenment itself a product of the Christian concept of the soul: all beings have souls, they are equal before God, therefore, all should be considered equal in the eyes of human authority—the law—as well. In the Christian tradition, souls were so valuable in the sight of God that they were worth saving at great personal cost. The Christian church taught that those who had received the gospel were obligated to share it with others and thus the notion of the need to "save" the non-Christian world or, in Enlightenment terms, to promote some universal idea of "progress."

Early Movements for Human Solidarity: Sixteenth Through Nineteenth Centuries

By the beginning of the sixteenth century, Christian missionaries were sailing on the ships of the conquistadors. However imperialistic their protectors and paternalistic their own attitudes, missionaries came to the colonies with the idea that even savages had everlasting souls of value to God and could, with the right instruction, be saved.

> ... missionaries managed to convince Pope Paul III to issue the bull *Sublimis Deus* in 1537, which declared that the Amerindians were rational beings with souls, worthy of conversion as well as protection rather than the slaughter that was being brought down upon them by Christian soldiers. (Willinsky, 1998, p. 93)

Close to the concept of saving was the idea of civilizing or indoctrinating the non-European world into Western culture. Willinsky, quoting Winks (1969), argues that it was the idea of exchange—that Europeans had a right to take away the material riches of the colonies in return for delivering to the colonies the sublime civilization of the West—that kept alive among some colonists a commitment to educating at least a few colonial subjects. A special provision was written into the notorious Berlin Act of 1884, which divided Africa among European nations "[a]ll the powers exercising sovereign rights or influence in the aforesaid territories . . . shall . . . protect and favor all religious, scientific, or charitable institutions . . . which aim at instructing the natives and bringing home to them the blessings of civilization."

While critical of colonial schooling in general, Willinsky also points out some of its unintended, salutary effects. For example, colonial elites who studied the storming of the Bastille in some detail, instead of simply admiring the revolutionaries, identified with them and found it easier to plan revolt against their colonizers. As another example, he cites the case of English women who worked in the colonies as schoolteachers and later returned to England. "They were in a far better position to understand [and publicize] the vile prejudices that infused the governing of the colonies, prejudices that remained largely invisible in Great Britain" (p. 105).

In addition to Catholic proselytization and European "civilizing" efforts in the colonies, many other events and movements in the eighteenth and nineteenth centuries, often associated with nongovernmental organizations (NGOs), contributed to the stirrings of international consciousness among groups in Europe and North America.

- Both the U.S. Bill of Rights (1781) and the French Declaration of the Rights of Man and Citizen (1784) asserted that certain rights were inalienable for all human beings, helped to raise questions about the institution of slavery, and inspired the first colonies to take up arms for independence in Latin America (Anderson, 1991).
- While not specifically religious, the Quaker leadership of the British and Foreign Antislavery Society (f. 1839), now known as Antislavery International (ASI), brought a common moral framework to the task and developed communication and cooperation among the society's members in several different countries. Later women formed the core of the anti–white slavery movement in an effort to stop the international trafficking of women and children for prostitution (Berkovitch, 1999). These global social reform movements increased a sense of responsibility among the general public for issues that transcended national borders.
- Protestant missionaries, lacking the resources of the Catholic Church, raised funds constantly, sending letters describing conditions in Africa, Asia, or Latin America to dozens, if not hundreds of individual and congregational donors each year. These letters represented an effort to expand the donors' sense of responsibility for those outside their own family, community, nation, and race.
- In 1859 Henry Dunant's *A Memory of Solferino*, written in response to the lack of medical care for some six to ten thousand Austrian and French soldiers wounded in battle at Solferino, Italy, brought the needs of the war-wounded, regardless of nationality, to the larger

world (Finnemore, 1996). Dunant's subsequent work led to the first Geneva Red Cross Convention in 1864, the founding of the International Committee of the Red Cross, and the establishment of the principle of neutrality for the wounded, prisoners, and relief workers. Based on this precedent, the principle of neutrality would later be extended to children and noncombatants.

- Socialist and communist workers' groups in the late nineteenth century emphasized the international nature of capitalism and provided a counterpoint to the rise of the capitalist philanthropists (see "Precursors" below). These workers' organizations worked to increase cross-national solidarity.

The Precursors of the International Development Field: Twentieth Century

Several factors in the first half of the twentieth century contributed to a growing appreciation that national development might involve something more than the enrichment of the state and/or elites, and that it might require international assistance. First, social science data collection in the 1930s first made possible international comparisons of living standards. For example, in 1935 the Food Research Institute, established by Herbert Hoover in 1921, joined with the League of Nations to undertake the first systematic study of the dimensions of worldwide hunger and malnutrition. The subsequent information about starvation in many parts of the world added to the emergency relief experience of the 1910s and 1920s and generated several responses in the industrialized world. For many people,

> ... the unequal distribution of this world's goods between a privileged minority and an underprivileged majority has been transformed from an unavoidable evil into an intolerable injustice by the latest technological inventions of Western man. (Toynbee, 1947)

Many more, however, ascribing to a deprivation theory of war, argued that people deprived of their most basic needs were bound to be driven to violence.

> The country needs and, unless I mistake its temper, the country demands bold, persistent experimentation. It is common sense to take a method and try it. If it fails, admit it frankly and try another. But above all, try something. The millions who are in want will not stand idly by silently forever while the things to satisfy their needs are within easy reach. (Roosevelt, 1932)

In this framework relief, and later development aid, could be rationalized, at least in part, as an exercise in self-interest or world peacemaking.

Second, in the late nineteenth and early twentieth century industrialists with strong Christian leanings, such as Andrew Carnegie and Nelson Rockefeller, became philanthropists who focused not just on saving souls, or on temporary relief of human suffering, but on using science to attack what was perceived to be the physical and intellectual causes of such human misery. The work of these wealthy philanthropists contributed to later rationalizations of international development in two ways: first, by supporting science-based approaches to global social problems, and second, by contributing to the idea that capitalism (like colonialism, above) entailed voluntary social responsibility. Medical research funded by these industrial philanthropists in the decades immediately preceding and following World War II led to hitherto inconceivable advances in medicine, such as the global eradication of several major diseases including smallpox, as well as the control of many others such as typhus, typhoid, yellow fever, and polio. These successes generated great hopes of what twentieth-century science might do to reduce human suffering.

Third, these public health campaigns demonstrated the feasibility of addressing peace-time problems on a global scale. This image was bolstered by experience with governmental and nongovernmental emergency relief organizations during and after both world wars, proving it was possible to address international disasters, such as famines and epidemics, on a massive scale.

Fourth, the prominent role of John Maynard Keynes and other like-minded macroeconomists during the Depression and World War II bolstered confidence in economists in general and in macroeconomic planners specifically. Economists played a key role in the Marshall Plan for the dramatic and relatively rapid reconstruction of Europe and its colonies after the war. The success of these large-scale programs convinced many that governments guided by well-trained economists were in a unique position to plan and promote this type of development.

Finally, Lumsdaine (1993) argues that the rise of the welfare state in Western Europe and North America in the late nineteenth and twentieth centuries prepared the way for considering welfare on a global scale to be a subject appropriate for international cooperation.

In January 1941, U.S. President Franklin D. Roosevelt declared in his Four Freedoms speech, that all people, not simply Americans, had a right to "freedom from want." This sentiment was echoed in the Atlantic Charter, in August 1941, which declared that all states should have equal access to trade and raw materials in order that "all men in all lands might live out their lives in freedom from fear and want." The 1948, UN Universal Declaration of Human Rights and its subsequent covenants echo these and earlier commitments to promoting human welfare.

Most historians of international development trace the present use of the word *development* to Point Four of U.S. President Harry Truman's ("Four Points") inaugural speech in 1949:

> We must embark on a bold new program for making the benefits of our scientific advances and industrial progress available for the improvement and growth of underdeveloped areas. The old imperialism—exploitation for foreign profit—has no place in our plans. What we envisage is a program of development based on the concepts of democratic fair dealing.

Note that democratic fair dealing has not necessarily characterized actual development practice, but its articulation here as a stated ideal creates a standard that makes all sorts of unfairness more visible.[1] This was also the role of various human rights declarations issued by the UN throughout the postwar period that laid out the universal nature of the development and education imperatives in increasingly specific terms.

UN Documents as Catalysts

Prior to World War II, the more industrialized countries of Western Europe and North America typically characterized the quality of life in less industrialized countries, most of them colonies, as traditional, backwards, uncivilized, poor, and/or underdeveloped. The United Nation's 1945 charter, however, makes no distinction among nation-states—poor or rich, more or less industrialized—when it declares as one of its principle purposes "to achieve international cooperation in solving international problems of an economic, social, cultural, or humanitarian character." Likewise, the UN's 1948 Universal Declaration of Human Rights establishes individual rights to a minimum standard of living, without reference to the preexisting quality of life in the country where an individual may reside:

> Article 25, Para 1. Everyone has the right to a standard of living adequate for the health and well being of himself [sic] and of his family, including food, clothing, housing, and medical care and necessary social services . . . .

Eighteen years later, in 1966, two new covenants attempted to translate the nonbinding 1948 declaration into binding international agreements. At the height of the Cold War, the United States promptly ratified and the Soviet

---

1. I do not argue that benign motives shaped the discourse; I do contend that the discourse was universalistic and benign. Its unintended consequence was to make less benign policies and practices easier to identify and critique. I thank Francisco O. Ramirez for this point.

Union rejected the first covenant dealing with civil and political rights. The two countries then reversed positions for the second covenant, which covered economic, social, and cultural rights. For those leery of entitlement programs, like many in the U.S. Senate, the second covenant opened the way for individuals to demand welfare improvements from their governments and for less industrialized states to demand assistance from wealthier states to meet those demands. For example,

> Part II, Article 2, Para 1. Each State Party to the present Covenant undertakes to take steps, individually and through international assistance and cooperation, especially economic and technical, to the maximum of its available resources, with a view to achieving progressively the full realization of the rights recognized in the present Covenant by all appropriate means, including particularly the adoption of legislative measures.
> Part II, Article 11, Para 1. The States Parties to the present Covenant recognize the right of everyone to an adequate standard of living . . . and to *the continuous improvement* of living conditions. *The States Parties will take appropriate steps to ensure the realization of this right*, recognizing to this effect the essential importance of *international co-operation* based on free consent [my emphasis].

The signers of this covenant collectively agree to provide not just for adequate standards of living for each citizen but also for continual improvements in everyone's general quality of life. Nonetheless, the immediate, de facto impact of this covenant should not be overstated. The Covenant acknowledges that such improvements will require "international cooperation," presumably between more and less wealthy nation-states. In fact, by the mid-1960s, when the wording for this covenant was being finalized, many industrialized countries were already formalizing bilateral "development cooperation" agreements with less industrialized countries. Commitments to these bilateral organizations tended to reduce the funding that the UN hoped to secure for UN-coordinated development activities. The "based on free consent" wording of the final phrase, acknowledged that in the mid-1960s, much like today, the UN did not have the authority or resources to compel signatories to "cooperate" in any specific manner.

Nonetheless, the UN Universal Declaration of Human Rights and the Covenant on Social and Economic Rights indirectly helped to create a dichotomized world: those nation-states that could ensure an adequate and continually improving quality of life for their citizens, and those nations that needed assistance in doing so. In addition, both these documents emphasize that the measure of development is not the national economy—the traditional "wealth of nations"—but "everyone."

According to these documents, individual development had become the primary means to national development and, in turn, many UN documents present individual education as a key component of individual development.

For example, at a time when the literacy rates in most of the less industrialized countries were less than 25 percent, the Universal Declaration of Human Rights nonetheless asserts,

> Article 26, Item 1. Everyone has the right to education. Education shall be free, at least in the elementary and fundamental stages. Elementary education shall be compulsory . . . .

In addition, Articles 13 and 14 expand on these themes at length.

In summary, since the end of World War II, the UN has helped to create a world in which development and education are prominent and closely linked concerns in international forums and documents. Regardless of their actual capacity to implement programs, all nation-states were de jure equally responsible for continuously improving the quality of life for all of their citizens. These responsibilities were to be financed by state revenues or by cooperation with other states. Few industrialized nation-states chose to use the UN as coordinator or broker for most of their development cooperation, rendering rhetorical many of the individual rights and national responsibilities articulated in UN declarations and covenants. Nonetheless, as the development agenda evolved, so pressure increased on both less and more industrialized nation-states to operationalize it. The next section examines some of the pressures—economic, cultural, historical, political—which have distilled the international development aid system.

The Origins of International Development Aid

The U.S. Point Four Program, started in 1943 and later merged with other U.S. foreign aid programs, offered technology and technical aid to less industrialized countries in Africa, Asia, and Latin America. These countries were seen as important in the emerging Cold War between the Soviet Union on the one side and the United States and its allies on the other. Britain followed suit with the Colombo Plan (f. 1950), later joined by the United States and Japan, to strengthen the social and economic structure of its soon-to-be former colonies. Belgium and France both launched new public investment plans for existing colonies, intending development as an alternative to demands for independence (Young, 1982, p.92). A stream of announcements of new bilateral aid agreements between industrialized and newly independent nation-states followed over the next four decades.

The Organization for European Economic Cooperation (f. 1948), originally set up to manage the Marshall Plan in Europe, became the Organization for Economic Cooperation and Development (OECD) in 1960. By the early 1990s, most upper-middle-income and industrialized countries were contributing to multilateral development aid funds, and all OECD member countries and several Arab countries sponsored bilateral development programs.

The OECD (1985) and others identified the key elements in the emergence of the current development aid system as follows:

1. the decision of the founders of the UN system to "employ international machinery for the promotion of the economic and social advancement of all peoples" (OECD, 1985, p.40), as well as sincere adherence on the part of some donors to notions of scientific progress and global responsibility as expressed in the UN Charter and other documents (Riddell, 1987);
2. the creation at Bretton Woods, New Hampshire, of the International Bank for Reconstruction (and Development) and the International Monetary Fund, and later of the International Development Association, collectively known as the World Bank;
3. the emergence of the concept of "technical assistance" or the transfer of know-how from industrialized to less industrialized countries;
4. efforts of individual nation-states to establish legitimacy in the world society; and
5. commercial and/or military self-interest (Goulet and Hudson, 1971).

The last point is a major one. International development aid was sometimes portrayed as an extension of World War II, or at least the prevention of what seemed an imminent World War III, as the capitalist core set about protecting the less developed periphery from Communist expansionism (OECD, 1985). As a result, in later years, the less industrialized countries would assert their independence from the capitalist First World and the communist Second World by designating themselves the nonaligned Third World.

In a world that privileges formal rationality and legitimates the nation-state as a primary actor, self-interest is one of the more compelling rationales for action. Some industrialized countries constructed development as means to transform newly independent countries into valuable new markets for trade or at least into partners in the Cold War. These often appeared as one among several rationales used to legitimize international development aid to skeptical constituencies in industrialized countries. In the United States, for example,

> [. . .] in 1960 it seemed that Asia, Africa, and Latin America would become the stage upon which Cold War politics would be played out, and U.S. attention shifted from the [Pacific] rim countries to the entire underdeveloped world.
>
> . . . U.S. President John F. Kennedy, for example, argued, "the economic collapse of those free but less developed nations . . . would be disastrous to our national security, harmful to our comparative prosperity, and offensive to our conscience." (Grant, 1979)

In the United States particularly, throughout the post-war period, development programs couched in security language found more support in the U.S. Congress than those framed in terms of progress and global responsibility. A retired senior official recalls:

> ... deciding we needed to change the name of the development agency to AID, so that it would sound helpful. I remember being visited by Averill Harriman, who said that we were crazy. "You will never get a dollar for that," he said, "why do you think we call it [development aid] mutual security?" (Bundy, 1989)

In both bilateral and multilateral organizations, discourse about development grew independently of funding for development activities, resulting in more discourse than action, an unstable state of affairs. Despite the many incentives for industrialized countries to commit resources to international development, few ever met the target of 1 percent of GNP endorsed by the World Council of Churches (1959), the UN General Assembly (1961), the UN Conference on Trade and Development (1964), and the OECD's DAC (1965). Beginning in the first half of the 1960s, UN meetings periodically estimated the additional financial and scientific resources that might be made available for development through disarmament,[2] proposing a link between development and peace.

If development in less industrialized countries was progressing more slowly than reconstruction in Europe had under the Marshall Plan, some argued that it was in part a problem of relatively lower volume of aid in both absolute and per capita terms. Nonetheless, lack of funding did not deter the UN from declaring the 1960s the Development Decade, and lack of progress in that decade did not deter the UN from declaring the 1970s the Second Development Decade, the 1980s the Third, and the 1990s the Fourth, all of them patently underfunded. Inflation associated with the oil crises of the 1970s eroded the real value of nominal increases in international development aid during the Second Development Decade, the increase itself, paradoxically, partly the result of new development programs funded by oil producing countries. The end of the Cold War in 1989 led some to speculate that decreases in military spending in the United States—until the 1990s the world's largest development donor—could result in a "peace dividend" that might increase real levels of development aid. In fact, the end of the Cold War simply eliminated one of the United State's major rationales for funding international development—halting the spread of Communism.

But with or without funding, the sheer quantity of discourse about development mounted steadily throughout the 1960s and 1970s, as reflected in the UN Yearbook. In the 1950s, the number of pages in the UN Yearbook

---

2. See especially UN Yearbooks 1963 and 1964.

devoted to international development as a percentage of total pages devoted
to the work of the Economic and Social Council is 20 percent or less. The
percentage rises, however, throughout the 1960s and peaks in the late 1970s,
at between 35 percent and 40 percent, only to decline to 16 percent in 1986,
and then to pick up again at the beginning of the 1990s. The rise in the 1960s
and 1970s reflects the UN's promotion of the First and Second Development
Decade. In the 1970s, at the height of the debates surrounding the New International Economic Order (NIEO), described in Chapter 3, the Table of Contents relates almost all activities of the Economic and Social Council to
international development. Then abruptly in 1981, for reasons discussed in
Chapter 3, the Yearbook's Table of Contents reverts from a complex to a simple structure, in which international development does not figure prominently. Instead the headings are truncated and politically neutral: "Science,"
"Food," and "Environment." "Development" only reappears in subheadings
of these truncated headings towards the end of the 1980s.

Conclusion: Origins of International Development Aid

By 1990, almost every industrialized country could point to a line item in its
national budget earmarked for international development aid. The motivation
for this funding was mixed; some offered aid in self-interested terms—security or trade—others believed in technology transfer as a means to create
prosperity for all, yet others had confidence in the power of large financial
institutions to determine the fate of small nation-states. But late in the century, the OECD began to press for more funding, more consistent with the
high goals established over the years, and with an eye to assembling a critical
mass of aid, able to make a significant dent in world poverty.

The next section illustrates how the logic of international development
and education resonated with leaders in the development field, and how they
translated the development imperative into a mandate to promote education
for all.

The World Conference on Education for All: The Role of Organizational Leaders

The World Conference on Education for All was not organized by nation-
states or by professional educators, rather it was conceived by the heads
of several large international development organizations and carried out
by international development professionals. Whereas most of this book is
concerned with the institutional effects of the structure of international
development organizations on the substance, format, and follow-up of an
international conference, the discussion that follows is more diffuse. However, it illustrates the implications of working out the cognitive models

described in the next chapter in a world that usually interprets itself in realist terms, emphasizing the importance of individual and organizational interests and action.

Responsibility for conceiving the World Conference on Education for All lies with the heads of three international development organizations: Federico Mayor of UNESCO,[3] Barber Conable of the World Bank, and James P. Grant of UNICEF. None of these three men had either an academic background in or professional experience with basic education. Mayor, a biology professor, had spent most of his career in and around universities in Europe and went against the advice of UNESCO's own education staff in promoting the WCEFA. Conable was a former U.S. Congressman from upstate New York prior to his appointment as World Bank president in 1986. James P. Grant of UNICEF was trained as a lawyer, not an educator, but was a career international development professional.

How did each of these men come to see promoting a world conference on Education for All as central to achieving their own organization's goals? In the case of Mayor, UNESCO had a long-term commitment to mass, particularly adult, education. In addition, UNESCO had several organizational problems that a successful, high profile, nonpolitical activity such as a world conference might have helped to address. As for Conable, Byers (1998) reports that, lacking either experience in banking or international affairs, he was nonetheless a Washington insider who could—and did—secure major increases in funds for the World Bank from the U.S. Congress. Funding was again an issue in 1988. The World Bank had recently completed a major study, *Education in Sub-Saharan Africa*, and was in the process of following up with a series of new sector loans. As explained in Chapter 3, the World Bank needed commitments from national governments to spend their own funds on education, as well as grant commitments from other donor organizations to supplement bank loans. The bank hoped a high-profile activity would mobilize both. In discussing his own motivations, however, Conable himself emphasized that he was simply convinced of the fundamental relationship between basic education and development.

Grant, on the other hand, was in the middle of what appeared to be a successful ten-year Child Survival Revolution, part of a multidonor effort to ensure Health for All by the year 2000. This effort was already stretching his modest organization to the maximum. The three leaders saw a synergy between education and health; to Grant, education was key to meeting Health for All goals, and to Conable and Mayor, the Health for All model was key to raising the profile of education on the world agenda.

---

3. Federico Mayor was the only one of the four heads of sponsoring organizations I was unable to interview. His role in the WCEFA is therefore apt to be understated throughout this account.

Grant's career is a study in the rise of development as an international activity. The grandson of medical missionaries and the son of a Rockefeller health advisor, Grant grew up in China and then attended the University of California at Berkeley. There he was active with co-ops and a group of students interested in the New Deal. During World War II he was assigned to Burma, then China, where after the war he worked with the Marshall Plan. Grant later helped establish the Joint Commission on Rural Reconstruction in Taiwan. After law school, he joined the first U.S. bilateral aid program in the 1950s and was involved in the creation of the Peace Corps in the early 1960s. In 1970, he helped found the principal international development think tank in Washington, D.C., the Overseas Development Council, and served as its first director for ten years, promoting the humanitarian and scientific base for international development. In the 1980s, he also served as the President of the Society for International Development.

Grant was appointed executive director at Unicef in 1980. A close friend and colleague explained Grant's interest in UNICEF:

> He has always seen children as [a] Trojan Horse for development, for equity, and for social justice . . . he felt children were the most universal "yessable" . . . nobody can refuse to do things on behalf of children. This enabled him to advocate and to urge others to join him because it was for the sake of the children, it wasn't for any partisan cause and therefore he has seen the case of children as that of development. (Rohde, 1995)

Although Grant inherited the ambitious Health for All by the Year 2000 goals from his predecessor, he manifested a personal interest in education through two actions early in his tenure at UNICEF. First, he recruited a former minister of education, Nyi Nyi, the director of a successful national literacy campaign in Burma, to be one of his senior managers. Second, he undertook a week of negotiations in Paris in 1982 in a failed effort to launch a major new education program with UNESCO (R. Jolly, personal communication, November 6, 1995).

Six months after the meeting in Paris, a consortium of intergovernmental organizations, including UNICEF, launched a global program for health, focusing on disseminating simple health technologies to decrease the rate of child mortality in less industrialized countries. This Child Survival Initiative (CSI) was an extremely visible and widely acknowledged public health campaign, but Grant viewed it in broader perspective:

> So children, even immunization, was [sic] not so much about immunization as it was about organizing society, about getting entire societies . . . together to do something for everyone, something of universal good. And then to use that to convince society that they could do many other things

and that if you can immunize everyone why can't you do "that" and "this?" (Grant, 1995)

In 1986, the UNICEF executive board declared that the education of women was the single most important factor for improving the survival and well-being of children (Phillips, 1987).

That same year, the United States, the United Kingdom, and Singapore quit UNESCO to protest what they portrayed as widespread corruption and waste under Director General M'Bow's leadership. This withdrawal left UNESCO without the financial support of two of its largest members. In 1987, therefore, newly appointed UNESCO Director General Federico Mayor, was looking for a way to reestablish UNESCO's credibility with these former members and to reestablish UNESCO's leadership in education. Mayor approached Grant about organizing a major initiative on education that would help generate some of the same goodwill fomented by the CSI (R. Jolly, personal communication, November 6, 1995). One of the outcomes of that meeting was a consultative meeting in February 1988 arranged by UNICEF's Nyi Nyi on "basic education" (described more fully in Chapter 5).

The paper prepared as an outcome of that meeting (United Nations Children's Fund, 1988) emphasizes the need for something like CSI in education and tries to tie this emphasis to UNICEF's mandate in child health in two ways. First, the paper claims, "unequivocal evidence has emerged to the effect that literacy of women is the most important single factor related to the reduction of the mortality of children" (p. 2).[4] Second, it argues that the key strategy in quickly implementing UNICEF's child health programs is social mobilization, which, in turn is much facilitated by literacy and numeracy.

Two World Bank representatives attended the February meeting and later played major roles in the preparation and follow up to EFA. Nonetheless, according to Grant (1994) and Conable (personal communications, July 31, 1994 and December 1995, respectively), the World Bank's interest in participating in a large-scale joint effort was initiated by Conable in April 1988, at a meeting of the Child Survival Task Force.[5] According to Grant, Conable was so impressed with the CSI momentum that he asked Grant if something like it could be done in education. Grant reports he told Conable that without

---

4. But does not provide a reference for this assertion.
5. The Child Survival Task Force was formed in the spring of 1984 by several organizations, including UNICEF, WHO, UNDP, and the World Bank, to enable heads of organizations to meet every two years with eight to ten key ministers of health in order to maintain momentum on the Child Survival Initiative. It is one more example of the increasing rationalization of joint activities that resulted in increasing interaction between both staff and senior management of international development organizations. The Brutland Report meetings described in the following paragraph are another illustration.

a conference to develop intellectual consensus on principles and methods—
as the Alma Ata Health for All conference in 1978 had done for health—it
was not possible. Such an intellectual consensus in education did not, in fact,
exist (see Chapters 3 and 5), but many, including the heads of organizations,
were convinced of the importance of education and hoped that the conference might produce such a consensus.

Within a few months of the April meeting, Grant, Mayor, and Conable
tentatively agreed to jointly sponsor a world conference on education. The
United Nations Development Program (UNDP) became the fourth sponsor
sometime late in 1988. In November 1988, the sponsoring organizations vet-
ted a revision of the basic education paper presented at the February 1988
meeting to a group of education experts from international development
organizations. In December 1988, the sponsors held an organizing meeting at
the World Bank in Washington, D.C., where each pledged US$ 500,000 of
in-kind and staff support for the conference preparation and implementation.
Senior staff from each of the organizations were assigned to work on the
executive committee of the Interagency Commission (IAC) and on the executive secretariat. The secretariat was set up in June 1989, with less than nine
months to prepare for a world conference.

In summary, the World Conference on Education for All was initiated by
the heads of three sponsoring organizations, with no prompting from individual countries, industrialized or not. Conable and Grant were convinced that
their responsibility as leaders of major international development organizations lay in inducing countries to undertake education programs clearly not
high on those countries' list of priorities. Mayor and Conable assumed such
strong cognitive links between education and development that they assumed
the existence of a key ingredient for the conference success—intellectual
consensus on a whole range of education issues—or assumed it could be
readily created. Based on this assumption, the heads of organizations put the
substantial resources of their organizations at the disposal of an interorgani-
zation task force with a modicum of time to produce a world conference.

Conclusion

This chapter has provided a brief look at some of the events and concerns that
shaped the current system of international development aid. Three points in
particular should be stressed. First, many of the early antecedents to development were religious and the development imperative grew out of nation-
states' highest values as well as their self-interest. Second, given that the
main precedent for international development aid was the Marshall Plan, few
were prepared to fund it for decades. Since such a broad program of international aid had never been undertaken before, all parties concerned hoped it
would require no more than a decade or two but in fact there were no prece-

dents. As a result, the system was never allocated resources commensurate to its lofty aims and the length of the effort.

The sequence of events in 1988 and 1989, as described above, provides little support either for an argument that nation-state interest initiated the World Conference on Education for All, or that this was the right stage in the evolution of development knowledge and process for such a conference to occur. Instead, while a Whiggish historian might argue this is a good case of the "great man" as catalyst for social change, an institutional sociologist sees in this picture a great deal of enacting: of what development organizations are supposed to do; of what heads of such organizations as progressive individuals are supposed to do; and of what nation-states should be held responsible for. The charismatic leadership of the three leaders described above triggers successful enactment by invoking highly legitimate ideas and blueprints for development. The dimensions of those ideas and blueprints are the subjects of the next chapter.

3
Discourse

This chapter explores the origins and evolution of international development discourse—where it comes from, what events and people shape it, how it has changed over time—in an effort to understand the development imperative that drives nation-states and the mandate that governs international development organizations, and to explore how these relate to education. "Discourse" in this context refers to the special terminology and language used to create identities, define structures, and explain behavior in a special domain. Studying discourse is important because in trying to express abstract concepts, people construct words and phrases that, once externalized, take on an outward objectivity, a reality, that causes them to forget the origins of these concepts. The internalization of this socially constructed reality causes many of these concepts to be experienced as facts, as forces outside individual or social control, or to be taken for granted as always having existed. In other words, discourse is one of the ways in which identities, structures, and behavior become institutionalized. For example, when someone in a position of authority discriminates against an individual on the basis of some personal characteristic, society applauds the individual who upholds his or her dignity by suing that authority. In the not-too-distant past, family honor was considered a compelling social obligation. When family honor was insulted, the family member designated to extract blood vengeance from the perpetrator were shown leniency in some courts. Today, someone who murdered to defend his family honor would receive no special consideration in any modern court, just as most current individual discrimination suits would have been considered frivolous in nineteenth century courts (Berger, 1992).

Prior to World War II, the word "development" had many definitions, none of which referred exclusively to improvements in economic or social conditions in less industrialized countries. However, since the end of World

War II, development has taken on a special meaning for a specific group working in a specialized domain, including both those who have engaged in efforts to increase economic growth or improve social welfare in less industrialized areas, and those who have critiqued those efforts. For the former, development is, ideally, objective, scientific, progressive, and politically neutral. For the latter, ideology, interest, and politics permeate all aspects of the development enterprise. In contrast, the institutionalist approach adopted here explores some striking aspects of international development that do not lend themselves either to technical or to interest-driven explanations.

The international development imperative for nation-states, for example, first appears in international discourse in the wake of the Universal Declaration of Human Rights in 1948. In the immediate postwar reconstruction period, this discourse aimed to undo the work of decades of nationalism and fascism in the former Axis countries, such as the notion that progress in one country could only be achieved at the expense of others. In immediate postwar documents, the word "cooperation" is often a coded reference to such aims.

Despite its original intent, in later decades "cooperation" has been more often applied to former colonies and less industrialized areas. Immediately after the war, international development discourse was broad and fluid, ascribing to individuals rights to social, economic, and political development, without specifying how those rights would be extended to the vast majority of the world's population who did not at that time enjoy them. Later, in the 1950s and 1960s, the discourse became focused on modernization and national economic growth as the fastest way to expand individual social, political, and economic development to the greatest number of people. In the 1970s and 1980s, confidence in such "trickle down" approaches waned, and attention shifted to poverty reduction. In these decades many international development programs targeted the poor, women, and other historically disadvantaged groups, and focused on strengthening the social services—education, health, family planning—considered necessary to draw these groups into the mainstream of a growing economy.

From the 1970s onward, individual welfare, rather than absolute rates of national economic growth, became the principal measure of development and, with the rise of the human capital concept in the early 1960s, education was seen as the key to individual development. Each of these different discourses in international development, however, implied a different mix of educational activities in less industrialized countries: more or less primary education, more or less adult literacy training, more or less higher education, more or less technical or vocational training, and so forth.

Economics has played a leading role in international development discourse throughout the postwar period, in part because that discipline has been more adept than other social sciences in applying the scientific method to social problems. Economists have pioneered ways of translating key aspects or components of development into quantifiable indicators, for example, defining economic growth as the increase in gross national product (GNP). Economists have also been flexible in adapting the data at hand (such as industrial and agricultural output) to approximate those indicators. As a result, by the late 1970s, economists had developed statistical models to explore relationships between various aspects of development, such as literacy and industrial production. Resistance to the dominant economic discourse has drawn attention to the poor quality of the official statistics in less industrialized countries used to generate these models. Others have criticized economic models for not incorporating many important aspects of economic and social life, such as the value of women's unpaid labor as a contribution to national output or the quality of life of individuals. For many reasons discussed here and in the next chapter, economics remains at the center of international development discourse, even as over time the narrow, materialistic focus on economics comes into tension with broader notions of progress and justice.

The next section of this chapter traces the increase in and content of discourse about individuals' rights to development and education in the post–World War II era and the responsibilities of nation-states to address them. Throughout this discourse, the conceptual link between national development and individual education has two strands. One strand constructs education in somewhat instrumental terms as a means to individual and collective development, first in economic terms and later in political and social terms. The second strand constructs social and economic development as a human right, part and parcel of development, and a human right in its own right.

The Development of International Development Discourse

From 1945 to 1990, the international development discourse did not so much evolve as accrete. Old ideas did not go away entirely as new ones were added on top, creating a great amalgam of good and not so good ideas, none of them fully implemented (Grant, 1979). The central goal of development changed once in these 45 years. Until the early 1970s, national economic growth and modernization was the principal goal of development and the chief measure of progress was GNP or GNP/capita. From the 1970s through the 1990s, the main goal of the largest donors was poverty alleviation or reduction and the chief measures of progress focused on individual welfare. The case for a strong relationship between education and economic development first appeared in the 1960s, in the form of human capital theory. That theory remains an important justification for investments in education to this day, but since the 1970s increasing concern with poverty reduction has led to greater focus on the poor and the marginalized, and with access to education as the key to individual development.

Table 3.1 presents summarizes the major themes that accumulated around development and educational development over the last 50 years.[6] Each decade is reviewed in some detail, since historical trends in the international development discourse help to explain trends over time in the growth and focus of international development organizations, professionals, and conferences analyzed in later chapters.

The 1950s

As shown in the second column of Table 3.1, both capitalists and communists advocated "comprehensive economic development planning" in the 1950s. Classical economists such as Paul N. Rosenstein-Rodan (1944) theorized about *The International Development of Economically Backward Areas*, while Ragnar Nurkse (1953) addressed *Problems of Capital Formation in Underdeveloped Countries*, and W. Arthur Lewis (1955) outlined *A Theory of Economic Growth*. These approaches focused on determining the appropriate balance between industrial and agricultural growth, the modern and the traditional sectors, foreign and domestic investment, all with an eye to maximizing the rate of growth of the industrial, or modern, sector. Their works bristle with input-output tables and explanations of "the vicious cycle of poverty," "low-level equilibrium traps," and the imperative of "a big push" before "takeoff" into a period of sustained economic growth. Few assumed that newly independent nation-states were in a position to be fully autonomous, but most treated prudent management of domestic resources and international trade—however difficult—as within each country's grasp and defined industrial growth as the key determinant of development. According to this approach, development could be achieved with little help from the outside world beyond expert advice—technical assistance, some technology transfer, loans for capital investments in infrastructure, and increased trade.

For models of growth, many theorists looked to the histories of already industrialized countries. Others built on these histories, but took into account factors considered unique to certain colonies, such as unlimited supplies of labor, thereby distinguishing development economics from classical economics (Lewis, 1955). Some sociologists, such as Levy (1972), even assumed there might be some advantages to being a latecomer to industrialization. Levy argued that whereas industrialized economies had to develop sequentially, discovering efficiencies by trial and error, the less industrialized countries could start out with tried and true economic models and technology and therefore advance more quickly.

But there were also dissenters, among them Gunnar Myrdal, quoted earlier. Albert Hirschman (1958), for example, argued "that both the theorist and

6. For much more detailed and contrasting perspectives on development discourse, see Escobar, A. (1995), and Lumsdaine, D. H. (1993).

Table 3.1. Themes in International Development and Educational Development Discourse, 1950–1995

Decade/ Development Indicator	DISCOURSE		EDUCATION PRIORITIES
	International Development	Education and Development	
	Modernization and Critiques		
1950s GNP	Comprehensive economic planning Technology transfer Community development *Deteriorating terms of trade* *Import substituting industrialization*	Manpower planning Fundamental education	Expansion of formal education, particularly primary Technical training Rural extension training Adult education for health and agriculture
1960s GNP per capita	Economic growth Stages of development Capital accumulation Appropriate technology *Development of underdevelopment*	Stages of educational development Human capital theory Human resource planning Functional literacy	Technical education and vocational training Teacher training Formal secondary and higher education Vocationally oriented literacy

*Italics indicate critiques.

Table 3.1. (cont'd)

Decade/ Development Indicator	DISCOURSE		EDUCATION PRIORITIES
	International Development	**Education and Development**	
	Poverty Reduction and *Critiques*		
1970s **GNP per capita**	Poverty alleviation Redistribution with growth Bottom-up development Community-based strategies Basic human needs Family planning *Dependency* *New International Economic Order*	Equalizing educational opportunity Basic education Rural development Community schools *De-schooling* *Cultural imperialism* *Conscientization*	Incorporating "neglected groups" Nonformal education for adults and children Agriculturally oriented vocational school curricula
1980s **PQLI** **LSMS**	Structural adjustment Poverty reduction Social dimensions of adjustment Decentralization Participatory development *Dependent development*	Human resources development Educational effectiveness and efficiency Local administration of schooling Endogenous education	Community financing of education Training for local and regional education administrators
1990s **HDI**	Sustainable human development Environmental protection	Education for all Female education Eradicating illiteracy Quality learning for all	Universal primary and secondary schooling Female secondary school scholarships Education for special populations Classroom pedagogy and curriculum

GNP = Gross National Product

PQLI = Physical Quality of Life Indicator (Morris, 1979)

LSMS = Living Standards Measurement Surveys (World Bank Poverty Reduction Handbook, 1980)

HDI = Human Development Index (United Nations Human Development Report, 1993) the practical policymaker could and should ignore the pressures to produce buttoned-down, mathematically consistent analyses and adopt instead a sort of muscular pragmatism in grappling with the problem of development" (Krugman, 1994). They questioned both the historical appropriateness of industrial growth models based on the European and North American experience and the ability of nascent national governments to implement complex formulas for optimizing growth, not to mention the weakness of the statistics available to arrive at such formulas.

These were not the only defectors from the modernization camp; some economists began to recognize that conditions both internal and external to less industrialized economies were different in the twentieth than in the nineteenth century. Raul Prebisch, the first director of the UN's Economic Commission for Latin America (ECLA), and his colleagues reported that many newly independent countries were facing deteriorating terms of trade (United Nations Economic Commission for Latin America, 1949). Over time the price of their primary exports such as copper and wool deteriorated while the price and proportion of their manufactured imports rose, keeping less industrialized countries in a dependent position. Although the deteriorating terms of trade argument is sometimes considered the first manifestation of the dependency approach (Meier, 1995), ECLA prescribed remedies considered within less industrialized countries' control, such as import-substituting industrialization, rather than worldwide reform of the relationship between more and less industrialized countries.

Despite ECLA's insights, by the end of the 1950s, most external donors still expected less industrialized countries to cover the costs of industrialization with trade receipts and the costs of human services by concessional loans and domestic resources. Those human services were often packaged as community development programs, consisting of building latrines, schools, and farmer cooperatives in the rural areas, where most of the population of less industrialized countries still lived. These community development efforts were generally applauded by external donors but not well funded. In the eyes of the external donors, community development activities, after all, needed no modern technology or imports and were therefore considered to be within the scope of the national government's domestic resources.

The 1960s

By the beginning of the 1960s, with the escalation of the Cold War, the struggle for the hearts and minds of citizens of newly independent countries began in earnest. Many less industrialized countries had defined themselves at the 1955 Bandung Conference as "nonaligned" with either the communist or capitalist world, but popular pressure was on leaders of these countries to produce rapid economic development. Leaders in the First, Second, and Third Worlds all had strong motivation to increase the flow of international development aid to signal to their respective citizenry that they were taking positive action. All three groups therefore supported the UN in declaring the 1960s the Development Decade and set ambitious goals for development cooperation.

In 1960, Walter Rostow, a U.S. economist, proposed in *The Stages of Economic Growth: A Non-Communist Manifesto* (1960) the levels of domestic savings and public and foreign investment levels needed to enable less industrialized countries to "take-off," that is, to achieve high, sustainable levels of economic growth within a relatively short period of time. This period marked the height of modernization theory, and 1970 was set as the target for achieving a host of development goals. Since technology and technology transfer lay at the heart of so many industrialization plans in the 1960s, much discourse in the 1970s revolved around the quality and source of that technology. Must less industrialized countries depend on industrialized countries for all new technology? Was the latest technology appropriate in less industrialized countries (Schumacher, 1973)? Was less expensive, second-hand machinery more appropriate for newly industrializing countries than state-of-the-art equipment, or did it simply ensure that the newer countries would remain unable to compete with industrialized countries (Goulet, 1977)?

By the early 1960s, both economists and psychologists in the modernist camp, looking for reasons why more less industrialized countries were not "taking off," turned their attention to the role of individual attitudes. Early in the 20th century economist Josef Schumpeter had called attention to the important role of entrepreneurs in his book, *The Theory of Economic Growth*. In 1961, psychologist David McClelland published *The Achieving Society*, suggesting that the need to achieve or to perform well or to strive for success in the face of obstacles, was more prevalent in fast developing societies than in slower developers.

By the mid-1960s, some less industrialized countries were considering the possibility that not only technology or the individual psychology of their citizens, but also the entire organization of aid, trade, and resources on a global scale might need to be reordered. Later, in the 1970s, their perspectives on the immutability of global inequities would translate into demands for a New International Economic Order, a complete revamping of relations between more and less industrialized countries, as a prerequisite to national development. All this discourse, emphasizing foreign investment, imperialism, trade, and external dependencies, plus the technology transfer issues, undercut earlier images of less industrialized nation-states as autonomous and largely in control of their own development. At the same time, the discourse retained earlier ideas that the state should, nonetheless, be held accountable for prudent management of domestic resources and of foreign relations.

By the late 1960s, the economic growth rates of more than half of the 60 countries that gained independence after World War II compared favorably with European countries in the early stages of industrialization during the eighteenth and nineteenth centuries (Pearson, Boyle et al., 1969, p. 27). Nonetheless, these rates fell short of the ambitious targets set at the beginning of the decade. The fifteen or so major reports commissioned to analyze the state of development and the role of development cooperation at the end of the 1960s and the beginning of the 1970s all came to three broad conclusions. First, economic growth was much slower than projected and, when calculated on a per capita basis, was drastically reduced by population growth. Second, the benefits of that growth were not trickling down to the poor majority. Third, the distribution of income between rich and poor both within and among less industrialized countries was more uneven at the end of the First Development Decade than at the beginning. Despite the increase in critical voices in the development community Goulet and Hudson (1971) argued that all these reports reinforced the status quo: 1) "development ought to take place within existing world market frameworks" rather than socialist ones; (2) the goals of development did not need to be re-examined; and (3) structures of dependency did not need to be addressed.

However, in spite of their gloomy analysis of development progress in the 1960s, most of these reports included recommendations to increase, rather than to reduce, international development cooperation. Perhaps the best known of these reports, the Pearson Commission on International Development's report to the World Bank (Pearson, Boyle et al, 1969), titles the first subsection of its first chapter "Crisis in Aid," not "Crisis in Development." The thrust of this report is to convince international donors to give more, not less, aid. The report makes its case by appealing to moral considerations and self-interest, and by "increasing interconnectedness/internationalism." It argues that

> [B]oth sides have learned that cooperation for development means more than a simple transfer of funds. It means a set of new relationships which must be founded on mutual understanding and self-respect . . . The development relationship which is at the heart of efficient aid policy must be based on a clear division of responsibilities which meets the needs of both partners. (p. 6)

This excerpt from the Pearson report exemplifies how mainstream development discourse would adapt to address ambiguous progress in future decades. First, neither the goals nor the fundamental structures of the development field were seriously questioned. Second, the absence of a significant number of comparable instances of success in any discreet activity—given the finite number of aid donors, the finite number of less industrialized countries, and general agreement on the failure of most development projects—did not deter the authors from drawing "lessons learned." Moreover, baseline data collection did not become a standard startup activity in development projects until the 1980s. Lacking both a significant sample size (of more than 30 reasonably comparable countries) and consistent, valid baseline and trend statistics, determining the success or failure of development in the 1960s and

1970s was largely anecdotal. Throughout the next three decades, as a type of ritualized rationality, international development organizations and practitioners would assert that failures to date had generated "lessons learned" that would inform and improve future development efforts. This served both to reassure funders and to suggest that methodical, rational deliberations were steadily improving the outcomes of development activities. Third, the Pearson Report's emphasis on mutual understanding, self-respect, and partnership reflects the ritual importance of invoking de jure equality among states, regardless of their level of development, particularly in the face of enormous disarticulation between the aid programs of the industrialized countries and the needs of less industrialized countries.

Several of the reviews at the end of the First Development Decade explained the failure of many development activities in terms of lack of participation by the intended beneficiaries in the design, implementation, and evaluation of development projects. Although social activists and field workers had been talking since the 1950s about participation as a key ingredient of successful development projects, it wasn't until the late 1970s and early 1980s that the concept became widely accepted as an integral part of good development practice. The difficulties in measuring the outcome of development projects on intended beneficiaries were formidable, particularly with respect to previously disadvantaged and therefore hard-to-reach groups. Moreover, the participation norm, requiring that input from these groups be incorporated at all stages in the project process, was practically impossible to implement, given that the target group was, by definition, generally beyond the administrative reach of many large international organizations and of many less industrialized states. Yet the concept became one of the most well-established in development discourse and influenced several generations of international development organizations and their standard operating procedures.

By the time of the Pearson report, the word "crisis" had begun to appear regularly in international development discourse. Crises were used to explain the failure of many development efforts, tending to focus on a single domain or sector, extrapolating current conditions several years into the future and predicting disaster, which might be averted only by increased international development funding. For example, until the last half of the twentieth century, population growth was generally associated with increasing national wealth and power. After World War II, however, improvements in public health and nutrition increased child survival rates, which, without commensurate decreases in fertility rates, contributed to rapid population growth. Population growth was the first narrowly defined crisis to appear in the development discourse (Mudd, 1964; Coale, 1963) and rapid population growth was subsequently used to motivate arguments for other crises (Barrett & Frank, 1999). For example, the education crisis (Coombs, 1968), described in greater detail in the next section, "The 1970s," was defined by comparing the projected rate of expansion of school systems with the projected rate of population increase in less industrialized countries. The environmental crisis (Kay & Skolnikoff, 1972) and the food crisis (World Food Conference, 1974) were also driven by this type of calculation.

The 1970s

In response to the Pearson Report, even before the Second Development Decade had started, the new president of the World Bank, former Ford Company executive and U.S. Secretary of Defense Robert McNamara, instituted a new focus on poverty that coincided with the new national War on Poverty in the United States (Finnemore, 1996). As shown in Table 3-1, from the 1970s on, poverty reduction replaced modernization as the overarching theme in international development discourse. This focus on poverty reduction meant that the impact of most development activities, even infrastructure projects involving hundreds of millions of dollars, was to be defined not simply in per capita terms, but also in terms of impact on the poor. This required, on the one hand, that other quality of life indicators be constructed and, on the other hand, that the poor be identified, enumerated, and systematically studied.

During the Second Development Decade, the 1970s, development discourse attended less to industrialization and more to agriculture, the sector where a majority of the poor continued to be employed. Development donors used the terms "bottom-up," "community-based," "grassroots," and "participatory," to signal their intentions to incorporate more input and feedback from the poor. These approaches resonate with several key Enlightenment values, including individualism and equity. These approaches were—and are—extremely difficult for large international organizations to operationalize, which makes all the more remarkable the development field's determination to invoke these terms more frequently over time.

The International Labor Organization (ILO) introduced its definition of Basic Human Needs (BHN) in 1974, placing minimum requirements for shelter, food, drinking water, sanitation, health services, and education within the broad framework of fulfilling basic human rights. Subsequently in the 1970s, in an effort to create an indicator of development encompassing more than economic growth, the Overseas Development Council proposed an alternative to GNP per capita. The Physical Quality of Life Indicator (PQLI) (Morris, 1979) was a composite index of life expectancy, infant mortality rate, and literacy rate. The new measure was not widely adopted, but was a precursor to the creation of the more popular Human Development Index (HDI) in the 1990s, which incorporated life expectancy, educational attainment, and income adjusted for purchasing power in different countries.

Alternative measures of development, such as the PQLI and the HDI, attempted to measure quality of life and helped to raise the status of health and social welfare activities in which women traditionally played a more central role: family planning, nutrition, child welfare. The new focus on women was reinforced by the rapid growth of the women's movement in the United States and other industrialized countries and increasing interest on the part of this movement in the fate of women in less industrialized countries. The UN's International Development Strategy for the Second Development Decade included a specific reference to the "women's component." Beginning with the First UN Decade for Women (1976–85), the statements of international organizations expressed a clear causal link between development and women's rights. By the end of the decade, development projects routinely gathered, or requested local officials to produce, statistics disaggregated by gender. These data were needed to differentiate the impact of development activities on men's and women's output and benefits, thus making gender inequities easier to identify.

Finally, during this same decade, children were identified as a category of persons especially vulnerable to poverty. Poor prenatal and postnatal care contributed to high infant mortality and child morbidity rates, not to mention weakened or stunted adults. Children's rights to development began to be articulated separate from those of their families (if not those of their mothers), and were central to the mission of the international development community. In recognition of this, the UN General Assembly appointed the United Nation's Children's Fund (UNICEF) the lead UN organization for promoting basic services mandated by the BHN approach.

Also in the 1970s, as concern was growing about inequality and more vulnerable groups within countries, a coalition of less industrialized countries began to focus on *international* inequality among countries and the structures that reproduced this. Proposals for a New International Economic Order (NIEO) proliferated in UN forums. By the early 1970s, the UN Annual Report devoted at least half of the Economic and Social Council's section to development. In contrast with BHN, which appealed to the humanitarian instincts of former colonial powers and other industrialized countries, the NIEO represented a demand for political and economic justice and, in effect, for reparations for colonialism and neocolonialism from the industrialized countries.

Although both the poverty reduction and NIEO discourses emphasized radically different issues and remedies, the discourses share several assumptions of interest to world society scholars. First, the autonomy and sovereignty of nation-states although not entirely revoked, were further constrained. Both BHN and NIEO approaches argue that outside intervention is in many instances necessary for development. Second, these approaches buttressed less industrialized countries' demands for preferential trade relationships, a fundamental reordering of trade relationships, and minimum levels of aid from industrialized countries. However, BHN also legitimized demands for increased accountability for less industrialized countries, placing the burden of proof on less industrialized countries to demonstrate that

BHN projects were both targeted at and reaching the poor in order to secure continued funding.

Throughout the 1970s, development discourse continued to accrete. Earlier ideas were not entirely abandoned; instead, new and sometimes not entirely consistent ideas were added to them. For example, since the 1960s, national development had been talked about as something that governments in less industrialized countries needed to promote through careful economic planning. But in the 1970s, without entirely abandoning the comprehensive planning concept, the discourse acknowledged the important role of factors beyond the control of individual states, factors that could not be controlled through national planning. Although the term modernization receded from the center to the margins of development discourse, it did not disappear. The central new caveat of the 1970s was the emphasis on poverty reduction and the insistence that development efforts must not exacerbate existing inequalities among nation-states or groups within nation-states. National governments came under increasing scrutiny as identifying and monitoring the effects of development projects on the poor became a major preoccupation for many international development organizations.

The 1980s

In the 1980s, the debt crisis and the introduction of World Bank and IMF structural adjustment programs in heavily indebted, less industrialized countries reinforced the interdependence of national and international financial markets. Many structural adjustment programs required governments in less industrialized countries to dismantle the bureaucracies that had grown, at least in part, to handle the demands of integrated development, basic human needs, and other earlier government-sponsored development approaches. As part of structural adjustment programs, less industrialized countries were required to let the value of their currencies fall and to cut the size of the government workforce, simultaneously triggering substantial inflation and unemployment, respectively.

At the same time, recessions in industrialized countries resulted in demands for greater efficiency and effectiveness in all government-funded programs and prompted decreases in funding for development in less industrialized countries. A resurgence in faith in market forces and skepticism about the efficiency of government as a provider of social services or as a monitor of markets led donors to emphasize local financing for development and nongovernmental organizations (NGOs) as social service delivery agents.

Surveying both the expected and actual effects of these changes in development approaches, some long-term development professionals labeled the Third Development Decade the lost decade for development (Grant, 1988). Nonetheless, the World Bank and other donors continued to talk about poverty reduction and by the end of the decade were tying Social Dimensions of Adjustment projects (SDAs) to their structural adjustment programs.

SDAs were supposed to improve the recipient government's ability to monitor the effects of large-scale adjustment program on the poor through Living Standards Measurement Surveys (LSMSs) and to promote grassroots NGO programs to mitigate negative effects. Women and children continued to be considered the most vulnerable and needy groups, but increased attention was also directed to historically disadvantaged minorities. Though many of these groups were engaged in marginal economic activities, international development discourse soon included rationales justifying how improved health and education would increase their productivity, lower their fertility, and improve their quality of life. In 1987, a special internal task force constituted by the World Bank produced an action plan that combined growth policies and poverty reduction efforts and proposed to "eliminate poverty in the world by the year 2000" (Salda, 1997, p. 149).

That same year the World Commission on Environment and Development issued a report, *Our Common Future*, calling for a new type of development that "meets the needs of the present generation without compromising the needs of future generations." The head of the commission, Norwegian Prime Minister Gro Harlem Brundtland, warned,

> After a century of unprecedented growth, marked by scientific and technological triumphs that would have been unthinkable a century ago, there have never been so many poor, illiterate, and unemployed people in the world, and their number is growing. . . . This situation is a feeding ground for conflict and violence. . . . In the twenty-first century, violence emanating from such sources may be a more serious challenge to our sense of security than the more traditional threat of war between nations. (p. 13)

In the 1990s, the sustainable development approach grew out of the Brundtland Report and promised to address two of the most successful crises highlighted in earlier development discourse—population and environment. Appeals to reduce poverty and inequity were also added in. Both the population and the environment crises—the survival of the planet—appeal to self-interest in the more industrialized countries. Both are associated with clear courses of action that resonate at both policy and grassroots levels, capturing the attention of ecologically-oriented Green movements throughout the industrialized world. At the same time, the discourse promoting sustainable development does not release either nation-states or international development organizations from any of their previous mandates.

Conclusions about Development Discourse

By the mid-1990s, all nation-states were responsible for

- efficient management of domestic resources;
- generating and implementing coherent, multiyear development plans covering all sectors of the economy;

- producing steady improvements in individual welfare;
- monitoring development efforts to ensure that earlier inequities were not exacerbated; and
- securing the necessary outside resources and state-of-the-art development theories from the rest of the world.

By 1993, the World Bank President Lewis Preston claimed that "sustainable poverty reduction is the World Bank's fundamental objective" (World Bank, 1993). By this point in the middle of the Fourth Development Decade, the discourse suggests all nations in the world are responsible for reducing poverty globally over time and they are also responsible for minimizing both the global and local impacts of environmental degradation and population growth.

This list of responsibilities—built up over time, rational, consistent with the world cultural values described in Chapter 1—is patently impossible to implement within the limits of resources historically available to many less industrialized countries and international development organizations. As a result, both nation-states and international organizations pick and choose which mandates they will respect, where, and when. There is therefore much loose coupling between, on the one hand, international and national development policies and, on the other hand, what occurs on a daily basis in organizations attempting to implement those policies at the national and local level in less industrialized countries.

Although these approaches and themes have dominated development discourse since World War II, they have not gone uncontested. The dependency critique first introduced by Latin American economist Raul Prebisch in the 1950s and 1960s has already been mentioned above. Along similar lines, Escobar (1995) and Sachs (1991) critique the Euro- and econo-centric power and knowledge structures that created what they characterize as the neoliberal, hegemonic discourse. Deeply embedded in this critique is skepticism about the scientific knowledge claims put forth by international development organizations and professionals, though not necessarily with science and technology themselves. Likewise, anthropologists such as Ferguson (1990) and Hill (1986) play up the inadequacy of universal knowledge claims in light of the particularistic nature of economic relations in less industrialized communities.

While much of what these writers have to say is important, two particular points are relevant here. First, most of these writers consider as unacceptable the treatment of less industrialized countries as less than entirely autonomous, sovereign nation-states, regardless of their resource base, their administrative capacity, and the logic—or lack of logic—behind their current borders. Second, many of these writers perceive as detrimental to the interests of the poor majority in less industrialized countries the existence of an international development industry, with its agenda tied to elites in both more and less industrialized countries, somewhat independent of any nation-state. While there is merit in each of these critiques, what is of most interest here is the extent to which they confirm the existence of strongly held world cultural standards. These standards insist upon the de jure equality of nation-states and the elevation of the individual—even if poor and not terribly productive in modern economic terms—to the status of most important subject for development.

In summary, this review of the international development discourse highlights three trends over time. First, development becomes something that every less industrialized nation-state must promote and that, in the absence of domestic means, more industrialized nations must fund. Development becomes a global phenomenon, not simply because it is an activity in which all nation-states are involved, but also one for which world society is responsible. The French, for example, are not simply responsible for the French, nor even just for their former colonies, but for South Africa and Bolivia and every other country that manifests shortfalls in Basic Human Needs.

Second, the level at which development is measured has shifted over time from the national to the individual level, from growth in national economic output to improvements in the welfare of individuals. Development is increasingly judged in terms of its ability to deliver a better quality of life to the poor majority, to deliver a "continuous improvement of living conditions" to everyone. Over time, the legitimacy of individual nation-states depends, in part, on their effectiveness in promoting this globally established vision of national development—a vision which does not necessarily correspond to local conditions or resources. Finally, there is an increasing concern for broadening participation in development beyond just those who have somehow found their way into the modern sector. This broadening participation is difficult to imagine without increasing access to education.

Educational Development Discourse and Activities

This section highlights similarities over time among the development discourse just described, discourse about education in less industrialized countries, and the educational activities those discourses encourage. The work of the United Nations Education, Scientific, and Cultural Organization (UNESCO) figures prominently in this discussion, since UNESCO was de jure the lead UN organization in educational development activities throughout the postwar period. Other better-funded UN organizations, such as UNICEF and the World Bank[7], were required to seek UNESCO participation in all of the education components of their activities. As education grew to be

---

7. A formal agreement in 1947 established the World Bank as a specialized agency of the United Nations and an independent international organization.

a more important part of their portfolios in the late 1980s and throughout the 1990s, both UNICEF and the World Bank achieved some independence from UNESCO. Non-UN organizations also had education strategies, but less influence on the global discourse, for reasons discussed in the Chapter 6.

Notions of educational development arise in an organizational environment already filled with discourse about development, making some education approaches seem more rational than others do. In addition, educational development concepts incorporate an amalgam of ideas drawn from the study of international and comparative education. In borrowing from these two sources, what persists and what perishes over time appear to coincide with the world cultural concepts described in Chapter 1. For example, vocational training and adult literacy classes seem logical responses to the lack of skilled labor and the persistence of illiteracy in many countries. Nonetheless, time and time again adult training and education, however excellent their intrinsic merits, are pushed off the educational development agenda in favor of administratively more complex and sometimes more costly compulsory primary education programs. In part this is because primary education represents a more egalitarian, universal approach to education than the highly differentiated technical training and literacy programs that often do not allow for access to higher education.

Because these norms change over time in the way education and development are talked about do not necessarily reflect empirical advances in our understanding of the relationship between the two. In the absence of empirical evidence, much confidence about education—as in many other fields— is the result of repeating seemingly logical rationales in many different settings simultaneously. Eventually these become conventional wisdom or standards and thereafter taken for granted, that is, socially constructed institutions. Similarly, educational activities do not necessarily rise and fall on their own merits, rather they may be prematurely bolstered or undercut by broad frameworks embedded in Western culture or by historical contingencies.

The roots of international comparitive education lie in the industrializing world of the nineteenth century, when individual nations looked abroad for ways to improve their national education systems by imitation. During the same period, a few educators also saw in international education a way to promote international peace and understanding. These moral educationists perceived schools as powerful socializing institutions, able to tame aggression and nurture peaceful, productive citizens. They warned that uneducated children grow into socially inept adults, unable to make their way in the world, deprived, alienated, and therefore potentially dangerous.

By the time the UN was established in 1945, there was widespread support for an organization that would promote science, universal education, cultural understanding, and intellectual cooperation. The Allies were particularly eager to reconstruct and remove the more nationalistic components of the education systems of the former Axis countries (Jones, 1990). An emphasis on psychology and international peace carried over into the philosophy of UNESCO, whose first director, Julian Huxley, popularized the notion that "war is made in the minds of men."[8] As in the development discourse, in the interest of spurring the more industrialized countries to open their treasuries, the education discourse is not above making drastic predictions about the dangerous effects of neglecting education in less industrialized countries.

The third column of Table 3.1 summarizes the main themes in the educational development discourse in the post–World War II era by decade, with the recommended education activities associated with that discourse shown in column four. To the extent possible, the educational development discourse in column three is also lined up with the development discourse in column two to which it is most closely related.

The 1950s

In many less industrialized countries, independence brought the release of an enormous pent-up demand for formal schooling. Formal schooling and entrance into the colonial service had been an important means of upward mobility during the colonial period; now citizens demanded that their new governments facilitate upward mobility for all through universal primary education (UPE). Newly independent countries had many reasons to oblige this demand. In some countries, such as Kenya and Zambia, the leadership of the independence movement included many former schoolteachers who were strongly committed to education. Many countries, lacking literate, native-born candidates, staffed their new governments with Europeans, many of whom were former colonial officers. Not surprisingly, Myrdal (1970) reports,

> The Indian Constitution of 1950 bravely stipulated that within 10 years' time compulsory education should be the rule for children up to 14 years of age; in 1951 the Indonesian government set as its goal universal elementary schooling by 1961. (p. 182)

In the 1950s, several prominent development economists, such as W. Arthur Lewis and Frederick Harbison, had strong opinions about the role of education in economic growth. These ideas were often featured at regional UNESCO conferences (see Chapter 6). In 1961, Lewis, recently returned from three years in Ghana as an economic advisor, warned a conference of African ministers of education:

8. The source of this famous epigram is unknown, but most sources agree it was not Huxley.

Many of the newer governments [including Ghana] had given absolute priority to primary education . . . [but] those who make primary education their first priority are asking for trouble, and get it. Their budgets are strained by teachers' salaries, their towns are disordered by the influx of primary school graduates seeking clerical jobs, and their lives are harassed by irate parents demanding secondary, university and other superior training facilities to which similar priority has not been accorded. (as cited in Bartels, 1983, pp. 6–7)

However pragmatic, such arguments, though raised repeatedly over the following 40 years, did not prevail. Reproducing the slower educational growth patterns of nineteenth century Europe was not an option. After the framing of the Universal Declaration of Human Rights in 1948, anything less than immediate universal formal schooling was not politically palatable at the national level, nor, at times, at the international level.

As comprehensive economic planning became the watchword in the 1950s, UNESCO and its advisors urged newly independent countries to focus their education efforts on developing needed skilled labor identified in manpower development plans. Manpower planning used various forecasting techniques to generate estimates of numbers and types of critical "technical skills" theoretically needed to ensure economic growth, as well as the types of training such workers needed. These estimates were then used to generate projections of the size and type of training facilities needed in various countries. Not all countries had the national statistics necessary to generate projections; yet national plans provided a veneer of rationality to what might otherwise appear to be ad hoc decision-making in young ministries of industry and education.

To meet the continued popular demand for schooling for children in the 1950s, UNESCO and other international organizations advised newly independent countries to undertake community-based, "fundamental" education programs, focusing on literacy and numeracy and practical skills for rural life and agricultural occupations. Margaret Mead, as part of a task force assembled by UNESCO to help it define its mission, wrote:

The task of Fundamental Education is to cover the whole of living. In addition, it is to teach, not only new ways, but the need and the incentive for new ways . . . if the new education is to fill the place of the old, it has to cover all areas of living . . . . In many countries new fundamental education is carried on by teams including social workers, graduate nurses, agricultural assistants, home economists, hygiene experts. (as cited in Jones, 1988)

Jones (1988) explains that in the late 1940s and early 1950s, UNESCO, with its fundamental education programs so central to rural development and its mandate so broad compared to other existing UN organization, attempted to become the UN's lead organization in socioeconomic development. As described in Chapter 4, this role for UNESCO did not materialize, but its aspirations are an indication of the pride of place given to education within the development strategies of the time.

Fundamental education was not such a radically new concept, rather it derived from the only primary educational development strategy available at UNESCO's founding conference: the British Colonial Office's 1944 report, *Mass Education in Africa* (Jones, 1988). The British Colonial Office had earlier developed its education programs based on advice from the Phelps-Stokes Fund, an organization that specialized in promoting education for "Africans," both in Africa and the United States, in the form of agriculturally/vocationally-oriented, nonacademic school systems similar to the Tuskegee-Hampton model. While Phelps-Stokes claimed this nonacademic approach to education was adapted to the special needs and situations of Africans, later generations would judge it an inferior education and a tactic for pacifying Africans and African-Americans while depriving them of access to higher education (Bude, 1983). Similarly, however "appropriate" the UNESCO's community-based fundamental education might appear, it was not widely adopted since it neither looked like formal schools of the colonial era nor provided access to higher levels of formal schooling.

As Cold War rationales seeped into educational development discourse, manpower planning also provided a relatively uncontentious domain in which several UN organizations could expand or redirect their education work. A researcher at ILO—an organization that funded vocationally and technically oriented training—wrote of this period:

> Trade unions became highly politicized in the Cold War, their international policies polarized on the issue of anti-Communism. The emphasis by the ILO Director General on manpower put to the fore a technical matter which . . . was able to maintain trade-union support as being useful and noncontroversial. The program also found favor with ILO Employer delegates and some governments not only for its own merits but because it represented a shift away from ILO's traditional work of drawing up legal standards of labor legislation. . . . Manpower activities thus, for ILO, represented an important area of consensus in an environment bedeviled with ideological and political conflict and a significant expansion of ILO's tasks. This development has been so important that it would be difficult to imagine ILO today sustaining sufficient support for the residue of its programs (none of which have such broad appeal as the manpower program) and maintaining its place in the world if its manpower activities were to cease. (Cox, 1968)

The 1960s

In the late 1950s and early 1960s, as the focus of development discourse shifted from industrialization to agriculture and then to balanced economic growth, discourse about education also shifted to "human capital" and its contribution to growth. Schultz (1961) argued that rather than simply a means of individual mobility, a consumption good, education should be considered an investment that, relative to other investments such as capital equipment or infrastructure, could yield high returns to both individuals and the national economy. Like the development economists around him, Schultz used time series data from the industrialized world to demonstrate that historic trends in economic growth in industrialized countries could not be accounted for entirely in terms of material inputs. He attributed the residual growth in productivity to human factors, or "human capital." The human capital concept provided justification for broad support for all sorts of education, though throughout most of the 1960s, human resource planning, the successor to manpower planning, continued to privilege secondary and higher education as the appropriate levels for international development aid.

Mass education and formal primary school languished somewhat during the 1960s, although UNESCO regional conferences for ministers of education set 1970 as the target for UPE. Echoing Rostow's *Stages of Economic Growth* (1960), prominent international education scholar C. E. Beeby published "Stages in the Growth of a Primary Education System" (1962). Meanwhile UNESCO shifted its mass education emphasis to "functional literacy" or pilot literacy projects intended to make a direct contribution to worker productivity.[9]

By 1968, in synchronization with the larger development field, the education sector was discovered to be in crisis. A systems analysis by Phillip Coombs (1968) highlighted the large gap between widely adopted education goals, such as UPE by 1970, and the financing necessary to meet such a goal. Coombs highlighted the importance of "nonformal education"—adult education, community-based schools, on-the-job training—to help close the gap between the demands for formal education and the resources available. With respect to training farmers and rural leaders, he notes:

> The problem . . . is less one of knowing what is needed than of achieving the proper organization and staff for getting it done. . . . The lack of economic resources is often far less of an obstacle than the tangled maze of conflicting jurisdictions and uncoordinated efforts by numerous agencies having a hand in agriculture and rural affairs. . . . One gets the distinct impression from very sparse available evidence that in most developing countries, too small a share of total educational resources has been allocated to nonformal education. (p. 144)

Myrdal (1970), drawing conclusions from his three-volume opus on development in South Asia, comes to quite a different conclusion:

---

9. This does not imply a unique concern with adult education. Typical of reports of this period is "Preparation of the Child for Modernization: Skills and Intellectual Requirements" (Geneva: United Nations Research Institute for Social Development, 1969).

> Education statistics are probably even less satisfactory than statistics in almost every other field pertinent to underdevelopment and development.... Literacy figures for underdeveloped countries generally overestimate the actual spread of literacy.... The main reforms needed in education in all underdeveloped countries are of a qualitative nature. (pp. 164, 165, 169)

Coombs and Myrdal predictably differed on the appropriate response to this crisis. Coombs estimated 60 to 70 percent of all the external aid to education was accounted for by personnel, "mostly teachers, educational experts, and advisers sent to assist less industrialized countries. In 1965, over 35,000 technical assistance teachers and another 8,000 volunteer teachers were serving in less developed countries" (pp. 150–151). To Coombs, this suggests a much greater need for external aid to train local educators and education planners. Myrdal, on the other hand, asserts:

> In the educational field there is, therefore, no real counterpart to the technology of birth control which researchers in the developed countries could experiment with and then offer to the underdeveloped countries for immediate action.... Education experts from the West are, more often than in other fields, misfits in these [underdeveloped] countries . . . foreign aid can be of only marginal importance. Of overwhelming importance is what the underdeveloped countries themselves decide to do, and succeed in accomplishing in regard to educational reforms. (p. 207)

Among these reforms Myrdal includes more attention to universal adult literacy, more funding for elementary schools and vocational training, less funding for academic secondary and higher education, more equitable access to education, and fundamental curriculum reform. Note the importance that Myrdal attaches to the lack of a modern, easily transferable, universally applicable technology that the industrialized countries might provide to the less industrialized. Without such a transformative, transferable technology, Myrdal questions whether there is actually much that international development aid can do for education in less-industrialized countries. Such an approach places him outside the mainstream of positivist educational development discourse.

The 1970s

About the same time dependency theorists were taking the broader development field to task for fostering underdevelopment, promoting dependency, and spreading neocolonial ideas, critical theorists began to highlight the ill effects of promoting Western models of schooling in less industrialized areas. Ivan Illich's *Deschooling Society* (1970), Martin Carnoy's *Education as Cultural Imperialism* (1974), Ronald Dore's *Diploma Disease* (1976), all focused on the debilitating effects of expanding access to education without reforming the curriculum and structure of the colonial schooling system to reflect the class structure, culture, and goals of the newly independent countries. At the same time, the broader development community was beginning to fixate on "the poor" as an object of development. Paolo Freire's (1972) theories of "conscientization" argued that liberating the poor would involve more radical change than their children's simply gaining access to existing primary schools. Freire suggested those changes might begin by the poor developing their own concepts about their problems and solutions, and in the process developing their own literacy materials. All of these writers would be much invoked throughout the following decades, but no large-scale educational development projects based on their ideas would be supported by international development organizations. The structure of the larger development organizations, as described in the next chapter, precluded such a radical reorganization.

When the UN shifted to a Basic Human Needs approach in 1976, education gained the status of a "basic human need." Early definitions of "basic education" focused on numbers of years of primary school or on a set of skills, such as literacy. (Allen & Anzalone, 1981). The term "basic education," however, fell out of favor in some development circles as many of the nonformal and other nonacademic forms of education were judged second rate. Some educators accused donors of using the term "basic education" to justify providing the masses with a minimalist education with no possibility of moving on to higher education. A differentiated core education—practical for the poor and academic for the rich—was anathema in a world where formal equality of persons needed to be reflected in education systems.

The 1980s and 1990s

The debt crisis and austerity measures introduced by structural adjustment programs in the 1980s renewed interest in more efficiently managing resources, including the education system. The World Bank began urging countries to decentralize in order to reduce the size of the workforce in central ministries of education, and to encourage local communities to find local financing for their schools. At the same time, education ministries improved their statistical offices in order to be able to demonstrate the reach of the national school system and to be ready to measure improvements in the wake of various reforms.

The introduction of the Human Development Index (HDI) in the early 1990s renewed interest in "human resources development," giving a boost to human resource planning. Emphasis on "participation" led to greater efforts to measure exclusion and to incorporate more children into formal schooling, particularly girls and ethnic minorities. With endogenous education, UNESCO made one more effort to help countries develop curriculum and education structures "appropriate" to their particular needs and independent of international standards. However, resistance prevailed to anything that deviated from the world cultural norm of a formal education system: graded classes; certified teachers; formal classrooms with desks, chairs and black-boards; state-approved textbooks; standardized curricula; and formal assessments of achievement.

In the late 1980s and early 1990s, ongoing concerns with women's rights and the importance of their role in family planning and in the acceptance of modern contraceptives led to increased interest in the gap between female and male literacy and primary enrollment rates. The emphasis on curtailing population growth in the new sustainable development approach led to increased investments in both primary and secondary education for girls: the first for literacy and the second to delay teenage marriages, in an attempt to reduce the number of childbearing years.

Conclusions: Educational Development Discourse

The educational development discourse described above closely follows the logic and emphases of the international development discourse since the end of World War II. Like development, education was included as a human right in the 1948 Universal Declaration of Human Rights and the 1966 Covenant on Social, Cultural, and Economic Rights, yet access to education is still not universal.

In the 1950s, government investments in education were targeted to develop skilled manpower sufficient to fuel the drive to industrialization and modernization. In the 1960s, investing in human capital was to produce dramatic increases in labor productivity and national economic growth. In the 1970s, education was to increase individuals' abilities to contribute to growth in the agricultural or industrial sector and to ensure their ability to meet minimum standards of living. In the 1980s, education was key to incorporating more of the historically disadvantaged and women—as the primary care-givers for children and as household income contributors—into the benefits of development. Throughout this time, the status of education as a human right came increasingly to the forefront of its justification. By the 1990s, that right had become institutionalized, even as the number of illiterate adults and children with no access to primary school totaled more than one billion. (World Conference on Education for All Inter-Agency Commission, 1990a).

Over time, the potential contribution of education to development may have been exaggerated in part as a result of efforts to assure everyone a right to education. By 1981, Allen and Anzalone (1981) reported that, though this exaggeration rarely succeeded as a call to action, it nonetheless

> . . . has led many people to equate the ability to read and write with the ability to think, and it has led others to believe that literacy is absolutely necessary for the "functioning" of society. . . . It requires the conclusion that the

majority of the people in developing countries cannot think and are socially
dysfunctional, and that the historical achievements of the centuries before
Gutenberg were not even possible. (p. 223)

Given that literacy has preceded its perceived economic and political
"need"—in terms of employment in the modern sector, of access to newspa-
pers and books, and of minimal opportunities to participate in democratic
governance—Bray (1986) has asked, "If universal primary education is the
answer, what is the question?" Many nation-states are indeed faced with the
situation described earlier by W. Arthur Lewis: "their budgets are strained by
teachers' salaries, their towns disordered by the influx of primary school
graduates seeking clerical jobs, and their lives are harassed by irate parents
demanding secondary [and higher] education." Yet in light of current development discourse, no country can do less than redouble its efforts to provide
universal primary education. And the bar to accomplishing this continues to
be raised. First, it was adequate to reach those in urban areas with formal
schooling, then nothing less than formal schooling would do for rural areas
as well, then girls had to be included, then minorities, then other historically
disadvantaged groups. Second, population growth indeed created a crisis in
education systems facing exponentially increasing cohorts of students

None of the education approaches described above (fundamental education, functional education, and basic education) was ever implemented on a
large scale and therefore the postulated contribution of education to development was never conclusively proved or disproved. However, these theories
about the relationship between education and development were asserted and
reiterated at hundreds of international conferences in the post-war period,
many of them aimed particularly at officials in less industrialized countries
and in international development organizations. By the 1990s, however, other
world conferences were still focussing their bid for legitimacy on their link to
development—for example, the Population and Development Conference
(Cairo, 1994) and the Environment and Development Conference (Rio de
Janeiro, 1992). But the world conference on education was titled not Education for Development, but rather Education for All.

The 1990 World Declaration on Education for All

The World Declaration on Education for All was first drafted in 1988 and as
such incorporates many concepts from both the international development
discourse and the educational development discourse introduced above. Its
preamble begins with reference to the Universal Declaration of Human
Rights: "Recalling that education is a fundamental right for all people,
women and men, of all ages, throughout our world . . ." (p. 2). In keeping
with the spirit of the discourse of the 1980s, the declaration immediately

mentions the millions who are presently neglected by existing education systems, particularly women and girls. The declaration then identifies the obstacles to broadening access to education, reflecting the development discourse of the day. These obstacles include national debt burdens, rapid population growth, widening economic disparities among and between nations, preventable deaths of children, and widespread environmental degradation. The subtitle of the declaration, "Meeting Basic Learning Needs," puts the emphasis on basic needs and on learning rather than on basic education or schooling. Basic learning needs are defined as those

> . . . required by human beings to be able to survive, to develop their full capacities, to live and work in dignity, to participate fully in development, to improve the quality of their lives, to make informed decisions, and to continue learning (p. 3).

The Declaration of Education for All and the Framework for Action for Education for All, direct products of the 1990 WCEFA, are relatively modest in asserting education's potential connection to development:

> . . . education can *help* ensure a safer, healthier, more prosperous world, while simultaneously *contributing to* social, economic, and cultural progress, tolerance, and international cooperation. . . .

Nonetheless,

> . . . sound basic education is fundamental to the strengthening of higher levels of education and of scientific and technological literacy and capacity and thus to self-reliant development. . . . (World Declaration on Education for All, Preamble).

The declaration puts forward a variety of means to meet basic learning needs for everyone:

> To serve the basic learning needs of all requires more than a recommitment to basic education as it now exists. What is needed is an "expanded vision" that surpasses present resource levels, institutional structures, curricula, and conventional delivery systems while building on the best in current practices . . . the expanded vision encompasses:
> - universalizing access and promoting equity;
> - focusing on learning;
> - broadening the means and scope of basic education;
> - enhancing the environment for learning; and
> - strengthening partnerships.

Under the heading of universalizing access, consistent with development discourse in the late 1980s, the declaration identifies girls and women as the most urgent priority, with the underserved and disabled close behind. Anticipating the temptation some schools will face to meet targets by simply increasing enrollments, the declaration endorses "active and participatory approaches" to learning. Broadening the means and scope of basic education calls for primary education as the main delivery system for children, but also includes a call for early childhood education and a variety of delivery systems for youth and adults. The declaration calls attention to the social environment for learning and, finally, emphasizes the importance of "partnerships" between different government ministries, the public and private sector, government and NGOs, and religious groups. According to the declaration, all of this requires developing more supportive policies at the national level; mobilizing resources at the local, national, and international levels; and strengthening international solidarity.

Echoing general international development discourse in the late 1980s, this declaration emphasizes the importance of incorporating all individuals, particularly those traditionally left out, such as females and minorities. Although direct, "whole class" teaching has been historically and continues to be the most common pedagogical approach in most countries, the declaration specifically recommends more individually oriented, progressive "active and participatory approaches." While endorsing customized delivery systems for young children, adults, and youth in each country, the declaration endorses formal primary education as the main delivery system for children. Creating custom delivery systems requires time, so already existing primary education systems provided the most immediate site for international donors to quickly increase their funding to basic education, contributing to what later would be seen as a bias towards primary education in the EFA initiative. The importance of "partnerships" hearkens back to the 1968 *Partners in Development* report, and highlights nongovernmental approaches. In addition, the conference issued "A Statement of Principles on the Involvement of NGOs in WCEFA Follow-up Activities with Non-NGO Bodies," declaring,

1. NGOs shall be part of all formal structures for the implementation of EFA at all levels: local, national, regional, and international . . .
. . .
7. Subsequent major international meetings and conferences relative to the Education for All movement shall include NGOs as full delegates . . .

The generality of most of the recommendations in the Declaration on Education for All is striking. The three concluding articles, dealing with the requirements necessary for bringing about EFA, contain few words specific to education, such as "school" or "literacy." Almost all of these requirements deal with factors outside the school, the community, and, for the less industrialized countries, the nation-state; the emphasis in these articles is on external, international factors. The word "health" might be substituted for most instances of the word "education" in these last three articles. In fact there is very little in this list that is particular to education; it is another "sector" of development that can be addressed with a similar framework for action, and with additional international development aid. The last article in the declaration specifically foresees a major role in EFA for "substantial, long-term increases" in unselfinterested international aid, with priority given to least-developed and low-income countries.

UNICEF executive Director James Grant pushed aggressively for targets, arguing that it would be impossible to raise the funds needed to make the sort of progress described in the declaration without such targets, preferably associated with measurable interventions, with specific price-tags attached to each. The drafting committee, however, staunchly resisted, insisting that differences between countries required each to tailor its own targets to its own national strategy. As a result the 1990 declaration contained no targets and the 1990 Framework for Action gently suggests, "Countries may wish to set their own targets for the 1990s in terms of the following proposed dimensions. . . ." The dimensions included expanding early childhood care (no suggested target), achieving UPE by 2000, reducing adult illiteracy by half by 2000, among others.

At the World Education Forum in Dakar in 2000, the approach to targets changed dramatically. The results of 10 years of EFA were "uneven and far too slow" (United Nations Educational, Scientific and Cultural Organization, 2000):

	1990[10]	2000 (predicted)	2000 (actual)
Children out of primary school	100m	160m	113m
Adult illiterates	960m	NA	880m

Although the absolute number of children out of primary school increased between 1990 and 2000, the increase is much less than was predicted without EFA and less than half what might have been expected given the population growth rate in the 1990s. The number of adult illiterates did not decrease by 50 percent between 1990 and 2000, as suggested by the 1990 framework but the number did decrease, again, despite a positive population growth rate throughout the 1990s. The World Education Forum says that children out of school and adult illiterates

. . . represent an affront to human dignity and denial of the right to education. They stand as major barriers to eliminating poverty and attaining sus-

10. Source: 1990 actual, 1990 *World Declaration of Education for All*; 2000 predicted, 1990 *Framework for Action*; and 2000 actual, 2000 Dakar *Framework for Action*.

tainable development, and are clearly unacceptable. (United Nations Educational, Scientific and Cultural Organization, 2000, para 6)

In a global synthesis report sponsored by the EFA Forum (Skilbeck, 2000), the author acknowledges some progress in the 1990s, but the word "failure" appears repeatedly in the text. The report concludes:

> The Jomtien movement cannot be judged a failure simply because targets have not been achieved although that must be of great concern when little or no progress has been made. Worse, there have been serious losses. What is important, however, is to reach a conclusion about whether the effort has been worthwhile. . . . [Indeed] the effort has been worthwhile, indeed necessary, and . . . the mission of EFA must again be taken up, with strengthened resolve and renewed energy. Too much is at stake for anything else. (p. 81)

In its emphasis on the need to go on in spite of much "failure," this report on the first decade of EFA efforts is similar to the dozen or so reports chronicling the "failure" of the First Development Decade. As in those reports, this failure is not interpreted to mean that the international community should give up trying to promote educational development, or completely reassess its approach, but rather that it should redouble its efforts. For example, in the face of failing to meet even the country-specific, flexible targets of the 1990 framework, the 2000 Dakar framework establishes concrete international targets. These targets include achieving UPE by 2015, reducing adult illiteracy by half by 2015, eliminating gender disparity in primary and secondary education by 2005, and achieving gender equality in education by 2015. This new framework does not allow for failure, only for adjusting how long it will take to achieve education for all.

Conclusion

By the last decade of the twentieth century, the discourse around development had transformed the idea of development into a national imperative, and had legitimated claims for transfers of resources for international development from more to less industrialized countries. The recommended approaches to development varied over time but they increasingly privileged individual welfare over national growth as the more appropriate measure of development. Improvements in individual welfare, so consistent with world culture and so linked to new human capital theories, were much more difficult to measure than indicators of national industrial output, and numerical measures of progress were dragged downward over time by an ever increasing denominator: population growth. Trends in educational development discourse tended to lag slightly behind trends in international development discourse. The amount of international development discourse escalated in the 1960s and early 1970s, reaching its highest levels in the 1970s, with the Basic Human Needs (BHN) and New International Economic Order (NIEO) discourse. With the failure in the early 1970s to muster either the resources necessary to fully implement an integrated BHN approach or the political support to keep NIEO on the global agenda, the development discourse changed gears and began expressing itself in more disaggregated, sector by sector terms: agriculture, health, education, environment. Sectoral strategies circumvented the more complex NIEO issues raised in general discussions of development by associating development with particular areas of scientific expertise. Moreover, in several sectors—such as health and agriculture—with better-established scientific bases and broader stockpiles of technical innovations and improvements in delivery systems, progress was indeed tangible. The discourse also focused on special disadvantaged groups—such as children, women, and minorities—whom no development organization wanted to be accused of depriving.

In one sense, this is not a story about progress, in the terms defined in Chapter 1. Discourse in education changes over time, but the fluid nature of education, the lack of robust statistics in less industrialized countries and the difficulties in identifying reasonably comparable countries, from which trends can be projected or generalizations drawn, all complicate efforts to measure success. The relationship between education and economic development and the efficacy of education activities in less industrialized countries remain in dispute among scholars (Chabbott & Ramirez, 2000). But, at a policy level, this relationship remains indisputable. The idea that a country might develop without educating its citizens is a non sequitor; the notion of education for development is thoroughly institutionalized.

On the other hand, the conclusion that international development as an endeavor is a failure may be premature. At the end of the 1960s, as reports documenting the failutre of international development multiplied, one of the founders of development economics, Albert Hirschman (1968) suggested that three factors contributed to the tendency for international development experts to suffer from "fracaso-mania" or "failure-mania," or the tendency to declare failure too soon. First, he pointed out that most development planners, lacking any objective basis for determining a reasonable rate of growth, had chosen overly optimistic targets for the First Development Decade. Second, he claimed it was in the interest of many less industrialized countries to hide their development successes in order to ensure a continuing flow of external funding. Third, Hirschman suggested that perceiving change in less industrialized countries is difficult because development in dependent countries is not likely to look like development in dominant countries nor will it follow the path predicted by various ideologies.

Hirschman chides international development theorists for institutionalizing a model of the development process divorced from history and from the particularity of nation-states in distinct eras.

At an earlier time, contempt for the countries designated as "rude and bar-
barous" in the eighteenth century, as "backward" in the nineteenth century,
and as underdeveloped in the twentieth had taken the form of relegating
them to permanent lowly status . . . the underdeveloped countries were
expected to perform like wind-up toys, and "lumber through" the various
stages of development, single-mindedly; their reactions to change not to be
nearly so traumatic or aberrant as those of the Europeans, with their feudal
residues, psychological complexes, and exquisite high culture. In
sum . . . these countries were perceived to have only interests and no pas-
sions. (p. 9)

In this, the first decade of the twenty-first century, both international
development discourse and educational development discourse lend legitimacy to statements like the Declaration on Education for All and set major
national and global initiatives in motion. These statements and initiatives are
difficult to align with the interests of any particular nation-state or block of
nation-states, and are better understood as products of institutionalized ideas
about development, nation-states, and international development organizations. The discourse is both an instigator and a product of international organizations, professionals, and conferences, all of which bring international
pressure to bear on nation-states to take actions that they, the nation-states,
might prefer to avoid.

For industrialized nation-states, this means committing more development aid to activities for the poor and marginalized, scrambling to rationalize
it in self-interested terms for domestic audiences, but actually with little hope
of quick return in terms of military or commercial gain. For less industrialized nation-states, this means committing more funds to "soft," non–revenue
producing activities and accepting responsibility for a far broader range of
social welfare goals than their resources can cover. The institutional mechanisms which propel nation-states in these directions are wrapped up in the
structure, governance, and belief systems of the international development
field, the subject of the following three chapters.

4

International Development as an Organizational Field

The purpose of this chapter is to explore how development discourse called into being a host of international organizations, both governmental and non-governmental, to carry out the international development mandate. World leaders talk of serious matters—of human rights, of human development—they formulate goals, they propose agenda, and increasingly they come under pressure to take action consistent with that agenda. In the post–World War II period, such talk, or discourse, has been associated with global fund raising, with the hiring of experts to design, and advise and of managers to implement development activities. To coordinate—and control—this activity, individuals and states create formal organizations.

The growth of the international development field since the end of World War II has been dramatic. Although some organizations previously involved in disaster relief or colonial affairs switched over at least part of their operations to development after 1945, most of the 3000 plus organizations described in this chapter are less than 50 years old. Yet in that time, they have built enormous coherence and a sense of historical continuity that defies both their relatively young age and their relatively disappointing performance in each of the development decades since 1960. They have, in a sense, taken the international development mandate—the responsibility for operationalizing the international development imperative—and run with it. Without much intentionality on the part of dominant nation-states or more powerful organizations, international development organizations have taken on a life of their own far beyond what their founders imagined for them and have gained some measure of influence over their current funders. This chapter looks at how these organizations multiplied and how they reinforced and supported each other in their efforts to translate their mandate into concrete action, into development and, by extension, into education for all.

Conceptualizing International Development as an Organizational Field

"Organizations are social units (or human groupings) deliberately constructed and reconstructed to seek specific goals" (Etzioni, 1964, p. 3). This definition of organizations is simple, straightforward, and incomplete. Etzioni defines the role goals play in organizing and reforming organizations, but does not define the role those goals play in organizations' day-to-day operation or in their long-term survival. In fact, in recent years, sociologists who study organizations have downplayed the role of goals in determining what organizations do. These scholars instead focus on the interests of those working inside the organizations and the environment created by the organizations around them. The environment determines what organizations—particularly those producing things that are relatively hard to measure, such as schools and government—decide to do and how they do it. They define organizations in much more complex terms.

> Organizations are systems of interdependent activities linking shifting coalitions participants; the systems are embedded in—dependent on continuing exchanges with and constituted by—the environments in which they operate. (Scott, 1992, p. 25)

This suggests that over time, many organizations may secure a measure of independence from their stockholders or, in the case of international development organizations, from the nation-states and private citizens who fund them. Organizations may also develop significant interdependence among themselves. These two effects draw attention away from the stated goals of these organizations and towards the environment, or organizational field, in which they operate. Scott and Meyer (1983) define an organizational field as

> (1) a collection of organizations operating in the same domain, as identified by the similarity of their services, products or functions, (2) together with those organizations that critically influence the performance of the focal organizations: for example, major suppliers and customers; owners and regulators; funding sources and competitors.

The study of organizational fields provides many insights into the operation of international development organizations, both individually and as a group, and suggests several ways that these organizations may play a major role in formulating agenda at the global level.

This is because though international development organizations have—or can formulate—fairly clear goals, the means to achieve them is unclear. As a result, within the international development field as a whole, two types of organizations have become more central: (1) those able to produce scientized rationales for implementing development one way and not another and (2) those able to work the grassroots. These types address two persistent themes within world culture: the need to scientize action and the determination to foster equitable progress at the individual level.

The first section below outlines the components of the field, its activities and how these activities promote interdependence among various types of international development organizations. In particular, the discussion of interdependence links the increase in the number of international nongovernmental organizations founded in the late 1970s and early 1980s to shifts in the international development discourse described in the preceding chapter. The following section describes how governance, the belief system, and hierarchies within the international development field help to mediate conflicts and competition among member organizations. The final section then analyzes the role of the international organizations involved in the World Conference on Education for All, contrasting the interdependence of the sponsoring organizations with their relative independence of the nation-states that fund them. This section suggests that the conference, on the part of the sponsoring organizations, included mixed motives: both self-interest in increasing public support and governmental funding for these organizations' activities, and also strong normative beliefs in the mutually reinforcing relationship between education and development. As much as these organizations recognized that their current funding levels could not support education for all, their mandates could not support anything less.

Components of the Field

The task of cataloging the members of the international development field is a daunting one. Using the Scott and Meyer (1983) definition above, the complete field includes permanent and temporary organizations in almost every country of the world. For example, in each donor country—and most high- or upper-middle-income countries are now donor countries—this includes:

- the committees in charge of defining and providing direction to the international development program in both the executive and legislative arms of government in donor countries;
- the bilateral organizations those donor countries create to execute bilateral development programs;
- the intergovernmental development organizations (development IGOs) those countries contribute to and participate in, including UN organizations, regional organizations, and international development banks and funds;
- private contributors to and constituencies for international development;

- nongovernmental international development organizations (development INGOs);
- training and research centers for international development; and
- suppliers and contractors for both governmental and nongovernmental
  development organizations.

In recipient countries—and most of the less industrialized countries were
recipient countries by the end of the 1980s—the list is even longer. It
includes all ministries that receive international development assistance,
along with national nongovernmental development organizations (development NNGOs) and local community-based organizations (development
LNGOs), national training and research centers that interact with the international development community, and more. Finally, the field also comprises
the intended beneficiaries (end users) and freelance consultants.

Because of the practically infinite number of organizations at the
national and local levels, this analysis focuses on formal international development organizations, though it may refer to national or community-based
organizations from time to time. By the late 1980s and early 1990s, information on many of these organizations was available in specialized directories
and databases of international organizations. Appendix A explains the protocol used for identifying international development organizations in these
directories and databases. Table 4.1 presents a composite typology of all
development organizations with the sources and estimated funding levels (as
of 1991), and their approximate numbers (as of 1990). Graphs 4.1 and 4.2
summarize the frequency of foundings of several types of governmental and
OECD-based non-governmental international development organizations,[11]
respectively, as listed in development directories published in the late
1980s and early 1990s.[12] Bear in mind, many of the organizations founded
before 1960 did not start out primarily as "development" organizations,
rather they engaged in work that would be later defined as development work
or they carried out activities that would later be classified as "development
education."

Graph 4.1 shows that after the end of World War II and the creation of
the first cohort of UN organizations, the number of foundings of IGOs
dropped to zero until the 1950s, then grew steadily through the last years of
the 1950s and the early 1960s, with peaks in foundings in 1948 (6), 1962 (8),

---

11. As explained in Appendix A, the OECD-based international non-governmental development
organizations (development INGOs) accounted for most development INGOs in 1990. Since
that time, there has been a dramatic growth in regional organizations based in non-OECD countries, that may also be considered INGOs in future analyses.
12. These graphs do not include organizations that were founded and shut down before these
development directories were published. The effect of leaving out these organizations may be to
overstate the increase in organizational foundings in recent years.

and 1971 (9). Beginning with a low of three in 1969, the foundings increase
at the fastest rate of the post-war period and peak in 1975 (14).

In contrast, some of today's development INGOs were founded as early
as the eighteenth century, having started out as mission organizations, and
turned in part or in whole to development work after World War II. Graph 4.2
provides a summary of development INGO foundings between 1900 and
1989. INGO foundings peak just after World Wars I and II and then begin a
dramatic upward climb, peaking a second time in 1981 with 118 new INGOs.

Graph 4.3 compares the post-war foundings of both IGOs and INGOs.
The peak for the IGOs in 1975 precedes the peak for the INGOs in 1981 by
six years. In addition, the growth of INGO foundings is much more dramatic:
the number of INGO foundings in 1981 is almost four times the peak in
1947. In contrast, the IGO foundings increase by only two-fold between

Table 4.1. Types of International Development Organizations, 1990

Type, with roles	Source of funds	US$ in millions (1991)	# of orgs.
Multilateral Agencies (Intergovernmental Organizations):			
Development banks and funds	Government contributions, interest on loans	7,227	< 40
United Nations agencies and private contributions	Assessments, government	5,364	< 70
Other multilateral development organizations	Assessments, government contributions	3,630	< 140
Bilateral Agencies (Governmental Organizations with International Mandates):			
Donor agencies surplus	Taxes, government	50,926	< 40
International Non-Governmental Organizations:			
Research, training, and professional organizations	Private and public grants, dues, fees	N/A	< 1000
For-profit firms with governmental contracts	Fees	N/A	< 1200
Nonprofit groups based in high-income countries	Private and public grants, dues, fees	5,403+	> 2500
Nonprofit groups based in low-income regions	Private and public grants, dues, fees	NA	< 300

Sources of organizational data: East, Smith-Morris, & Wright, 1990; Eurofi, 1988; Korsmeyer, 1991; Organization for Economic Cooperation and Development, Development Centre, 1990; Organization for Economic Cooperation and Development, Development Centre, 1991; Organization for Economic Cooperation and Development, Development Centre, 1992; Organization for Economic Cooperation and Development, Development Centre, 1993; Union of International Associations, 1993/94, Vol. III, p. 1754; World Bank, Operations Policy Research and Planning Group, Operations Policy Department, NGO Unit, 1996. Organization for Economic Cooperation and Development, Development Assistance Committee. 2002.

Source of funding data: OECD, Development Assistance Committee, 1994.

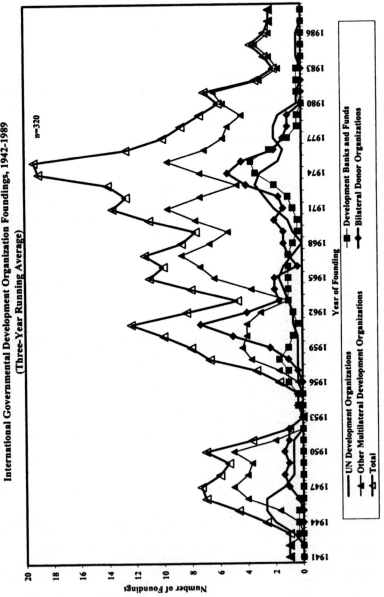

Graph 4-1
International Governmental Development Organization Foundings, 1942-1989
(Three-Year Running Average)

n=320

Number of Foundings

Year of Founding

—— UN Development Organizations
—▲— Other Multilateral Development Organizations
—△— Total

—■— Development Banks and Funds
—◆— Bilateral Donor Organizations

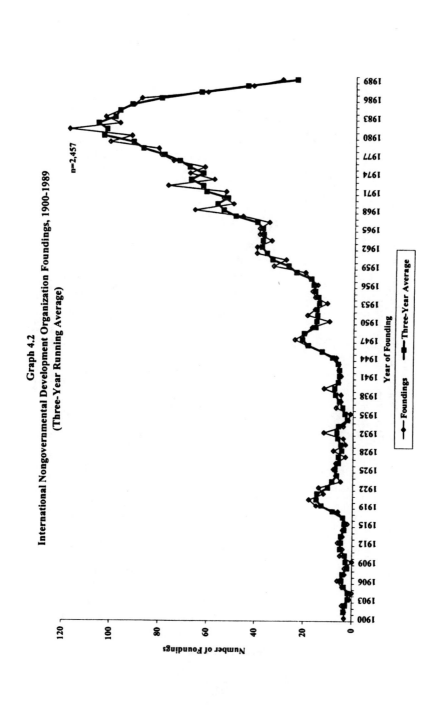

Graph 4.2

International Nongovernmental Development Organization Foundings, 1900–1989

(Three-Year Running Average)

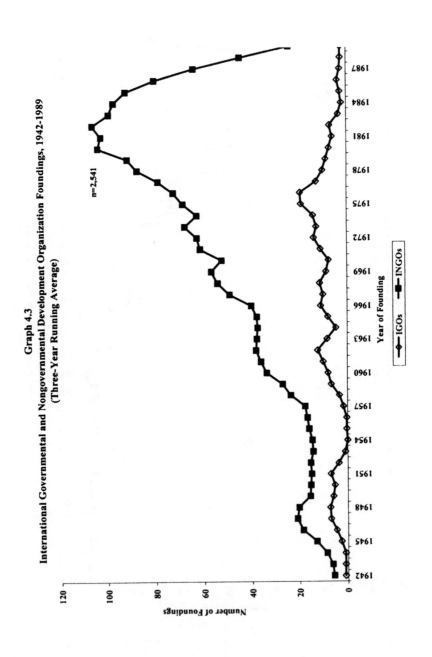

Graph 4.3

International Governmental and Nongovernmental Development Organization Foundings, 1942-1989

(Three-Year Running Average)

n=2,541

Number of Foundings

Year of Founding

IGOs INGOs

1948 and 1975. Overall the increase in the number of INGO foundings since World War II, in comparison with IGO foundings, appears to be larger, more homogeneous, and more robust. On the other hand, the increase in funding for development represented by each new INGO tends to be a fraction of the income introduced by each new IGO.

These patterns of IGO and INGO foundings reflect trends in development discourse and in the evolution of the field. Specifically, these patterns mirror increasing concern in the 1970s with the welfare of all individuals, particularly the poor, and with the need to design development activities to address their needs. Traditional development IGOs continued the large-scale, trickle-down approaches for which they had been designed but they also fashioned new alliances with INGOs better able to access the individual or grassroots level. The discourse sometimes reconciled these two activities by emphasizing how upgrading living conditions for the poor would result in upgraded human resources and thus national economic growth. Other strands of the discourse, emphasizing individual development as a human right, created relatively more tension, as development banks and other organizations tried to estimate how loans to education might be repaid.

The next section highlights components and structures of the field of international development organizations. The section following it provides a brief description of the different types of organizations introduced in Table 4.1 and how various field characteristics promote interdependence among these types.

Structuring the Field

> The UN has defined development activities as those "operational activities of a development cooperation character that seek to mobilize or increase the potential and capacities of countries to promote economic and social development and welfare, including the transfer of resources to less industrialized countries or regions in a tangible or intangible form." (United Nations, 1992, p. xii)

International development organizations support or implement several types of activities, including construction, research, advice, and training. The basic unit of development assistance is usually a multiyear *project* consisting of one or more of these activities in one or more *sectors*, such as health, education, or agriculture. For example, a multisector women's income-generating project might combine loans for microenterprise with literacy training (education) and the distribution of modern contraceptives (health/family planning). Donor support for development activities or projects comes in the *form* of loans, grants, and/or commodities (food, contraceptives, fertilizer).

International development organizations conduct their activities on one or more *levels*: world, national, local, and/or individual. Prior to the 1970s, some multilaterals and many bilaterals worked on the top three levels. However, in recent decades shifts in the development discourse altered the role of the end user, at the local or national level, from passive recipient to that of active participant in the design and delivery of development activities. As a result, few international governmental organizations now work at the local, let alone the individual level, in less industrialized countries. Instead most depend on arrangements with local governments, INGOs, and LNGOs to enable them to incorporate grassroots participation in their poverty reduction projects.

Organizations play various *roles* in international development including recipient, lender, donor, enduser, intermediary, professional support, or interest group. Organizations may play more than one role, even within one country. CARE, for example, operates as an intermediary for U.S. government funds and commodities; as a donor, using private contributions, to smaller NGOs in less industrialized countries; and as an end user for the delivery of emergency relief.

Organizations in the international development field face a broad range of uncertainties not unique to the field but nonetheless constraining. The output of many organizations in the international development field is difficult to describe, let alone measure. In recent years, identifying objectively verifiable indicators of "participation" and "empowerment" have occupied much organizational resources. The unit by which many organizations organize their work—projects—may take two to three years to plan and five to ten years to implement, although even 15- to 20-year projects are not unusual. During this time, staff may turn over many times and national governments may change as well. Large gaps in time and geographic space—particularly between project designers and implementers—mean that it is difficult for organizations in the international development field to "learn." Systematic evaluation of development projects within many organizations was only introduced in the late 1970s and in the early 1990s many organizations were still experimenting with ways to formulate conclusions and circulate them in ways that promote organizational learning (Riddell, 1987).

For example, various characteristics noted above make loose coupling endemic to the field: the distance between levels of the same organization, the time between the conceptualization of a project and its completion, and, perhaps most important, the ambiguity of output (Weick, 1976). Loose coupling inevitably appears in the gaps between the policies issued by donor head offices and projects designed by donor field offices thousands of miles away, between the directives issued by a ministry of education and the programs carried out in schools hundreds of miles away. Yet many evaluations of international development projects identify loose coupling as an individual project management failure rather than a feature common to almost all international development activities (Hossain, 1994; Meyer, 1994).

The following brief description of each organizational type explains the various roles each plays and describes how the structural characteristics of the international development field propel various types of organizations into collaborative arrangements with one other.

Types of Organizations

International development organizations may be divided into eight types: development banks and regional funds; UN donors; regional organizations; bilateral donors; quasi-nongovernmental research and training organizations; for-profit international nongovernmental organizations; nonprofit INGOs based in industrialized countries; and INGOs based in less industrialized regions.

The development banks and funds shown in Table 4.1 are conventional IGOs, established by intergovernmental agreements. Together, they account for a larger proportion of total international development assistance in dollar terms than any other type of multilateral development organization. Most of this assistance is given on "soft" terms, at below-market interest rates, with significant grace periods, and long amortization schedules. Nonetheless, the loan funds shown in Table 4.1 represent only a fraction of the development lenders' financial influence since less industrialized countries' access to conventional international loans and capital is often tied to performance on development bank loans. For example, the World Federation of Development Financing Institutions (f. 1979) claimed 349 members in 1990 (East, Smith-Morris et al., 1990), the majority of which are commercial, for-profit organizations. The development banks typically grant voting rights to members according to their relative capital contribution and their policies therefore tend to reflect the economic perspectives of the higher-income capitalist countries.

The International Bank for Reconstruction and Development (IBRD, f. 1945), also known as the World Bank, was the earliest development bank. The Bank began making a substantial portion of its loans to less industrialized countries as early as 1949 (Lumsdaine, 1993), but its "soft loan" window, the International Development Association (IDA), was not founded until 1960. Indeed, three-quarters of the other organizations in this category were formed since 1959.

The banks and funds serve two primary functions in the international development field. First, they provide concessional loans for large-scale projects, such as regional dams, that are beyond the means of most other individual donors. Second, in more recent years they have carried out and disseminated much of the economic research that lends scientific legitimacy to other bilateral and multilateral programs. The rise of their analytical

capacities, particularly in "soft" sectors, such as education, parallels the rise
of the discourse on basic human needs and poverty alleviation that increased
the demand for noneconomic indicators of human welfare.

In their early years, both banks and funds focused on infrastructure
development and took a relatively hands-off approach to recipient government management. When many projects failed to become profitable, however, some development banks adopted a more hands-on approach,
requiring recipient governments to hire "technical assistance," that is, foreign experts, to help plan and monitor projects. Since many recipient governments were loathe to use scarce foreign exchange to hire these relatively
expensive foreign experts, other donors provided grants to cover these
costs, increasing ties between the banks and other development organizations. The changing development discourse, with its increased emphasis on
social sector development, also produced a demand for intermediary organizations—in many cases national or INGOs—that could work on a relatively small scale, in soft sectors that do not traditionally generate income
or government revenue, such as health and education. Again, since recipient
governments in less industrialized countries were reluctant to use loan
funds for activities with no immediate economic returns and also to support
organizations somewhat outside their control, grants from other donors
were often used to fund INGO activities in these sectors. In this way, cofinancing arrangements between donor and lender organizations proliferated
in the 1980s and 1990s.

The United Nations donor organizations,[13] the second organizational type
shown in Table 4.1, outnumber the development banks but work from a much
smaller funding base. In 1949, the UN created the Expanded Program of
Technical Assistance (EPTA) to help coordinate the development efforts of all
the UN organizations in less industrialized countries. The program included
activities in seven organizations: the World Health Organization (WHO); the
Food and Agricultural Organization (FAO); the International Labor Organization (ILO); the International Civil Aviation Organization (ICAO); the International Bank for Reconstruction and Development (IBRD); the International
Monetary Fund (IMF); and the International Refugee Organization. In the
1960s, consistent with the UN's new emphasis on development, a new specialized UN organization, the United Nations Development Fund (UNDP),
took over this function.

By charter most of these organizations, and the other UN organizations
that began to form, give each nation-state equal representation, regardless of
size or wealth. Since the ratio of low- and middle-income to industrialized
member-states has always been greater than one and has increased over time,

---

13. The World Bank is officially part of the UN system, but it is a lender not a donor organization.

powerful countries such as the United States and the United Kingdom have less control over UN organizations than they are accustomed to exercising in some other IGOs, such as the OECD. This principle of "participatory equality" of less industrialized nation-states (United Nations, 1984) contributed to the growth of the international development field in at least two ways. First, the predominance of less industrialized country members meant that almost all UN forums and organizations, even those founded pre-1945, such as FAO and WHO, turned into de facto international development organizations. Second, their inability to control UN organizations disposed some wealthier countries to establish bilateral organizations and send more of their development funding through them, rather than through multilateral organizations.

This issue of control first arose at the end of World War II, when a U.S. review of the state of the United Nations Relief and Rehabilitation Agency's (UNRRA, f. 1943) global operations determined that although the Western alliance contributed most of UNRRA's funding, Eastern Europe received most of its assistance. With the Cold War looming, the review suggested U.S. contributions to UNRRA were being used to prop up Communist regimes in Eastern Europe and recommended that the bulk of future U.S. foreign aid be channeled not through multilaterals, where its destination was difficult to control, but through bilateral programs, such as the Marshall plan, and through U.S.-based INGOs. At U.S. insistence, UNRRA was indeed dissolved in 1946, and its functions were divided among several UN organizations (Black, 1986).[14]

The UN's first attempt at coordinating UN development efforts in 1949 involved nine organizations, ranging from the International Civil Aviation Organization to the International Refugee Organization. By 1992, more than 32 UN organizations were involved (United Nations, 1992). Since the late 1940s, underfunding of the UN and its affiliated organizations relative to their mandates has been a chronic feature of the development field. Budget constraints have forced many UN organizations to limit their operations in less industrialized countries and to focus on information collection and dissemination activities, such as sponsoring conferences and producing specialized publications. In general, their meager resources restrict UN organizations' operations in less industrialized countries to pilot projects; in order to participate in large-scale projects, UN organizations must usually collaborate with better-funded donors and lenders and raise funds through social service NGOs operating in more industrialized countries.[15]

---

14. Most notably UNICEF (f. 1946), an organization whose ability to weather the storms of the Cold War and later anti-UN sentiment rests to a large extent on its association with a highly legitimate, nonpolitical target group. See Black, M. (1986).

15. For more details, see section below on nongovernmental organizations.

In the 1960s, the UN began establishing affiliated organizations exclusively devoted to international development, such as the UN Industrial Development Organization (UNIDO, f. 1966) and the UN Conference on Trade and Development (UNCTAD, f. 1964). The main growth of UN organizations involved in international development comes in the 1970s.

The UN and its affiliated organizations were involved in the founding of at least half of the other multilateral development organizations formed since World War II. A small group of these—such as the West Africa Rice Development Association (f. 1970)—are designed to further the commercial development of resources and trade considered key to regional development. The titles of these organizations suggest, however, that most deal with training, science and technology policy, educational innovation, research, and information sharing.

The funding problems of the UN organizations are directly related to the proliferation of bilateral aid organizations. By the early 1990s, almost all industrialized countries, in addition to contributing to UN development activities, had established bilateral donor organizations, such as the U.S. Agency for International Development and Sida (the Swedish international development authority). As shown in Table 4.1, these organizations collectively provided more international development assistance than any other type of development organization. Founding dates for bilateral organizations are often difficult to distinguish from the dates a country begins making contributions to (1) UN development organizations; (2) INGOs working in less industrialized countries; and/or (3) colonies in transition to independence. The pattern of founding dates in Graph 4.1, showing that most bilateral organizations formed during the 1970s, should therefore be considered provisional.

In 1990, budgetary commitments from individual donor countries to their bilateral aid programs ranged from about US$ 8.4 billion for the United States to US$ 7 million for Algeria. A few bilateral donor organizations—such as Japan's—can dwarf most UN donor organizations, but no individual bilateral organization can match the resources of a single development bank. Although by the early 1990s, China, India, and various Arab countries had established bilateral aid programs, the majority of and largest bilateral donors are funded by Western nation-states and are members of the Organization for Economic Cooperation and Development's Development Assistance Committee (DAC, f. 1960). Unlike the development banks and funds, bilateral organizations have tended to move in and out of the donor/implementer role over time, sometimes channeling aid through recipient governments, for-profit contractors, and/or INGOs, at other times staffing and running their own projects.

Quasi-nongovernmental research, training, and professional organizations provide much of the infrastructure necessary to give the international development field credibility with the general public and its funders. Some of the major subtypes within this category of organization are described in greater detail in Chapter 5. These organizations also provide much of the formal and informal networking that makes the interdependent field run more smoothly than it might otherwise. For example, the Interregional Coordinating Committee of Development Associations (f. 1976) set up the International Development Information Network (f. 1976) to exchange regional and interregional information about research and training institutes, research projects, and researchers and specialists. Consistent with norms in the international development field, the network began decentralizing in 1985 to five regional associations.

The for-profit, private firms that proliferated in response to the governmental organizations' needs for logistical support and technical expertise since the late 1950s bring no independent funds to the international development sector. There are probably fewer than 1200 of these organizations,[16] including large multinational firms, such as Arthur Andersen Consulting, and smaller "body shops" that pull together teams of freelance consultants for both long-and short-term contracts. Presumably they proliferate and decline in number based on demand from governmental organizations, and they provide an employment source outside of governmental and nonprofit organizations for international development professionals. Their role is restricted to implementation and mediation as they construct buildings and lay electrical grids, for example. Since the purpose of these firms is clearly to make a profit—functional self-interest—their work in international development does not raise the same kinds of institutional questions as the work of nonprofit and governmental organizations, and as such they will not be discussed here.

International Nonprofit Nongovernmental Organizations (INGOs) Based in Industrialized Countries.

The OECD-based INGOs have the distinction of being the oldest type of international development organization. They vary in size from the Aga Khan Foundation (f. 1967) with a budget of US$ 52 million (1992) to the Malayam Association of Vienna (f. 1974) with a budget of US$ 1,106 (1993) (OECD, 1995). Despite the emphasis on governmental action and responsibility up to this point, in fact many of the scientific breakthroughs that proved the feasibility of international development—the Green Revolution, the vaccine for smallpox—were sponsored by private foundations in the first half of the twentieth century. Missionary societies established the earliest Western-style schools and hospitals in Africa and Asia in the eighteenth and nineteenth centuries and these, in turn, educated the first generation of national leaders of former colonies in the twentieth century. Many development INGOs incorpo-

16. See Appendix A.

rate literacy training into all sorts of development projects: microlending, maternal-child health, community development, for example.

As shown in Table 4.1, private nonprofit organizations outnumber all other types of international development organizations and are the third largest funders of international development activities. This type includes organizations that carry out activities in less industrialized countries, as well as a wide range of other organizations, including: those that promote education about less industrialized countries for the public in industrialized countries, those that provide emergency relief operations, and those that serve as UN fundraising organizations. In addition, a variety of regional associations promote and coordinate development banking. Great variations in terms of the size and goals of the various organizations, the geographic spread of their activities, and competition for governmental funds, however, resulted in a wide range of concerns and little cohesion among development INGOs for many years.

The experience and perception of the work of NGOs have played a major role in the formation of many of the principles underlying the development discourse. The next section explores this role in greater depth.

INGOs and Development[17]

In recent years claims about the potential of INGOs to replace IGOs and bilateral donor organizations and to carry the development field into a new era of participation and justice have generally been overstated. At the same time, the role of INGOs in helping to establish the moral, scientific and operational basis for international development, and the support they have provided to other organizations from the 1950s to the 1970s has been somewhat understated. The founding dates of many development INGOs precede World War II, and some were founded in the nineteenth century, a hint that their original goals preceded—or presaged—current notions of development.

Development INGOs Founded Prior to 1945.

The development INGOs with the oldest founding dates tend to be religious; over two-thirds of those founded before 1900 include reference to a religion, denomination, or sect in their names. Many of these organizations' staff went into Asia, Africa, or Latin America as missionaries, some proselytizing, others establishing the first Western-oriented schools and hospitals, both to attract potential converts and to serve new native Christian communities. Chapter 2 highlighted how these missionaries, in writing letters to small contributors, helped to expand the scope of these funders' contact with others beyond their family or country. Similarly organizations such as the British and Foreign Antislavery Society focused on raising awareness in then-industrializing countries of moral concerns

---

17. For an expanded discussion of this topic, see Chabbott, C. (1999), pp. 222–248.

in places beyond the boundaries of kin and race. At the same time, the best known secular humanitarian INGO listed in several development directories, the International Committee of the Red Cross (ICRC, f. 1863), succeeded in classifying new categories of persons, independent of their nationality—the war wounded, refugees, prisoners of war—who deserved international help.

In the period from World War I through World War II, three new types of INGOs were founded that would later play a major role in the international development field: private philanthropies, specialized sectoral organizations, and emergency relief organizations. American industrialists Andrew Carnegie and John D. Rockefeller, while outspoken sectarian Christians, focused not on saving souls or ministering to the sick and helpless but on attacking what they perceived to be the roots of human misery. They and their fellow industrialists helped to establish graduate schools of public health or tropical medicine in the then British Empire. The research funded by these industrialists helped to control a wide variety of tropical diseases and produced vaccines for small pox and other life-threatening diseases. After World War II, private philanthropies also helped to set up several centers for international agricultural research that played a major role in the Green Revolution, and established the Population Council to begin the serious study of population growth throughout the world. In addition these groups established dozens of development economics departments, development policy research centers, and centers for the study of education in less industrialized countries. The idea that problems on a global scale might be ameliorated by science grew in large part from these efforts.

Following on the success of the ICRC, individuals such as Eglantyne Price and Herbert Hoover began founding private relief organizations, such as Save the Children (f. 1919) and the Committee for the Relief of Belgium (f. 1914), respectively, to address the physical needs of noncombatants and to assist with relief and reconstruction following these wars. The foundings of such organizations mushroomed during and after World War II; some of the better known ones include Oxfam (f. 1943), Catholic Relief Services (f. 1943), World Relief (f. 1944), and CARE (f. 1945). All of these organizations increased the awareness of individuals and groups in industrialized countries of suffering in foreign countries, and engaged many individuals from industrialized countries in both paid and volunteer work abroad. Moreover, these organizations worked to convince the public that if the means existed to alleviate suffering wherever it might be, this alone constituted a responsibility to respond (Toynbee, 1947).

Development INGOs Founded From 1945 to 1985.

In the post–World War II period, hundreds of additional INGOs were founded to respond to perceived needs in the less industrialized countries. Many of these organizations, directly or indirectly, supported the postwar development regime. For example, when governments in industrialized countries began establishing bilateral aid programs, some chose to channel that aid through INGOs already established in the donor country and working in the target less industrialized country. In contrast, some UN organizations used national NGOs in industrialized countries to raise funds for UN development activities. Some new INGOs formed around issues such as the environment or population. Others were founded based on ties of friendship and solidarity between specific places in industrialized and less industrialized countries, such as the Danish-Gambian Friendship Society (f. 1975). Finally, IGOs played a role in establishing some regionally based development INGOs in Africa, Asia, Latin America, and the Middle East; others were local initiatives.

In the decades immediately following World War II, because of their small budgets and their mostly volunteer staff, the work of development INGOs was sometimes characterized by the larger IGOs as "band-aids" rather than serious treatment, and their workers characterized as "amateurs" or "bleeding hearts" rather than as professionals (Sommer, 1977; Smith, 1990). Over time, however, the development discourse has carved out a more important role for INGOs in the international development field. As shown in Table 4.2, by the late 1970s, as poverty reduction came into vogue, INGOs' potential to carry out small-scale pilot projects for service delivery to disadvantaged groups was recognized, and bilateral, if not multilateral, IGOs began to develop more collaborative arrangements with INGOs. This coincided with a sharp increase in the founding of development INGOs in the early 1970s, as shown in Graph 4.2.

This trend continued in the 1980s and 1990s, as donor organizations became more dissatisfied with the administrative capacity of many governments in less industrialized countries to manage structural adjustment programs and, simultaneously, to deliver services to disadvantaged groups. By the late 1980s, therefore, the INGOs, as well as the national development NGOs emerging in the less industrialized countries, had become the social service delivery agents of choice in some sectors for many donors. In the 1990s, discourse on sustainable development—combining concerns for population control, the environment, and respect for microcommunities—called for the development and grassroots dissemination of environmentally sound technologies and modern contraceptives. At this point, the INGOs are no longer marginal in the development field; rather the areas in which they have established their comparative advantage are now at the very center of the field's approach to development.

By 1990, all OECD-member countries had standing agreements to collaborate with development INGOs. The UN's Nongovernmental Liaison Service, the World Bank's NGO Unit, and the OECD's Development Centre compiled databases and produced directories of thousands of INGOs and NGOs based in less industrialized countries. Some OECD members were even channeling up to 25 percent of their development assistance through INGOs and NGOs (Smillie & Helmich; 1993). Similarly, INGOs' presumed backward linkages to grassroots constituencies and funders in industrialized

Table 4.2. Roles for International Nongovernmental Development Organizations, by Development Approach, 1950–1990

Decade	Development Approach	Role for NGOs
	Modernization	
1950s	Comprehensive economic planing Industrialization and community development	Minor: emergency relief
1960s	Economic growth Dependency	Limited: emergency relief + technical assistance, schools, and hospitals
	Poverty Reduction	
1970s	Equitable Growth Poverty Alleviation Basic Human Needs (BHN) New International Economic Order (NIEO)	Limited: emergency relief + technical assistance + small scale rural social service delivery + pilots and development advocacy
1980s	Structural adjustment Social dimensions of adjustment	Significant: emergency relief + technical assistance, schools, and hospitals + small-scale rural social service delivery pilots + development education + social service delivery to the poor
1990s	Sustainable development	Major: emergency relief + technical assistance, schools, and hospitals + small-scale rural social service delivery pilots + development education + development and dissemination of environmentally sound innovations and modern contraceptives

countries have made them a focus of governmental development education activities,[18] designed to inform citizens in industrialized countries of the importance of supporting international development. Themselves unable to lobby their national legislatures or parliaments for more funds, many governmental development organizations depend on NGOs and INGOs to establish

---

18. See Chapter 5 for more details on the growth of development education in industrialized countries.

and/or maintain a "constituency" for international development in industrialized countries.

INGOs Based in Less Industrialized Regions.

Although the importance of NGOs based in less industrialized countries has been growing since the 1980s, as of 1990, fewer than 600, and perhaps as few as 200, of these organizations might be considered INGOs, or NGOs that work in more than one country.[19] Among these, the General Arab Women's Federation (f. 1944), the Inter-American Planning Society (f. 1956), and the Afro-Asian People's Solidarity Organization (f. 1957) are some of the oldest.

Similar to the pattern described above regarding bilateral IGOs and INGOs based in industrialized countries, some of the growth of regional INGOs in less industrialized regions is closely related to the mandates and initiatives of IGOs. Multilateral IGOs play an important role in the emergence of NGO networks in many less industrialized countries and in the building of regional INGO networks in Africa, Latin America, and Asia (UNESCO, 1991; UNESCO 1992). For example, the UNESCO-sponsored *African Development Sourcebook* (UNESCO, 1991) documents 174 networks of development NGOs; however, fewer than 70 are clearly regional and many are the direct product of INGO/IGO donor-funded conferences or ongoing projects. In development discourse, supporting domestic NGOs in less industrialized countries is sometimes referred to as promoting the development of "civil society" and "democratization," (Smith, 1990; Clark, 1991; Fisher, 1993) both presumed necessary elements of well-functioning nation-states. In recent years, too often INGOs and NGOs have been designated "The Third Sector," and touted as the answer to inefficient government social service delivery. In fact it is impossible to make generalizations about the role of NGOs in less industrialized countries, given tremendous variations in the scope, maturity, and effectiveness of regional, national, and local NGOs from one country or region to another.

The increasing dependence of governmental organizations on INGOs and NGOs within the international development field has won the latter a seat at the development table. In 1963, 1,000 NGO representatives were invited to participate in a parallel meeting held simultaneously with the World Food Conference. Thirteen years later the 6,000 NGO representatives attending the parallel meeting to the World Conference on Habitat in Vancouver outnumbered the official delegates. By 1995, 30,000 NGO/INGO participants attended the parallel meeting to the Fourth World Conference on Women (Alliance for a Global Community, 1996).

Both local and regional NGOs are used as stand-ins for the poor and disadvantaged, enabling international development conference organizers to claim that they have listened to the voices of the poor and marginalized. As a

---

19. Estimated from World Bank (1996).

result, the NGOs invited to participate in conferences may not include all the most active, well-organized, or articulate organizations because relatively small organizations may be invited to ensure representation for some special marginalized group. The drawback of this approach for NGOs is that the sponsors of the conference may report the same number of NGOs invited, but those invited may be among the least articulate and the least able to construct alternatives to platforms offered by the IGOs.

Since the mid-1990s, interest has mushroomed in NGOs and particularly in their role as "transnational advocates" of social development. In the run-up to the WCEFA, as described later, the NGO community was not so prominent.

Summary: Organizational Types

The emphasis in the preceding section on structural features that promote interdependence between governmental and nongovernmental organizations should not lead one to conclude that the international development field works mainly on a cooperative basis. Within specific geographic areas, INGOs, both for-profit and nonprofit, may compete for funding and/or contracts from the same governmental organizations (Sanyal, 1991). IGOs and bilateral organizations also compete to establish preferred models within sectors that better fit their own national experience or the structure of the assistance they are able to provide. For example, UNESCO education efforts tend to focus on adult literacy, whereas World Bank projects tended, until the 1990s, to focus on secondary and higher education. These dynamics occasionally make it possible for recipients to play one or more donor organizations off against each other. Finally, in some less industrialized countries with less articulated administrative and financial capacities, donor organizations may compete for the privilege of sponsoring one demonstrably effective local organization. Donors may also compete to work with one of the few organizations, either governmental or nongovernmental, with the bureaucratic apparatus (Rueschemeyer & Evans, 1985) necessary to implement development projects consistent with donors' monitoring and audit requirements.

In summary, the international development field is comprised of both governmental and nongovernmental organizations, working at the international, national, and local levels, as well as individual beneficiaries, and consultants. This chapter, however, focuses predominantly on the formal international organizations that engage in or support one or more development activities, such as providing commodities, technical assistance, training, research, construction, or advocacy. These activities are often organized into multiyear projects. Many organizations play more than one role and are dependent on other organizations for providing funds or organizing activities essential to the completion of these projects. This interdependence does not necessarily imply the absence of conflict within the field because cooperation is often of necessity, rather than by choice. Competition, on the other hand, is the rule, not the exception among many governmental and non-governmental organizations. The next section describes the way centrality, governance, and belief systems mediate conflicts and competition within the international development field.

Governance, Jurisdiction, and Hierarchies

Scott (1993) suggests that, in addition to the structure variables described above, two other broad categories of variables help to define organizational fields/industry systems: (1) the nature of their governance systems and (2) the jurisdiction of their belief systems. The following two subsections explore the governance and jurisdiction variables in the international development field. The third subsection demonstrates how these variables, combined with the other structure variables, can be used to create measures of centrality or status for organizations within the field.

Governance Variables

Organizational fields usually fall under the jurisdiction of just one national legal system. The international development field diverges from this pattern, since it is not, as a whole, subject to any one national legal or regulatory system. Instead, international development organizations must conform to the legal requirements of the countries of origin of their funds, as well as to less binding guidelines established by various coordinating groups within the field, and to the unwritten mores of world culture. All three of these types of governance are discussed below.

The more binding forms of governance placed upon international development organizations are explicit directives from funders who (1) regularly audit for compliance with those directives and (2) base future funding on compliance with those mandates. In this regard, bilateral organizations with a single, governmental source of funds, such as the Japanese International Cooperation Agency (f. 1974), the U.S. Agency for International Development (USAID, f. 1952) (Shapiro, 1996), and the Canadian International Development Agency (f. 1960) (Mundy, 1995), must be relatively responsive to their national funding authorities. In addition, organizations with annual reviews of their programs by those authorities must be relatively more responsive than those with less frequent reviews. In addition, the mandates of national funding authorities may have repercussions beyond the organizations they fund directly.

For example, in the early 1970s, the U.S. Congress ordered USAID to channel more of its funds through NGOs, in an effort to ensure that more international development assistance benefited the poor at the grassroots level. "Congressional debate made it clear that support for official aid, having significantly declined, would decline further, or even disappear, unless it could be shown that poor people, rather than the rich elites and military causes were benefiting from it" (Sommer, 1977).

In order to comply, USAID subsequently promoted the use of NGOs in all its activities, including those it undertakes in partnership with other donors. In some cases this has caused partner donors to increase support to NGOs more than they might have otherwise, but in some cases USAID's influence has actually decreased donor support. For example, in the 1980s, the U.S. Senate added clauses to USAID's annual funding resolution that prohibited the Agency from supporting any organization that performed abortions anywhere in the world. In addition to curtailing many of USAID's independent family planning activities, these anti-abortion clauses had dampening effects on many other organizations as well. These included: the UN and bilateral donors with which the US collaborates on funding large family planning/population projects; the INGOs that serve as intermediaries for those projects; and the national governments, NNGOs, and LNGOs in less industrialized countries that depend on project funds to operate national family planning programs.

In a less binding form of governance, the OECD's Development Assistance Committee (DAC, f. 1960) explicitly provides several types of guidelines for international development policy and implementation to member nation-states. First, the Committee issues nonbinding guidelines and handbooks and offers seminars on a wide variety of operational issues, such as aid evaluation (1970, 1984), aid management procedures (1977–79), guidelines for improving aid implementation (1979), and recommendations on environmental assessment of development assistance projects (1985). Furthermore, the DAC adopts formal recommendations for member-states' development programs. Examples include: endorsing the UN Conference on Trade and Development's target for development assistance as 1% of national income in OECD countries (1965) and urging members to provide the bulk of that assistance as grants, not loans (1969, 1972), to the least developed, rather than to the most politically or economically advantageous countries (1981), without restricting the source of goods and services to the donor country that provided the assistance (1973, 1974). Finally, the DAC places normative pressures on OECD members with its regular reports on the levels and distribution of international development assistance by member countries.

Strong core nation-states, such as the United States, are in the best position to resist pressure to conform to the DAC's recommendations and guidelines, whereas weaker nation-states can use compliance, among other things, to increase their legitimacy. This is the type of governance that leads to discussions of aid as a "regime, . . . [that is,] principles norms, rules and decision-making procedures around which the behavior of nation-states converge" (Lumsdaine, 1993). While Lumsdaine characterizes the aid regime as driven by the moral vision of the wealthier nation-states, Thérien (1991) describes it as ". . . a political institution which is gaining in importance because it fits with the dominant hard-core interests and ideologies [of individual nation-states] at the individual level." Yet there is much that occurs at the international level that is difficult to account for in terms of either moral or hard-core political interests and ideology.

Other types of international development organizations have their own coordinating organizations that play both a governance and a promotional role. For example, the first regional association of development financing institutions was formed in 1968, followed by the World Federation of Development Financing Institutions in 1979 and four regional associations by 1986. The International Council of Voluntary Agencies (ICVA, f. 1962) serves as a coordinating body for INGOs. In addition, at the national level in most less industrialized countries, representatives of governmental donors meet regularly as a round table or consultative group, and LNGOs and NNGOs, often prompted by INGOs or IGOs, participate in permanent consortia. Even more so than the DAC, roundtables, consultative groups, and NGO consortia at the national level exercise some measure of governance, though manifest mainly through normative pressure, rather than through legal sanctions.

The UN organizations face additional restrictions on their activities. Various UN specialized organizations, such as UNESCO and FAO, have a mandate to coordinate UN activities in certain sectors; other UN organizations will not usually take up activities in any of those sectors without first establishing a collaborative agreement with the appropriate specialized organization. In addition, many activities of the United Nations as a whole serve to create standards governing the extent and types of international development assistance. For example, UNCTAD defines the "least developed countries" and the World Bank identifies the low-income (per capita) countries and these categories are used to prioritize nation-state's needs for international development assistance. The UNDP identifies the percent of the world's population living in absolute poverty and thereby determines whether international development efforts can claim to be making progress towards reducing or alleviating poverty. In the 1990s, the UNDP also began using the Human Development Index—a composite of life expectancy at birth; the adult literacy rate; combined first, second, and third level education enrollment ratios; and real GDP per capita—to rank the general quality of life for each country.

Finally, perhaps the most ubiquitous, though indirect, regulation of international development at the national and local level appears in the form of donor procurement and audit regulations. Donor governments fund by far the bulk of development assistance grants and a substantial portion of the loans, and both governmental and nongovernmental recipient organizations must conform to the procurement and audit regulations of their funders. As international development organizations collaborate on development activities—to span the international, national, and local levels and/or to consolidate scarce funding—their activities become subject to more than one set of governmental audit and procurement regulations. In these cases, the potential range of development activities may be restricted to those that may be carried out within the scope of the most rigid of the funding governments' regulations.

In summary, the international development field is not regulated by a single nation-state. Rather each individual international development organization—and sometimes each international development activity involving more than one organization—operates under a somewhat unique amalgamation of the rules and regulations of its funders, and of the less binding standards established by the coordinating organizations in which it participates.

Jurisdiction of Belief Systems.

Whether the field has one dominant belief system, two competing ones, or a variety of alternatives helps determine the degree to which the field is tightly or more loosely structured (Scott, 1993). The dominant and, to some extent, the alternative development discourses described in the preceding chapter represent the belief system of the international development field.

Critiques of the discourse of development tend to occur outside the more central international development organizations (Harcourt, 1994), for the most part in academia, though some characterize the emphasis on sustainable human development in the 1990s as a triumph of a certain line of criticism (van Ufford, Kruijt et al., 1988). For reasons described in Chapter 5, the liaison between academics and professionals in the international development field, as in many other organizational fields, tends to be weak. Academic critiques, therefore, do not generally pose a challenge to the dominant belief systems of most development practitioners.

Nonetheless, the two most disputed aspects of the dominant international development belief system are its claims (1) to universally applicable scientific knowledge and (2) that such knowledge provides a basis for objective, essentially apolitical decision making (see Chapter 3). The research activities undergirding these claims to scientific knowledge, therefore, become extremely important to the construction of the field as a whole; those organizations capable of producing scientific research that expands the pool of scientific knowledge relevant to international development play a very important role in the field. Given the emphasis in international development discourse on serving the poor, combined with general shortages of funds, the number of international development organizations able to support either basic or applied research is small.

Instead, many international development organizations depend for applied research on a few scientific organizations that operate on the margins of the international development field. The quality and relevance of this research tend to vary by sector. In agriculture, a network of centers associated with the Consultative Group on International Agricultural Research (CGIAR, f. 1971) generates a steady stream of new technologies and basic research whose excellence is recognized both inside and outside the international development field. Nonetheless, the Green Revolution produced in large part by the CGIAR and its affiliates had many unforeseen negative repercussions; for example, improved crop varieties required irrigation that encouraged the spread of bilharzia and new varieties have sometimes contributed to the disappearance of drought-resistant native varieties. This experience has reduced the public's willingness to accept CGIAR innovations uncritically. In health, a loose collection of research institutes, such as the International Center for Diarrheal Disease Research/Bangladesh (ICDDR/B, f. 1978), the Dutch Royal Tropical Institute, and the Center for Disease Control in Atlanta produce demonstrably effective innovations on a fairly regular basis. Other sectors, such as education or public administration, however, lack such a convincing research base. As a result, these sectors have a harder time selling expensive long-term projects to potential funders.

For reasons unrelated to its initial mandate, the World Bank has become the de facto source of the most widely cited—and criticized—economic research in the field. Until very recently, most other donor organizations and recipient governments lacked the data and the economists necessary to challenge the research and models promoted by the few organizations able to engage in the type of quantitative approach favored by the Bank.

Professionals play a critical role in creating and codifying the belief systems that operate and create cohesion within organizational fields (Scott, 1993). The rise of professionals, including the professional schools, journals, and research centers that produce and support them, is discussed in Chapter 5. Chapter 5 also deals with a fourth indicator of field structuration identified by Scott (1993): the degree to which organizations in the field acknowledge each other and have more contact with each other than with organizations outside the field.

Measures of Centrality.

The size of an organization's budget is one important factor in determining its status in the field relative to other organizations. But the absolute size of the budget may be less important than the degree to which that budget matches the mandate of the organization and the organization's reputation for effective pursuit of its mandate (Abbott, 1988). Other factors that play a role in mediating an organization's relative status in the international development field or within a sector of the field include:

- governmental rather than nongovernmental status;
- activities at multiple levels;
- activities in more than one geographic area;
- activities in more than one sector;
- age of organization;
- mandate;

- participation in coordinating mechanisms; and
- extent and relevance of research and development activities.

All other things being equal, a governmental organization, working at more than one level, in more than one geographic area, with activities in more than one sector, established soon after World War II, that actively participates in coordinating mechanisms and produces relevant research, will be more central to the international development field than a nongovernmental organization, working at a single level, in just one geographic area, with activities confined to a single sector and established in the last two decades.

The World Bank has become increasingly central in the international development field during the last two decades due in large part to the size of its budget compared to those of all other development organizations, coupled with its ability to generate timely research. Previously, private foundations with large endowments, such as the Ford and Rockefeller foundations were central in the international development field, with their budgets matched to their mandates and their commitment to research and professional training. These foundations' continued effect on the belief system of the international development field remained strong through the late 1980s, even though their funding in many sectors has been much reduced.

The increased status or increasing centrality of the NGOs in recent decades is at least in part related to the field's perceived need to reach out to the tax-paying, charity-supporting public in the industrialized world. Abbott notes a peculiar paradox: "Professionals admire academics and consultants who work with knowledge alone; the public admires practitioners who work with clients" (1988, p. 119). Of course, Abbott also warns that the status of clients also rubs off on the professionals who work with them. The centrality and legitimacy of development banks are enhanced by the fact that at least some of their staff work with ministers of finance, while many NGO staff work with illiterate day laborers. On the other hand, the work of the NGOs is often more photogenic and more comprehensible to the general public. As a result, since the 1980s, large, professionally prestigious IGOs have gone out of their way to prove to the public that they work closely with publicly admired NGOs, even when their size precludes this.

Implications.

"One effect of field structuration is that isomorphic processes are likely to occur more frequently, and with greater force" (DiMaggio, 1983). DiMaggio and Powell distinguish between two types of isomorphism: competitive and institutional. Competitive isomorphism occurs in fields with clear output and much competition, where all organizations adopt the same technologies and/or structures, because the effects on output and profits are fairly transparent. In fields such as international development, however, profitability is often irrelevant, output—let alone efficiency—is hard to measure, and interdependence is high. In such cases, at least three distinct types of institutional processes encourage organizations to adopt similar structures and technologies.

First, organizations that depend on each other for resources—i.e., cofinancing, basic research, markets—may be *coerced* by the real or imagined threat of the withdrawal of access to those resources. The international relations theory underlying many analyses of foreign aid tends to assign overriding importance to this effect, but coercion plays a less decisive role in organizational theory. Complex organizational fields, with many different types of organizations and some interchangeable roles, allow for much dodging and feigning among their members. In fact different organizations at different points in time manage their resource dependencies—or their susceptibility to coercion—more or less effectively (Oliver, 1991).

Second, organizations may simply *mimic* what other, apparently successful organizations around them do. This is a particularly likely outcome when measuring the impact of various alternatives on output is difficult and the range of potential responses is limited (Cohen, March et al., 1976).

Finally, the more organizations interact, the more they are likely to develop similar standards over time. For example, professionals in organizations facing similar uncertainties can, in effect, determine how success or productivity will be measured in fields with ambiguous outputs. They do this by setting standards for ethics and fairness, by developing rules of thumb for making decisions with less than perfect information, and by designing acceptable responses to external dependencies (Scott, 1992). "Bridging" activities, such as conferences, bring the field together to establish reasonable standards to which most organizations agree to be accountable. Also, professionals help organizations "buffer" important activities from the changing whims of outside funders by altering discourse or structures but leaving the core activities intact. In all these ways, professionalism encourages individuals to establish frames of reference somewhat independent of the stockholders of the organizations that employ them.

In the international development literature, the first or coercive type of influence is often ascribed to nation-states or to financial heavyweights such as the World Bank. For example the impact of the U.S. Congress's abortion clauses is a good example of coercive isomorphism. There is no question coercive isomorphism is indeed salient among international development organizations, since all are supposed to be making data-based decisions, yet few have the resources to gather or even to analyze the necessary data. Their individual mandates are much larger than their financial resources and they must collaborate to achieve their goals. Nonetheless, given that international development is a complex organizational field, the opportunity for coercion should not be confused with its effective use. For example, a development bank may coerce country X into accepting an enormous loan for an activity relatively low on X's priority list; X, however, may then place the loan in an interest bearing account and never draw upon it for the "agreed upon" activities.

The second, mimetic, type of organizational influence is less widely recognized but may well be as common. Organizations as diverse as Save the Children, the World Bank, and the National Rural Electrification and Cooperative Association share common project design protocols, strategic objectives, monitoring and evaluation plans, logical frameworks, and other standard operating procedures. The third, normative, type of organizational influence has increased with the rise of international development professionals, who among themselves determine priorities, what is do-able, which organizations have more legitimate status, how relations with different types of governments should be managed. Normative isomorphism occurs when professionals designate some activities as more effective than others and agree upon the "right" ways to pursue those activities. In the last two decades, world conferences have become an increasingly legitimate mechanism by which international development professionals can press their norms upon nation-states.

This analysis highlights the way the structure, governance, and belief systems of the international development field promote interdependence among its members. This interdependence, in turn, generates a narrower menu of development models and options than one might expect, given the number and variety of organizations in the field. The description emphasizes the strong isomorphic pressures in this organizational field, the first step towards understanding the way international development organizations carry fairly uniform blueprints of development and education. To illustrate the isomorphic effects of structure, governance, and belief system on the operation of the international development field, this section describes the role of multilateral and bilateral international development organizations in generating and conducting a world conference on education.

The Field in Action: The World Conference on Education for All

As shown in Table 4.3, the four central sponsoring organizations— UNESCO, UNICEF, UNDP, and the World Bank—are multilateral organizations that appear consistently in all international development directories. Of the four sponsoring organizations, UNESCO alone specializes in education and the focus of much of its work, throughout its history, has been on less industrialized countries. Only one of the 16 cosponsoring organizations comprising the International Steering Group represented a national government and its domestic ministry of education. The rest of the Steering Group was composed of representatives of international development organizations.

Although King (1991) identified fewer than 20 INGOs in his overview of educational development organizations, in keeping with the trend in the late 1980s for IGOs to collaborate with NGOs, 125 NGO delegations participated

Table 4.3. Sponsors of the World Conference on Education for All: Representatives on International Steering Committee

	Sponsors	Cosponsors	Associate Sponsors
Multilateral lenders (2)	World Bank*	Asian Development Bank*	
Multilateral donors (7)	UN Development Programme (UNDP)* UN Educational, Scientific, and Cultural Organization (UNESCO)*ᴱ UN Children's Fund (Unicef)*	UN Fund for Population Activities (UNFPA)* Islamic Educational, Scientific, and Cultural Organization (ISESCO)ᴱ	Economic and Social Council for Asia and the Pacific (ESCAP)* World Health Organization (WHO)*
Bilateral donors (10)		Denmark: Ministry of Educationᴱ Finland: Finnish International Dev Agency (FINNIDA)* Japan: Ministry of Foreign Affairs, Technical Cooperation Division* Norway: Norwegian Agency for Development Cooperation (NORAD)* Sweden: Swedish International Development Authority (SIDA)* U.S. Agency for International Development (USAID)*	Canadian International Dev Agency (CIDA)* International Dev Research Council (IDRC)* Italy: Ministry of Foreign Affairs, Education, and Training Cooperation* Switzerland: Federal Department of Foreign Affairs, Development Cooperation, and Humanitarian Aid*
International nongovernmental organizations (1)			Bernard van Leer Fdn*ᴱ

* international development organization

ᴱ specialized education organization

Source: World Conference on Education for All Interagency Commission, *Final Report: World Conference on Education for All* (1990).

in the WCEFA. Of these participating NGOs, approximately 24 were national in scope; 34 were regional in scope, based in less industrialized areas; and 67 were international in scope, based in industrialized countries. Consistent with the earlier suggestion that estimates of international development organizations based on directories might be low, only 42 percent of the NGOs attending WCEFA appear in an international development directory as of 1995.

The EFA conference was initiated and conducted entirely by international development organizations, with no formal initiative on the part of nation-states. Realist international relations theorists would argue, nonetheless, that nation-states were still the principal actors in the conference, assuming that nation-states play a determining role in the formal ideology and routine decision making of the international development organizations they fund. However, the evidence from the WCEFA suggests otherwise. The following analysis reviews the evidence that organizations, not nation-states planned and implemented the WCEFA.

Three Original Sponsoring Organizations.

The United Nations Educational, Scientific, and Cultural Organization (UNESCO, f. 1946) holds the UN mandate to promote education as a human right for individuals of all ages. UNESCO's educational development programs are the oldest of any multilateral organization, having pioneered fundamental education in the 1950s (Jones, 1988). UNESCO's budget, unlike that of UNICEF, is funded from fixed assessments on member states, and as such is buffered somewhat from direct interference in its day-to-day policies.

UNESCO, however, was one of the big losers when, shortly after World War II, the United States and several other Western powers decided to channel the bulk of their international development budgets into more easily controlled bilateral rather than multilateral aid programs. As a result, UNESCO ended up with an extremely ambitious mandate and a paltry budget. In 1984, the withdrawal of three nation-states that together accounted for a major portion of its budget, in response to what they perceived as the politicization of UNESCO, did not leave the organization with a free ideological rein. Since 1988, UNESCO has been attempting to woo these financial heavyweights back, by diluting its ambitious NIEO-oriented programs and trying to improve its public image by associating with the World Bank and UNICEF through activities such as the World Conference on Education for All.

UNESCO's efforts to maximize its influence within its budgetary constraints consist of sponsoring "information sharing" and "coordination" activities in the science, cultural, and educational communities. UNESCO routinely collects more educational statistics from more countries than any other organization. These statistics are essential to efforts by international development organizations to determine whether educational access is expanding or quality is improving in various parts of the world. Yet the quality of this data varies enormously from country to country. In the less industrialized countries, as noted by Myrdal in the last chapter, the capacity to gather and analyze education statistics is often limited and the quality of statistics poor. Nonetheless, much of the World Bank's research in education at least through the 1980s rested on this dubious database. In the 1990s, the World Bank funded a study by the National Academy of Sciences made a series of recommendations to improve UNESCO's education data gathering and analysis capacities (Hansen & Guthrie, 1995). By strengthening UNESCO, rather than collecting its own data, the World Bank avoids the appearance of being a vertical monopoly—producing its own data for its own models—and cultivates the image of being one among several donors who have arrived independently at similar conclusions about the progress of education in less-industrialized countries.

Furthermore, UNESCO's regional offices provide a logistical base for operations outside headquarters, and these offices, as part of their agreements with the local government, have the right to host international conferences. International conferences and compendia of cross-national statistics (Finnemore, 1991) and policies (McNeely & Cha, 1994) are indeed UNESCO's forte. In addition, as the one UN organization with a direct mandate to address education until the early 1980s, UNESCO provided most experts for all UN education activities, including those funded by the World Bank, UNDP, and UNICEF. Since the end of World War II, UNESCO has been, therefore, positioned to play a more important role in international education discourse than its budget might suggest.

The World Bank (f. 1944, soft-loan window f. 1960) obtains most of its funds from international capital markets. Until the early 1990s, the United States was the single largest nation-state contributor and the president of the Bank is always a U.S. citizen; in realist terms, the World Bank might be expected to reflect simply the interests of the United States and international capital markets. The World Bank, however, has more resources—both in terms of funding and research—than any other single international development organization. In addition to creating the potential for influence with other less well endowed organizations, these resources, combined with relatively secure funding sources, protect the Bank from too-frequent interference and fine-tuning by individual nation-state funders, including the United States (Jones, 1992).

The Bank's autonomy is further enhanced by its mandate to rationalize all lending decisions in economic terms. The Bank has consequently been in the forefront of the field in generating economic indicators in sectors, including education, that have proved historically difficult to model in empirical terms. The Bank has used its ample resources to assemble more sectoral experts and economists than any other international development organization. In the 1980s and 1990s it has invested significant resources in disseminating its expert research findings throughout the development community.

These same experts, however, are useful to the Bank only to the extent they are viewed as objective by the outside world. Maintaining some measure of intellectual independence is therefore essential. These experts help to ensure that, while the Bank's project documents remain focused on economic efficiency, some of its education studies, particularly internal ones, reflect a more socially oriented approach to development, for example, Basic Human Needs (Streeten, Burki et al., 1981). Nonetheless, Bank research is often criticized for its economistic bias, its tendency to use inaccurate cross-national data in econometric models, and thereby to generate questionable internal rates of return so that the Bank can have an "objective" basis by which to choose between investments in roads or schools.

The Bank started a small education projects division in 1962, but did not issue its first education policy paper until 1971. More importantly, until the early 1980s, the World Bank, as a UN affiliate, depended upon UNESCO for technical assistance in education—foreign experts to provide advice to the Bank and its less industrialized country clients—thereby ensuring UNESCO some influence on Bank education policies. Since that time, however, the World Bank's intellectual and financial investment in education has grown. With a larger research budget and publishing operation than any other international development organization, Bank influence on educational development policy increased in 1980s and, with large funding increases in the 1990s, that influence continued to grow.

For the last 30 years, the Bank has emphasized a relatively instrumental approach to education: education as an essential input into development, perhaps even a basic human need, but human rights did not figure prominently in its justification. Consistent with this approach, when reports surfaced in the 1980s about the backward trend in social indicators in many sub-Saharan African countries, the Bank identified education—particularly primary education—as the missing factor in its development investments and sponsored a report, *Education in Sub-Saharan Africa* (World Bank, 1988). According to many observers, the World Bank's interest in EFA was tied to its interest in finding partners to provide grants for the technical assistance needed to plan and implement the Bank's anticipated education loans in Africa, loans it hoped would revitalize African development efforts in general and restore investor confidence.

In contrast, by the 1980s, the United Nations Children's Fund (UNICEF, f. 1946) statements on education put primary emphasis on education's links to the Declaration of Universal Human Rights, rather than education's suggested contribution to economic development. Also in contrast to the World Bank, UNICEF raises most of its relatively small budget through annual voluntary contributions from nation-states, individuals, and nongovernmental groups. Until the 1990s, the United States was UNICEF's single largest contributor, but in recent years Nordic and other countries, acting as a block, have matched the U.S. contribution and thus its voting power.

UNICEF manages its financial dependency relatively astutely. Created as a follow-on to the UN Relief and Rehabilitation Agency (UNRRA, f. 1943)—an early organizational victim of the Cold War—UNICEF has cultivated an image as a nonpolitical organization, and has played a significant role in using global discourse to elevate children as a special nonpolitical category of persons deserving special assistance. (Black, 1986; Boli & Meyer, 1987). A comment made during a meeting to create UNICEF summarizes its basic approach to governments:

> ... one senior UNRRA official, exasperated and frustrated at the politics that were bringing the organization's operations to an end, exclaimed, "For God's sake, keep governments out of this as much as you can. Make it possible for the new show to give help to mothers and children directly. . . . The art is *not* to persuade governments to agree that UNICEF should undertake activities, but to ensure that the government does not say no and then, in the absence of prohibition, to get on with the job as quickly and discreetly as possible." (Jackson cited in Black, 1986)

In addition, UNICEF raises money directly by appeals through children's groups during holidays (on Halloween in the United States), sells greeting cards, and has established private fundraising UNICEF National Committees in member countries. Through these local and national organizations, UNICEF maintains an active, positive presence among the general public in many industrialized countries.

UNICEF had just three executive directors[20] through its first 49 years, while the World Bank and UNESCO had eight each. This helped UNICEF cultivate its somewhat unique image as a stable, well-managed UN organization. All its executive directors have been U.S. citizens, and the first two, moreover, were Republicans, providing additional credibility with conservative senior senators on the U.S. Foreign Affairs Committee so important to UN funding (Black, 1986). UNICEF documents strongly assert the rights of children and their mothers to basic social services, including education, despite close financial and organizational ties with the United States, a nation-state that periodically rejects the concept of entitlement programs at both the national and international level.

---

20. UNICEF's first three directors were also very personable and dynamic. In 1960, the Norwegian Committee for UNICEF had tried to nominate UNICEF's first Executive Director Maurice Pate, personally, for the Nobel Prize, but he insisted it must go to UNICEF, and in 1965 it did (Black, 1986). At his memorial in 1995, one speaker remarked that former Executive Director James P. Grant was survived by a wife, a sister, three sons, five grandchildren ". . . and several million children who would not otherwise be alive today." Note the similarity to a *New York Times* editorial eulogizing Pate, ". . . scores of millions of children in well over 100 countries have been fed and clothed because he lived."

UNICEF's role in education was subordinate to UNESCO's throughout the early development decades. For two decades, 1962 to 1982, UNESCO paid for an education advisor and liaison office located in UNICEF headquarters, to provide on-call technical assistance to UNICEF on education (Phillips, 1987). UNICEF focused more on issues relating to the health of mothers and children, and, within this emphasis, first on secondary, then later on nonformal education. In the early 1980s, in an attempt to maximize both organizations' limited resources in education, UNESCO and UNICEF entered into a collaborative pilot project to promote education and literacy in a few select countries and, also, in keeping with the era's emphasis on NGOs, cosponsored an NGO Collective Consultation on Literacy.

But by the late 1980s, the expansion of UNICEF's highly regarded Health for All campaign, emphasizing the introduction of four low-cost life-saving health technologies,[21] was slowing down and some senior officials at UNICEF associated this slowdown with high levels of illiteracy in high priority countries. Promoting literacy, therefore, came to be seen as a way to help meet the Health for All goals by the year 2000 and maintain both the credibility of UNICEF and a general public enthusiasm for international development programs such as Health for All.

In summary, the actions of these three multinational organizations are clearly more independent from nation-states' interests than their governmental funding base might suggest. Their education programs derive from different starting points and, without any conscious attempt to coordinate, emphasize different aspects of schooling: UNESCO, with adult literacy and work-related training; UNICEF, with nonformal education for mothers and preschoolers; and the World Bank, with formal education, originally secondary and higher education and more recently primary. In spite of these different approaches, the history of at least two of these organizations renders them keenly aware of the lack of public confidence and funding for the international development field. This awareness contributed, to some extent, to their interest in jointly sponsoring the World Conference on Education for All. None could have undertaken the conference alone, but together they held the essential ingredients for a major international initiative in education: UNESCO, the education mandate, regional infrastructure, and coordinating experience; the World Bank, the research and funding; and UNICEF, the model for the conference and public confidence.

Later in 1988, the three original sponsors would be joined by a fourth, UNDP, an organization with little education expertise, but with the broadest development mandate of any UN organization. The role of UNDP and the cosponsoring and associates sponsoring organizations listed in Table 4.3 are explored more fully in subsequent chapters.

---

21. Breast feeding, growth monitoring, infant immunization, and oral rehydration therapy.

Conclusion

The evolving discourse on international development supported the creation of thousands of organizations that today define their goals in terms of improving the welfare of individuals in less industrialized countries. These goals, and the international development programs they promulgate, are somewhat independent of the interests of the industrialized nation-states that fund them. The structure of this field of organizations creates substantial interdependence among organizations, and, since the mid-1970s, the discourse has promoted stronger alliances between governmental and nongovernmental organizations. The governance of the field cuts across national boundaries; the jurisdiction of its belief system varies, as some sectors are able to back up their claim to universally applicable scientific knowledge more credibly than others; and two types of organizations—those able to produce relevant research and those able to operate at the grassroots—each become central to the field.

In earlier years, this meant that the Rockefeller and Ford foundations, funding research in tropical medicine and founding international agricultural research centers were more prominent in the international development field. In recent decades, the World Bank has taken a more leading role in "knowledge production" in the field. But the Bank, like many of the larger IGOs, lacks a structure that allows it to work at the grassroots level demanded in more recent development discourse. During these decades, development NGOs have begun to be acknowledged more openly as important members in the international development field, as they are one of the few types of international development organizations able to work at the grassroots.

The World Bank lent its scientific legitimacy and funding weight to the WCEFA; UNICEF brought its good will and the operational capacity of all its field offices; UNESCO brought its education and conference convening mandate; and NGOs were invited to lend grassroots legitimacy to the WCEFA. All of these organizations represented not their nation-state funders as much as their clients: UNICEF, the children; NGOs, the poor and historically marginalized; the World Bank, higher education and research; UNESCO, higher education and literacy. With commitments and mandates like this, how could the conference affirm anything less than education for all?

Thus far, the main characters in the WCEFA story have been the leaders and the organizations. But this is not a story of great leaders or of peopleless organizations. The time and attention span of the leaders was limited and organizations generally need hands and arms and voices to come to life. The next chapter introduces the individuals who actually planned and executed the conference: the international development professionals.

5

Educational Development Professionals

The World Conference on Education for All as described to this point was an initiative not of states, but of the leaders of UN organizations and of other international development organizations. These organizations, however, did not spontaneously move to sponsor the conference on functional merits alone. Instead, professionals within these organizations, drawing on models and scripts generated over several decades, guided the sponsoring organizations into courses of action they knew to be acceptable to their funders and the broader international community. These models and scripts drew heavily on the international development discourse as well as on a partially established academic subdiscipline: international and comparative education. Compared to public health, however, education's claim to a universal scientifically-established knowledge base was relatively weak. Moreover education lacked consensus on a set of inexpensive technological innovations— such as immunization or oral rehydration therapy—that could speed the delivery of quality education to remote areas of less industrialized countries. The work of these professionals, therefore, was to reconcile the breadth of the development imperative and its insistence on "everyone" as the target, with the limits of international and comparative education as science and of the funds at development professionals' disposal.

The historical rise of the international development profession is evident in the establishment of specialized institutions, such as professional schools, professional associations, and professional journals. The profession also is strengthened by contacts created through an increasingly dense collection of less formal groups, such as those formed by users of specialized databases and projects. Some of these groups are mentioned in this chapter; formal sector-specific congresses and conferences are described in the following chapter.

The legitimacy that derives from this professionalism establishes for development professionals a frame of reference somewhat independent of the nationality of its members. Further, professionalism legitimizes various decision-making procedures, to the extent that these procedures become taken for granted as objective by many within the profession. Using these decision-making procedures, professionals in international development organizations who claim jurisdiction over and, in turn, apply supposedly universal standards to development activities are rarely challenged by nation-states. This chapter examines the extent to which international development professionals successfully exert a jurisdictional claim to specialized knowledge about the development of education systems in less industrialized countries and to the extent that those claims supported the idea of education for all.

International Development and Epistemic Communities

International development professionals are a relatively understudied phenomenon. There is some literature on consultants (Cleveland, Mangone et al., 1960; Benveniste & Ilchman, 1969; Fry & Thurber, 1989) and the "development set" (Hancock, 1989; Klitgaard, 1990). Many critiques of large international development organizations, however, tend to impute to their bureaucracies and, implicitly, to the people working in them, a degree of power, coherence, and efficacy (Hancock, 1989) that bears no relationship to the constraints that many of those professionals perceive. In fact, many international development workers sense that the range of their potential action is closely circumscribed by the bureaucratic logic of organizationally sanctioned processes, such as internal project reviews, logical frameworks, evaluations, and strategic plans. These processes, not individuals, appear to manufacture the organization's decisions (van Ufford, Kruijt et al., 1988).

However, international development professionals are in a strong position, not so much in terms of individual decisions, but in terms of their ability to define what is possible, reasonable, and efficient. Scott (1992) argues:

> More so than other types of collective actors, the professions exercise control by defining social reality—by devising ontological frameworks, promising distinctions, creating typifications, and fabricating principles or guidelines for action. They define the nature of many problems—from physical illness to economic distress—monopolizing diagnostic techniques as well as treatment regimes. They underwrite the legitimacy of providers as well as practices. (p. 139)

Researchers interested in international organizations, in an effort to expand their analyses to nonstate actors, have recently taken a new interest in professionals identified as epistemic communities:

An epistemic community is a network of professionals with recognized expertise and competence in a particular domain and an authoritative claim to policy-relevant knowledge within that domain or issue area. (Haas, 1992)

Haas argues that an increase in the role of science in policy making, together with increased complexity and uncertainty in the international arena, makes nation-states more willing to turn to self-styled, apolitical, epistemic communities for advice. Moreover, he suggests that the transnational span of international epistemic communities makes them much more powerful than national communities.

In Haas's terms, development professionals from diverse disciplines and nationalities do not share similar causal and principled beliefs, nor do they necessarily share the same interests and knowledge base; consequently, they are too diverse to constitute an epistemic community. However, a subgroup of development professionals that does share beliefs, interests, and an internationally recognized specialized knowledge base—such as the international development professionals who specialize in education, population, or environment—might well qualify as an epistemic community. The reputation of the scientific basis for their knowledge base will determine in part its ability to function as an epistemic community.

The next two sections examine how, over time, international development has taken on many of the characteristics of a profession and, at the same time, international and comparative education has been gaining academic credibility. The third section examines how professionals working on educational issues in international development organizations have tried to construct a new domain of recognized expertise and competence with an authoritative claim to policy-relevant knowledge about "educational development," that is the development of educational systems in less industrialized countries. The ability of a subset of these professionals to act as an epistemic community, however, is complicated by the relatively unscientized status of the academic knowledge bases on which they depend: international development studies and international and comparative education studies.

Abbott (1988) provides the framework for some of these analyses. He argues that most tasks have two qualities. One is objective, such as the technology and the organizations involved; the objective qualities of international development were discussed in the preceding chapter. This chapter deals with what Abbott calls a task's subjective qualities, defined by the way the profession currently holding jurisdiction over the task diagnoses, makes inferences about, and treats the problems associated with the task. Academic knowledge helps to legitimate a profession in a certain task by establishing its rationality and/or linking its foundations to widely-accepted cultural values. Haas observes similar processes at the epistemic community level, "It is the political infiltration of an epistemic community into governing institutions which lays the groundwork for a broader acceptance of the community's beliefs and ideas about the proper construction of social reality" (Haas, 1992, p. 27).

Abbott also provides additional guidance in evaluating Haas's somewhat normative distinction between bureaucratic and epistemic communities: "Bureaucratic bodies operate largely to preserve their missions and budgets, whereas epistemic communities apply their causal knowledge to a policy enterprise subject to their normative objectives" (Haas, 1992, p. 19). The description in the preceding chapter emphasizes that, given their strong resource dependence and concerns about generating more public support, many international development organizations are bureaucratic bodies. However, this section argues that epistemic communities, mainly experts grounded in academic and/or scientific communities, operate in a somewhat symbiotic relationship with the larger international development community. The experts formulate normative objectives and causal knowledge that in effect constitute important elements of world culture. Yet it is the bureaucratically organized international development organizations that carry and diffuse that culture on a global level. In this process, expert education knowledge may mutate to conform more closely to standards and concepts in the international development field. The case study at the end of this chapter highlights the role of international development and more specialized educational development professionals in the early preparatory stages for the WCEFA and illustrates how this mutated knowledge becomes codified in international declarations and plans.

International Development Professionals

At the end of World War II, several groups of individuals in Europe, North America, New Zealand, and Australia had preexisting interests in and familiarity with what were soon to be declared "developing" countries. This pool included:

- colonial officers, merchants, and their children;
- missionaries and their children;
- workers with governmental and nongovernmental relief organizations (Sommers, 1977);
- former military advisors; and
- others with technical expertise already working for foundations or multinational corporations in the colonies.

All of these groups figured prominently as consultants and staff in the early decades of international development. In addition, some donor countries, such as the United States, with no formal colonial experience, drew on individuals and organizations with technical expertise in areas that had been important in their own national development. Finally, all these groups were joined by a cadre of civil servants or academics from less industrialized countries who achieved senior status relatively young but who became expatriates, having exhausted career opportunities in very small countries, or because of political regime changes.

Eventually, specialized postbaccalaureate degrees in international development—and extensive overseas experience, often as a volunteer—became prerequisites for entry-level jobs in international development organizations. Long, back-to-back overseas assignments took young sectoral specialists— like epidemiologists or educationists—far from the academic communities and professional associations that might help them to maintain their particular skills and independent perspectives (Tendler, 1975). In some organizations, eligibility for promotion to midlevel and senior-level jobs became more dependent on satisfactory service in several different countries than on up-to-date sectoral or regional expertise.

International development professionals produced by this combination of schooling and work experience may spend their entire working lives in a series of assignments in global metropolises and less industrialized country capitols. At least one governmental donor uses mandatory transfers every two to three years to prevent staff in foreign posts from "going native" (that is, becoming overly sympathetic to local concerns, at the expense of the donor country's interests); yet such frequent transfers may well promote an equally antinational tendency to "go international." For example, a common peripatetic lifestyle tends to bind international development professionals more tightly together, promoting identification with the international development field as opposed to their technical specialization or even their nation-states. This lifestyle is similar to the one described by Anderson (1991) with respect to colonial administrators in Latin America, a lifestyle, he argues, that facilitated the social construction of the first "modern" nation-states.

The fact that Cold War arguments were used to justify much funding for international development work does not necessarily tell us anything about the motivation of Western development workers. In the eighteenth and nineteenth centuries, missionaries, themselves primarily interested in proselytizing but cognizant that London politicians had other interests, urged on the British Parliament the trade advantages of expanding contacts with Asia and India. Similarly, the degree to which international development workers motivated by essentially humanitarian and/or scientific concerns played upon Western alliance governments' fears of communism or propinquity for profits to increase international development budgets is unclear. Not just young Turks, but even very senior international development professionals sometimes refer to each other as "coconspirators,"[22] as though their true motives

---

22. See preface in Bienen, 1993. Also, in the same monograph, Gulick calls his colleague, "The archetypal Happy Warrior. His war is on global poverty; his enemies are ignorance, indolence, and indifference" (p. 39). Also see Chapter 4 for the idea of using children as a "Trojan Horse" for a larger development agenda.

for coaxing international development aid out of reluctant donor governments must be concealed. Similarly, Sommer (1977, pp. 18–19) argues that
the establishment of U.S.-based international development organizations in
the 1940s and 1950s generated

> . . . the institutionalization, for the first time, of a cadre of trained adminis-
> trators and overseas field workers. Given the consequently increased expo-
> sure to and knowledge of overseas conditions, it is not surprising that U.S.
> efforts then tended to aim at root causes of suffering as well as pure relief.
> (pp. 18–19)

More recently, Smith (1990, pp. 282–84) remarked on the tendency of the
staff of nongovernmental development organizations to focus on medium- to
long-term development activities, even when their private contributors in the
United States consistently contribute more funds in response to short-term
disaster appeals.

Perhaps no aspect of international development activities has been so
consistently misrepresented by professionals to their funders as the time
frame needed to achieve development goals. One professional who started
with the World Bank in the 1960s acknowledged,

> We were much too optimistic about the time needed to implement some-
> thing. The World Bank felt it had to tell the board it could accomplish
> something within five years. That was too short for "soft" components but
> board members didn't like to wait so long; they were happier when the
> hardware was dispensed.

The organizational affiliations of these early international development
workers—churches, the military, the colonial bureaucracy—brought with
them a certain culture. Most cherished science, preferred action to analysis,
and inclined more towards incremental change than radical reform. One
retired senior UN official reflected about his superior's strategy to international development, "He and I grew up in World War II. He used to say [with
respect to a difficult development problem], 'We need a Bailey Bridge.' "[23]
Another professional of the same generation confessed, "I'm for magic bul-
lets, for technical quick fixes," and contrasted himself with a younger colleague who he said was more concerned with systemic reform.

As international development became more professionalized, the search
for longer-term, systemic, empirical approaches became more common,
highlighted in the 1990s by the emphasis on "sustainable" development. One
senior manager at the World Bank acknowledged, "Our methods were too

---

23. Semi-prefabricated metal bridges designed to be constructed or taken down in a very short
time.

sophisticated, but when we tried to be more simple, we were accused of being second-rate." Another consultant preparing a report for the World Bank explained his supervisor ". . . insisted he wanted statistics, regardless of quality. Why? He did not want my report to be purely sermon . . . [rather he] wanted to show [the report] was grounded in reality [sic]." The search for scientific credibility was particularly important in light of the principal form of aid that professionals claimed to be able to offer to less industrialized countries: science-based technical assistance.

Technical Assistance

Development discourse in the 1950s and early 1960s emphasized that newly independent countries, many rich in raw materials and natural resources, needed only technology to industrialize their economies and some "technical" advice to install—or instill—it. "Technical assistance" became a euphemism for experts and trainers who could introduce this technology, be it modern machinery or management. Truman's Point Four speech, particularly the section, "We invite other countries to pool their technical resources in this undertaking" provided the rationale for the UN Expanded Program of Technical Assistance (EPTA, f. 1949). In its first report, the EPTA defined the forms of technical assistance as (a) technical advising services, (b) training, (c) pilot plans, (d) demonstration projects, and (e) dissemination of technical information (United Nations, 1949). By 1962, the International Institute of Administrative Sciences had expanded the definition to include:

> Technical assistance consists in the transmission of learning, knowledge, and techniques or material and human resources in order to help those who receive it to solve specific problems in a more suitable manner in keeping with their needs. It is an external contribution which assumes a very wide variety of forms: visits of experts and technicians, receiving fellowship holders, organizing courses and seminars, exchanging or disseminating information or documents, and supplying material and equipment, and occasionally financial means. (as cited in Sufrin, 1966, p. 44)

In the 1950s and 1960s, this concept of technical assistance provided part of the rationale for expanding scholarship and exchange programs in industrialized countries to residents of less industrialized countries, programs that themselves generated a new type of interest in international education (described in greater detail below). The concept also encouraged the use of many individuals with previous experience in less industrialized countries as advisors, trainers, managers, and demonstration project leaders onsite in less industrialized countries. The importance of technical assistance strategies that are "cooperative"[24] and "sensitive to local conditions" has

---

24. See Brown (1966).

been proclaimed in all decades; yet, the culture of expertise often makes such approaches difficult. Americans, in particular, have frequently been criticized for taking a salesmanlike approach to technical assistance.[25] One American international development professional said of his colleagues, "Everyone likes pushing ideas with missionary zeal."

After World War II, the international research work of the Rockefeller Foundation and the tropical medicine and agriculture institutes of the colonial powers generally continued along ongoing lines under the new rubric of international development. Although the Ford Foundation was a relative newcomer to international philanthropy at the end of World War II, its program of support to international development soon overshadowed that of all other private donors and that of many UN and bilateral donors as well.[26] Through its grants to the London School of Economics and many other economics departments in respected universities in both industrialized and less industrialized countries, the Ford Foundation played a particularly critical role in institutionalizing development economics as a subdiscipline of economics. Economists such as Sir W. Arthur Lewis, Sweden's Gunnar Myrdal, the United States's Frederick Harbison, and the Netherland's Jan Tinbergen were much in demand for international conferences and seminars. In the 1950s and early 1960s, they and other economists sometimes spent several years as resident advisors to newly independent countries, garnering experience that was then generalized to other countries at similar "stages" of development. The early investments of the Ford Foundation and these world-class economists helped to establish a credible economic base for much international development work in the following decades.

Terms of Service

By the early 1960s, new criteria for the selection of experts became widespread. Technical proficiency in a discipline relevant to development was a necessary but not sufficient condition for performing well as a technical assistance expert. A significant proportion of experts had proved unable to adapt to foreign cultures and unfamiliar living conditions and others seemed unable to tolerate the increasing bureaucracy in many international development organizations. Consequently, previous work in a less industrialized country, preferably associated with a reputable international organization, became an increasingly important criterion for securing long-term employment or contracts with international development organizations.

---

25. "Providing technical assistance always involves selling the other fellow on your point of view" Brown (1966).
26. According to Sutton (1987), a modest estimate of the value of Ford Foundation–held stock in 1951 totaled US$ 417 million, compared with the central regular budget of the UN in 1950 of US$ 43.7 million, or UNESCO's US$ 7.8 million.

In addition, with the proliferation of UN organizations in the 1950s and 1960s and the rise of bilateral aid organizations in the 1960s and 1970s, the new organizations looked for new professional administrative competencies, including the ability to formulate development activities into self-contained, time-bounded projects.[27] The ability to maneuver these projects through not just one governmental bureaucracy, but—with the rise of multidonor projects—two or even more bureaucracies was also important. Technical advisors representing donor countries—many of which had no national plans of their own—nonetheless encouraged recipient governments to develop national plans, clearly labeling priorities, so that the donor organizations might reference those priorities when justifying their own programs and plans to their funding bodies. Ironically, more often than not, expatriate technical advisors were needed to develop these "national" plans and priorities.

Some bilateral organizations—such as Britain's DFID[28] and Japan's JICA[29]—drew on career specialists in their domestic ministries for the prescribed combination of expertise and bureaucratic acumen. Other bilaterals, such as USAID, concentrated on procuring technical experts through short-term contracts—often with multiple extensions—while saving career slots for generalists. Long, consecutive tours of duty overseas tended to isolate specialists from their scientific communities and generalists from the interests of their headquarters. A Swedish economist reflects on his employment with the United Nations Technical Assistance Board:

> While I was stationed in Israel or Bolivia, it often happened that in my reports I referred to these countries as "my country." Maybe one of the problems of the international civil servant working in the field [that is, assigned to work in a less industrialized country] is that he [sic] must not lose his identity as an international employee—his friendly feeling towards the country where he works must not be so strong that he forgets his responsibilities towards his own. (Carlson, 1964)

Various governmental and intergovernmental organizations experimented with different strategies to forestall their professionals "going native." USAID, for example, discouraged its permanent staff from staying more than four years in one country. In addition, every seven or eight years USAID

---

27. The spread of a common project management structure in the international development field was facilitated by the large number of organizations that have worked with the U.S. Agency for International Development and its predecessor organizations, all of whom were working under the same Federal Acquisitions Regulations (FAR) as the Department of Defense. The effect of the Department of Defense on the spread of project management structures in the 1950s among its contractors is described in Wieland and Ullrich (1976).
28. Department for International Development, formerly the Overseas Development Assistance (ODA).
29. Japanese International Cooperation Agency.

recalled overseas staff to Washington for a two- to four-year tour, during which time they received short-term, in-service training to bring them up-to-date on new administrative procedures and/or technical subjects. Less attention appears to have been paid to the dangers of "going international." The same individual quoted above remarked,

> The fact that I was far away from home and that I felt a bit lost in a new social and cultural environment also promoted a strong feeling of fellowship towards my colleagues from the various international organizations. . . . Everyone feels like a member of a large and happy family. (Carlson, 1964, p. 6)

In addition, a significant number of international development professionals marry nationals in less industrialized countries, establish long-term ties with those countries, and may find a more supportive environment for cross-cultural marriages in expatriate communities overseas.

By the late 1970s, prior experience in a less industrialized country was a prerequisite for long-term overseas assignments with international development organizations. Entry to a career in development often started with a two- to three-year stint as a volunteer with one of many nongovernmental and governmental volunteer organizations, some established prior to 1945 as emergency relief operations. Some of these organizations worked closely on the technical assistance model and matched up experienced specialists from industrialized countries with small local organizations or communities in less industrialized countries. Others, like the U.S. Peace Corps, recruited generalists with bachelors' degrees in the 1960s and 1970s, then later focused on more specific degrees such as math and science. These returned volunteers provided a new cadre of applicants for postbaccalaureate programs in development and area studies, some of them specifically designed as preparation for a career in development.[30]

This combination of on-the-job experience and formal professional training provided relevant preentry service and became prerequisites for jobs with larger international development organizations. This long series of non-regulatory prerequisites to entry in the international development profession represents a major career investment for most international development professionals. Moreover, for many, this investment was nontransferable, since many employers in industrialized countries did not value overseas experience and seniority gained overseas did not translate into senior positions in domestic organizations.

---

30. For example, the two-year masters' degree in development policy program at Princeton's Woodrow Wilson School and the development studies programs at Harvard's Kennedy School of Government and the London School of Economics.

Professional Training and Research

Beginning in the 1950s, with the increased emphasis on the importance of planning for national development, and continuing in the 1960s and 1970s with the rise of bilateral and the proliferation of multilateral development organizations, three types of training for development professionals emerged. The first, oriented to training in-service officials from less industrialized countries, was usually provided over a three- to nine-month period in a nonacademic residential institute in an industrialized country.[31] In later years, some of these institutes took their short courses to less industrialized countries and/or helped to establish in-service training institutes for economists and planners in less industrialized countries.[32] Second, other public and private organizations offered short orientation courses for experts from industrialized countries assigned or aspiring to assignments in less industrialized countries. Finally, degree-granting programs appeared, usually of 9 to 24 months duration, targeting both aspiring young development experts from industrialized countries as well as career civil servants and young professionals from less industrialized countries.[33]

As part of their interest in promoting interest in world affairs in industrialized nation-states and the scientific study of development in less industrialized nation-states, the Ford and Rockefeller foundations provided much of the initial funding for development studies programs and research centers, as well as for area studies programs in Africa, Asia, and Latin America. The Cold War provided extra impetus to these interests for both the United States and U.S.-based foundations, leading Berman (1983) to interpret most of their activities as evidence of actual or desired hegemonic domination by the United States. The Ford and Rockefeller foundations, for example, supported the founding of the Institute for Development Studies (IDS/Kenya, f. 1961) at the University College of Nairobi, including funding more than 20 European and North Americans as resident scholars in 1970. Governmental organizations also chartered various development studies programs. The British Ministry of Overseas Development established the Institute of Development Studies at the University of Sussex (IDS/Sussex, f. 1966) as a focal point . . . gathering together in one organization experts in economics and the other main fields of development studies to do research and training.

---

31. Examples of these include the Economic Development Institute (EDI, Washington, D.C., f. 1956), associated with the World Bank, and the Administrative Staff College, Henley (UK, f. 1946).
32. For example, the Ford Foundation supported the work of Syracuse University's Maxwell School to set up the Pakistan Administrative Staff College (f. 1960, Lahore).
33. Examples of these degree-granting programs include the concentration in economic and social development offered by the Graduate School of Public and International Affairs (f. 1957) at the University of Pittsburgh and the Institute of Public and Business Administration (f. 1955) set up by the University of Southern California at the University of Karachi.

By the early 1990s, international development training and research centers were producing some 500 to 600 journals and serial publications.[34] In the United Kingdom, development studies as a field of academic study grew throughout the 1970s and 1980s (Association of Commonwealth Universities, various).[35] In the rest of the world, most of the growth of these programs in recent years appears to have shifted from industrialized to less industrialized countries. The Ford Foundation ended its funding for development studies in the early 1980s and the Rockefeller Foundation shifted to supporting research institutes in less industrialized countries. By the late 1980s, these latter two actions may have contributed to a decline in the number of international development programs in U.S. higher education institutions.

Some of these international development studies programs were actively involved in the production of research relevant to donor policy questions. Other institutes exclusively devoted to the study of policy-oriented international development research began appearing in the 1960s, also with substantial foundation aid. These latter include: the Overseas Development Institute (ODI, London, f. 1960), funded mainly by the Ford Foundation; the Overseas Development Council (ODC, Washington, D.C., f. 1969), with over half its operating budget from the Ford and Rockefeller foundations; and the International Development Research Centre (IDRC, Canada, f. 1970).

By 1976, the proliferation of international development training and research institutes called for more systematic cataloging. The government-funded Institute for Development Studies at Sussex and the OECD's Development Center[36] sponsored a series of conferences, resulting in the creation of the Interregional Coordinating Committee of Development Associations (ICCDA, f. 1976) and the International Development Information Network (IDIN, f. 1976). The latter organization created a database to promote the exchange of information about development activities on a regional and interregional basis. By 1988, the network covered training and research institutes, projects, individual researchers, bibliographic data, and referrals. It decentralized in 1985 into five regional associations and social science councils. The ICCDA in cooperation with these regional organizations periodically publishes directories that continue to chart the expanding boundaries of the international development field.[37]

34. See the bimonthly International Development Abstracts (f. 1982) and the Development Periodicals Index (f. 1991).
35. In 1982, Jackson (1980) listed 73 international development training programs, ranging in length from nine months to two years.
36. The Development Center (f. 1962), not to be confused with the OECD's Development Assistance Committee (DAC), carries out studies, maintains a library, and produces directories of organizations, and databases as a service to the development community, particularly for scholars and organizations in less industrialized countries.
37. Since the mid-1990s the number of websites that provide information about international development organizations has grown dramatically.

The Society for International Development

The professionals in governmental and nongovernmental international development organizations, academics and trainers in development studies programs, researchers in academic and policy-oriented research institutes, as well as short- and long-term expatriate technical assistance experts, began forming coherent professional groups as early as the mid-1950s. In October 1957, 60 individuals, of whom all but eight were Americans, met in Washington to formally draw up a charter and operating procedures for a new Society for International Development (SID). The preamble to SID's constitution expresses the fear of nuclear war as well as the positivist approach characteristic of that period:

> Science, the advance in man's knowledge of nature, by bringing man to the age of nuclear power and space conquest, has given international peace the new meaning of *a condition essential for the continuance of mankind.* By discovering new resources, inventing new products, devising new ways of production, and achieving new mastery over life and death, it enables more human beings to reach higher levels of well-being than ever before. By stretching a web of instant communication over the earth, it has opened men's eyes to new opportunities and stirred fresh aspiration for a better life. To fulfill this aspiration and make these opportunities real in a manner consistent with the growth of individual freedom is a major part of the dynamics of peace, requiring widespread international cooperation for technical development and economic advance . . . (Society for International Development, 1959)

Membership in the early years drew heavily from professionals working in the Washington, D.C., area, predominantly Americans. By 1959, the society had scraped together enough in membership dues to offer its first world conference (Washington, D.C.) and, with aid from the Ford Foundation, to publish the first issue of the quarterly *International Development Review.*

SID held annual world conferences between 1960 and 1969 and thereafter every two or three years. Efforts to internationalize the society led to the first world conference outside the United States in Milan in 1967, and the first in the less industrialized world in 1968 in New Delhi. By the time of the Delhi conference, SID's membership had grown to 5,100 members, only 50 percent of them Americans, and to 63 chapters, only 13 of which were in the United States. These trends were reinforced by new bylaws which elected members of SID's Governing Council on a regional, rather than an at-large basis and by other conscious efforts to diversify membership.

In light of its orientation towards less industrialized countries and its strong base in industrialized countries, SID has tried to play a bridging role in the international development community. In 1977, in a continuing effort to internationalize SID, the headquarters were moved to Rome and plans initiated for a "North-South Roundtable," intended as an informal place for dialogue about the type of issues the New International Economic Order proposals raised in formal intergovernmental forums. Along similar lines, SID, with the Brandt Commission, takes credit for initiating the call for the first summit meeting of political leaders from both North and South held in Cancun in November 1981.

In the larger international community, SID derives much of the legitimacy for such endeavors indirectly, through the stature of its individual members. SID International's recent presidents include an executive director of UNICEF and an executive director of UNFPA. Rice (1982) argues that SID did not secure the final stamp of legitimacy for a development NGO—formal consultative status with the UN—until 1970 because "to many SID leaders such a relationship had appeared redundant, given the unparalleled informal access which SID had through its own members."

Despite this apparent success in operating at the global level, SID remains relatively small—about 6,000 members worldwide in 1995—but not because its membership is exclusive. Specifically because of its small size and its perceived need to broaden the constituency for international development, the society has consciously chosen not to construct itself as a bounded professional organization. As part of its purposes, SID stated its commitment "to advance, through research, publication, and discussion, the science, process, and art of economic development and technical cooperation." In addition to publishing *Development: The Journal of the Society for International Development* (quarterly),[37] conference reports, and various newsletters, most SID chapters keep their membership open to anyone interested in development. SID's first and largest chapter in Washington, D.C., illustrates these features.

For most members, SID is a secondary, not a primary professional organization. In the early 1990s, the Washington chapter experienced a 50 to 60 percent turnover in membership annually as members left for and returned from overseas assignments. The Washington chapter is also located near some of the largest aid donors in the world—the World Bank, the Inter-American Development Bank, and USAID—and to the source of the bulk of their funding until recent years—the U.S. Congress. Since the 1970s, in light of shrinking U.S. government funding for international development aid, SID's Washington chapter has worked closely with the biannual International Development Conference (IDC, 1952 2001) and other NGOs to increase interest in international development. These efforts have included development education at the grassroots level in the United States in an effort to increase public support, and funding, for international development aid.

---

37. Succesor to the *International Development Review*.

INGOs—both missionary and emergency relief organizations—have traditionally played an important role in increasing the interest of citizens in industrialized countries in the welfare of less industrialized countries (see Chapter 4). These organizations typically portray their efforts as motivated by continuing and pervasive humanitarian concern for suffering or, in religious terms, "unsaved" humanity. The focus of some of the more recent development education campaigns into which governmental development organizations recruit NGOs, however, deviates from earlier campaigns. For example, the purpose of the Alliance for a Global Community (f. 1994), a project entirely funded by the USAID and run by a consortium of U.S.-based development NGOs, was "to persuade Americans not only that foreign assistance works, but that it works in their best interest" (USAID Administrator Brian Atwood, as cited in Alliance for a Global Community, *Connections 1*(1): p. 1). Each issue of the Alliance's newsletters dealt with a separate category of development issues such as the environment, women, children, or food. The newsletter emphasized globalization and the interdependence of the modern world, rather than more traditional notions of compassion; continuing and expanding international development efforts to promote human progress; and informing the public of the efficacy of ongoing international development activities.

These development education activities are designed, in part, to preserve the mission and budgets of existing international development organizations. As such, the development professionals engaged in these activities involved fit Haas's description of bureaucrats, rather than experts; these professionals are primarily concerned with keeping their organizations operating rather than with producing expert knowledge.

On the other hand, this description of international development professionals does include a role for experts with a particular area of expertise who maintain it through close ties with academic communities, research institutes, and other sites of expert knowledge production. These experts are more likely to be consultants than permanent staff with international development organizations (Tendler, 1975) or, if staff, then with a development research institute specializing in some recognized expert domain. Significantly, the organizations where such experts are trained and work are omitted from some international development organizations directories. These organizations include: the Consultative Group on International Agricultural Research (CGIAR, f. 1971) and its almost 20 affiliated centers specializing in different crops that have played a key role in carrying out the agricultural research essential to most agricultural development projects. Similarly, the International Center on Diarrheal Disease Research (ICDDR, f. 1978) which played an important role in developing the oral rehydration therapy that was key to the child survival revolution.

The ability of international development professionals to establish an "authoritative claim to policy relevant knowledge" (Haas, 1992) is therefore often based on the credibility of experts who usually work for organizations not solely or primarily focused on international development. Until recently, this was the case for development professionals working in the education sector. Linkages between the international development field and international and comparative education domain are explored in the following section.

Summary

An increase in the number of international development organizations has brought an increase in the number of individuals who spend much of their working lives in such organizations. The rise of the international development field created a unique career pattern for international development professionals. This pattern tends to distance them from their countries of origin, and to promote a sense of solidarity with other development professionals. A host of permanent and temporary organizations consequently emerged to service both international development organizations and international development professionals. These included research centers, professional training programs, and professional societies.

The definition of international development professionals used thus far incorporates both Haas's idea of bureaucrats—those primarily interested in preserving the mission and budget of their own organization—as well as experts—those who share beliefs, interests, and an authoritative claim to policy-relevant knowledge. Various subsectors within the international development field, such as public health and agriculture, have gained public recognition for their professional expertise while others are still struggling for both credibility and funding. The following section describes the struggle for credibility and jurisdiction in the international and comparative education discipline and how its interaction with the international development profession has strengthened but not yet established an internationally recognized expertise in educational development.

The International and Comparative Education Discipline

Lauglo (1995) describes the uneasy relationship between international development professionals and international educationists as a conflict between bankers/economists and pedagogues. The rise of international educationists, described below, traces the history of these pedagogues as well as that of a second group of educators—administrators—who perhaps find it easier to make common cause with international development professionals.

Historians of international education often trace the roots of their field to the 19th century, when Americans and other foreigner educators visited Prussian schools and representatives of the Meiji restoration traveled to Europe and the United States in the late nineteenth century. In both cases, the purpose of the comparison was to improve the educational systems in the visitors' home countries. Later in the nineteenth century, international conferences, such as the International Congress on Education in Philadelphia in 1876, offered educators the chance to learn something about several national education systems without having to undertake a multicountry study tour.

In the early twentieth century, the International Conferences on Moral Education (1908, 1912, 1922, 1927, 1929) attracted "progressive" or "new" educators, such as John Dewey, who were reacting against the Prussian-style/authoritarian pedagogy which had been widely diffused as a result of earlier study tours. The New Educationists promoted a more liberal, individualistic approach to education that emphasized child psychology and experiential learning. They interpreted World War I as an indictment of authoritative pedagogical methods and placed much hope in child-centered teaching as the key to world peace (Sucholdolski, Avanzini et al., 1979).

Various world federations of educators were formed in the first half of the twentieth century. For the most part their activities were limited to meetings and publications. For example, the World Federation of Education Associations (f. 1923, inactive) held biannual meetings and awarded a US$25,000 prize "for best feasible plan of promoting world peace through education" (Carr, 1928).[38]

The first permanent international institute to offer opportunities to study education internationally, the Institut Jean-Jacques Rousseau's (Geneva, f. 1912) School for the Sciences of Education, was firmly rooted in the New Education movement. Established on the 150th anniversary of the publication of Rousseau's *Emile, ou l'éducation*, the Institut took as its motto the first line from that book: "Begin ye preceptors by studying first your pupils, for most assuredly you are at present unacquainted with them." The Institut served as a school, research center, and dissemination point for ideas and information consistent with the New Education movement's commitment to the role of education in fostering peace. For example, in 1917, Institut director Pierre Bovet published *The Fighting Instinct*, in which he used psychology to explain the roots of aggression in adults and children and the role of schools and other progressive activities to channel, divert, sublimate, or harness "natural" aggression.[39]

Prior to 1920, efforts made to create an International Bureau of Information for Education and Instruction, an International Education Research Council, and a World Bureau of Education failed, as did proposals to incorporate education into the League of Nations. Instead, a donation of

---

38. The first prize was awarded to David Starr-Jordan, Chancellor Emeritus, Stanford University, for his plan for organizing the committees of the WFEA as follows: (1) international cooperation, (2) teaching of history, (3) use of international athletic contests, (4) current arguments for war as a cosmic necessity, and (5) methods of teaching facts about the present Court of International Justice.

39. Along these lines, Bovet would later become the founder and promoter of Baden-Powell's then recently conceived Boy Scouts in Switzerland.

US$5,000 from the Rockefeller Foundation to the private Institut Jean-Jacques Rousseau helped to establish the International Bureau of Education (IBE). While the Institut focussed on postgraduate study of education, with an emphasis on child-centered, activity-based primary education, the new Bureau was designed for information dissemination and scientific studies.

The Bureau struggled along on a financially unsuccessful private basis until 1929, when it was reconstituted as a governmental organization.[40] In 1934 it instituted the oldest extant intergovernmental education conference, the International Conference on Public Education.[41] With Piaget as the head of the Bureau (1925–1968), issues relating to child and adult learners' psychology and to improving pedagogy consistent with that psychology dominated the International Conference until the early 1950s. During the Piaget period, the Bureau did not promote scholarly study of education, rather it served as a clearinghouse for information.[42] The Bureau's compilation and dissemination of annual reports on the state of education in participating nation-states in an *International Yearbook of Education*, as well as its quarterly *Bulletin* (f. 1926), offered scholars and policy makers an opportunity to compare various education systems for the first time. The reports also expanded to scholars not physically located in Geneva[43] the opportunity to compare education systems.

The founding of UNESCO (f. 1946) did not immediately obviate the need for the Bureau, which remained semiautonomous until 1968 when it became a part of UNESCO. Today UNESCO's own education programs focus on promoting literacy in less industrialized countries (Jones, 1988) while affiliated organizations like the Bureau and later the Institute for Education (Hamburg, f. 1951)[44] address the needs of the scholarly education community in industrialized countries. By establishing information clearinghouses and directories of organizations involved in the same domain, these IGOs introduced some coordination and preliminary governance to the edu-

---

40. The first members included the Ministry of Education of Poland, the Government of Ecuador, the Department of Education of the Republic and Canton of Geneva, and the Institute Jean-Jacques Rousseau. By the beginning of World War II, membership grew to include most sovereign countries.

41. For more details on this conference series, see Chapter 6.

42. In later years, the Bureau began to produce a summary background paper on the subject of each conference, to be distributed to participants during the conference and to others afterwards. Aggarwal and Aggarwal (1982) assert these were widely used as models in newly independent countries.

43. Along similar lines, the International Institute of Teachers' College, Columbia University, published the *Educational Yearbook* (1924–44) organized around specific themes or levels of comparative education, and the University of London's Institute of Education published the *Yearbook of Education* beginning in 1932, interrupted by the war, later collaborating with the International Institute of Teachers' College.

44. UNESCO also started Institutes for Education in Munich and Cologne, but the Union of International Associations' Yearbook suggests that they are defunct.

cation sector in a nonauthoritative way. In their lack of binding jurisdiction, the development IGOs pose a minimal threat to the organizations that they attempt to document and, as such, almost any IGO at any level or status within the sector can offer these services. However, once created, such directories and the classification systems they use gain legitimacy over time.

An increasing interest in the formal study of international education in the United States begins about the same time as the founding of the Bureau. The Institute for International Education (IIE, New York, f. 1919) was established with a grant from the Carnegie Endowment for Peace (f. 1910) and another from the American Friends Service Committee (f. 1917) to promote the international exchange of students in the interest of improving international understanding and thereby promoting peace on an individual basis. In addition, these international exchange programs exposed a large number of Americans to foreign education systems and increased the pool of scholars interested in studying international education at an advanced level or choosing it as a career.

The first grants awarded by Rockefeller Foundation's International Education Board (IEB, f. 1923)[45] provided scholarships for foreign students at Teachers' College at Columbia University, New York University (f. 1923), and for study tours of African-American education for African leaders under the guidance of the Phelps-Stokes Foundation. The growing number of practitioners in foreign student exchange organizations, educational foundations, the U.S. Office of Education, and education experts within emerging development organizations, such as FAO, provided the critical mass for creating the first Comparative Education Society (CES,[46] f. 1954). Funding from the Ford Foundation enabled the society to publish the first professional journal of comparative and international education, *Comparative Education Review* (f. 1956).

In the 1960s, the society grew as both old and new comparative education programs and scholarships in Canada and the United States expanded, funded in part by the Ford Foundation, the U.S. Government's Fulbright Program, and the National Defense Act. While the Fulbright Program was explicitly designed to promote international understanding, both the Ford Foundation and the National Defense Act emphasized the importance of Americans acquiring knowledge about all parts of the world in order to maintain U.S. competitiveness in the Cold War.

---

45. John D. Rockefeller, Jr.'s international counterpart to the domestic General Education Board (GEB, f. 1903), created by his father, John D. Rockefeller, Sr., to promote advancement of education in the United States. Initially, the IEB and GEB shared a president and chairman and there was considerable overlap in their boards of directors.
46. Later to become the Comparative and International Education Society (CIES). More on this below.

Throughout the postwar period, British and American educators dominated the field of comparative education (Cowen, 1990; Wilson, 1994). Nonetheless, a Swedish psychologist headed one of the most influential comparative education institutions created in the postwar period. From 1962 to 1978, Torsten Husen lead the International Association for the Evaluation of Educational Achievement (IEA, f. 1960), a consortium of research institutes in more than 40 countries. Although established in Hamburg under the auspices of UNESCO's Institute of Education, the IEA moved to Stockholm in 1969 and later became one of the core activities of the Institute of International Education (IIE, Stockholm, f. 1971) before moving to the Hague in 1978. Thereafter, IIE, Stockholm focused on research and postbaccalaureate training for a new generation of comparative and international scholars based primarily in Europe.

Early cross-national studies by the IEA focused on determining the correlates of achievement in different countries, including pedagogy, class size, and curriculum.[48] The data produced by the IEA has provided the grist used by a generation of cross-national education scholars.

The study tour tradition of the late nineteenth and early twentieth centuries was reinforced in the 1960s with the creation of organizations such as the International Intervisitation Program on Educational Administration (IIP, f. 1966) by the U.S.-based University Council for Educational Administration (UCEA, f. 1959) and by the Commonwealth Council of Educational Administration (CCEA, f. 1970).[49] In the early 1990s an Intervisitation was held every four years, each one traveling to more than one location and producing a book of proceedings and papers. In addition, the two councils together produced three international periodicals.[50] The standardizing processes typical in most professional organizations are evident in one of the program's earliest publications, *A Glossary of Educational Terms: Usage in Five English-Speaking Countries* (edited by Walker, Mumford, and Steel, 1973). Because of the program's connections to the Commonwealth, an increasing proportion of the IIP participants have come from former British colonies, now less industrialized countries. As a result, issues relating to development have come to play a prominent role in the program.

The first World Congress of Comparative Education Societies (Ottawa, 1970) included participants from the societies based in the United States, Japan (f. 1964), Britain (BCIES, f. 1966), and Canada (CIESC, f. 1967). The

---

48. In fact, policy makers and educators often misuse the relative achievement of students on these assessments to evaluate the rigor of their own national education system.

49. Members of what would become the Commonwealth Council attended the first two IIPs and the creation of the council was a direct product of the second IIP. The council's creation spurred the establishment of several national societies, such as the British Educational Administration Society (April 1977), which, in turn, publish their own national journals.

50. *Educational Administration Quarterly* (f. 1965), *Educational Administration Abstracts* (f. 1966), and the *Journal of Educational Administration* (f. 1963).

congress resulted in the creation of a standing World Council of Comparative Education Societies (WCCES, f. 1970) supported by IBE and charged to produce a world congress every few years. While the main theme of the first national societies was post–World War II reform and reconstruction, one of the three themes of the first congress was "the role and rationale for educational aid to developing countries." By 1980, the entire fourth congress focused on "Education and National Development" and the council's major thrust in the following three years was "the extension of our field by means of professional organization of comparative educators in nations not yet represented" (Cowen, 1990, p. 341). By 1994, the council had 29 member societies.

Summary

Interest in improving national education systems stimulated the creation of an array of permanent organizations, including academic training and research centers, professional societies, and UN specialized organizations, as well as more transient organizations and communities, such as information clearinghouses, congresses, and loose networks of journal readers and contributors. International organizations formed to address the interests of professional educators became increasingly oriented to development, to the extent that they aspired to be global and to incorporate all countries and nationalities into their memberships and agendas.

In the nineteenth century, school-based psychologists and educators without governmental support initiated study tours to other countries, the first of a series of modern international development activities. These nongovernmental efforts became institutionalized in the first intergovernmental organization, the International Bureau of Education. In most nation-states, the state is involved in the licensing of teachers and the accreditation of primary and secondary schools. In many nation-states, however, the state does not regulate the right to do research or to teach at a higher level in education or any of its subfields, such as international and comparative education, with or without a specialized degree. Such regulation is left to the discretion of individual academic centers. Governmental and/or foundation funding of various programs within these centers plays a major role in which subfields thrive and which wither away. In the United States, both governmental and nongovernmental scholarship and research grants for international and comparative education, in part driven by Cold War concerns, fueled interest in comparative and international education as an academic field.

Professionalization within the field is not yet highly formalized. Most, if not all, of the international and comparative education societies mentioned above have no entry requirements tied to licenses or degrees.[51] Instead, these

51. This may not be true for all the European societies.

societies, like the Society for International Development described above, focus on including as many interested parties as possible, both in keeping with building a constituency for comparative and international education and consistent with world standards of equality of participation. This strategy leads societies like CIES and the CCEA to include more representatives from less industrialized countries and to encourage the formation of national chapters in less industrialized countries. The proportion of WCCES and CCEA members based in less industrialized countries has grown over time and hence development plays a major role in these organizations' agenda.

In general comparative and international studies remain a somewhat precarious subdiscipline within the precarious discipline that is education. Although comparative and international education departments in universities did not immediately disappear when their initiating grants from the Ford Foundation ended in the mid-1970s, the number of international courses in graduate education schools as a whole may be declining (Sutton, 1993).

The overlap between the international development field and the international education discipline is significant but not overwhelming. Foreign exchange students and trainees funded by international development activities contributed to the expansion of international and comparative education departments in schools of education. UNESCO provides some basic links between the international education community and the international development field. The World Bank has been encouraging the administration of international achievement tests in some less industrialized countries receiving education sector loans.

The next section describes how international development professionals have attempted to build a policy-relevant expertise on this somewhat fragile disciplinary base.

International Educational Development Professionals

Several overlaps between the fields of international development and international education have already been noted. The oldest organizations in the international development organization directories are the missionary societies that established schools and hospitals in Africa, Asia, and Latin America in the nineteenth century. The desire to save souls and/or civilize, rather than to promote scientific progress, motivated most of these early groups. Though these schools rarely tried to cover large populations comprehensively, the Western values that they imparted to emerging national elites in newly independent countries contributed to the later diffusion of a liberal rationalization of mass education, represented in Table 3.

The earliest—and continuing—support to higher education in less industrialized countries came in two forms: scholarships for individuals to study in Europe and the United States, described above, and support to

develop universities or specialized training centers. These scholarships contributed to the rise of Western-style research and higher education in less
industrialized countries, and created a Western-trained elite.

Professionals staffing new UN-based educational development programs after World War II came from a variety of backgrounds. A former
British colonial officer, John Bower, designed UNESCO's fundamental education program. Economists such as W. Arthur Lewis and Frederick Harbison
provided short- and long-term advice to newly independent countries.

In the course of promoting its educational programs, UNESCO set up a
series of centers such as the Arab States Functional Education Center
(ASFEC, f. 1952, later renamed the Arab States Regional Center for Functional Literacy in Rural Areas), founded under UNESCO's fundamental education program, and the International Institute for Adult Literacy Methods
(Tehran, f. 1968), founded in connection with the World Conference on Erad-
icating Illiteracy (1965). These centers primarily produced materials and
training for paraprofessional personnel for mass literacy campaigns. The
centers nonetheless offered sites where educational experts could begin to
specialize in issues specific to development.

The need for trained manpower planners, highlighted at a series of
regional conferences in the early 1960s, prompted UNESCO, the World
Bank, and the Ford Foundation to jointly establish the International Institute
for Educational Planning (IIEP, Paris, f. 1963). With the optimism of the First
Development Decade, the Institute was established as a temporary organization to address the training needs of newly independent countries; initial
pledges from the donors were for five years only. The Institute gave priority
to less industrialized countries in its research and training programs, since
many trainees could not afford the cost of in-house long-term courses in
Paris. Interest on the part of donor organizations was therefore key to funding
scholarships and maintaining enrollments. In the IIEP's first 32 years, 1,075
individuals participated in its eight-month course and 3,100 participated in
shorter courses. These former participants constitute a network that IIEP
endeavors to maintain through its *Newsletter* (f. 1982).[52] In addition, resident
scholars and consultants produce several series of widely circulated publications.

Because of the wide range of backgrounds of its students and the relatively short duration of its courses (two weeks to one year), the Institute
never became a degree-granting institution. Partly because of this and in part
because of its affiliation with UNESCO, the Institute remains closer in some
ways to the international development domain than to the scholarly international and comparative education domain.

---

52. The newsletter's circulation in 1995 was about 10,000.

In the industrialized countries, the Ford Foundation made major grants in the late 1950s to several education schools to establish special post-baccalaureate programs of research and academic training in international and comparative education focusing on less industrialized countries.[53] Like IIEP, these centers, under contract with a governmental donor or with scholarships from the Foundation, provided short-term, in-service training for educators. However, unlike IIEP, these centers also awarded master's and doctoral degrees and remained firmly grounded in the international and comparative education domain. As a result, in the 1970s, in keeping with broader trends in higher education, the centers in the United States began to pursue a line of critical theory more closely aligned with dependency theory than with liberal international development models (Carnoy, 1974; Arnove, 1980; Berman, 1983). Other scholars, influenced by social constructionist and post-modern theories, began to question the essentialist bias of international development organizations, problematizing the concept of development and education's contribution to it.

The dampening effects of these trends on the formation of a policy-relevant academic subdiscipline dealing with educational development may have been most pronounced in the United States. For example, throughout the 1960s, the Stanford International Development Education Center/Committee (SIDEC), under contract with the U.S. Office of Education, provided in-service training for foreign civil servants. However, in 1968, SIDEC merged with the international and comparative education program in the School of Education and curtailed its work with the U.S. government. Nonetheless, by the early 1970s, approximately one-third of SIDEC's doctoral graduates (1954–1972) worked for international development organizations. Throughout the 1970s and early 1980s, SIDEC was generally critical of international development organizations, though by the end of the 1980s the committee was providing short, academically oriented, in-service courses for World Bank staff and project participants. In the 1990s, SIDEC became the International and Comparative Education program, dropping the word "development" from its name.

Professional communities institutionalize themselves in part by defining a bounded domain of activities over which they exercise authority, by gaining exclusive right to define expertise within that domain and to limit the practice of that expertise to those upon whom the community confers licenses, diplomas, certificates, and/or degrees. Neither international development nor the narrower education for development domain has professionalized its expertise in this formal way. Hence in the United States, there is no permanent link between the professional development community and the academically

---

53. For example, the Comparative Education Center (f. 1958) at the University of Chicago and the Stanford International Development Education Center (1965–95).

based international and comparative education community. In larger academic and professional societies, the formation of a special section is sometimes used to indicate the growing legitimation of a particular specialty. The absence of a special section on international educational development in the Comparative and International Education Society may well be a function of the society's small size (about 1,200 members in 2001), but neither is there a special section in the 22,000 strong American Educational Research Association. The failure to make this linkage appears to extend beyond the United States; a 1995 "global" directory of 79 programs and centers in comparative and international education listed only one or two with the word "development" in their names (Altbach and Tan, 1995). On the other hand, academic communities in nation-states that did not experience as pronounced a clash of ideology between academics and government in the 1960s and 1970s, or those established after the first wave had passed, may have closer relationships with development organizations. Such may be the case with the Institute of International Education (Stockholm, f. 1977), which supplies most of the education staff and consultants for the governmental Swedish International Development Agency and, to a lesser extent, to some other Nordic bilateral donors. Donor/academic relationships on education issues are reinforced through organizations such as the Nordic Association for the Study of Education in Development Countries (NASEDEC, f. 1981), which hosts a biannual conference for staff, consultants, students of comparative education, and interested educators.

The development discourse in the 1970s and 1980s emphasized the importance of recipients' participation in the planning and implementation of development projects and in the production of empirically based strategic plans by recipient governments as evidence of their "ownership" of development activities. This discussion may have contributed to the decline of funding for international development education research in some industrialized countries. During this period, Ford Foundation resources dwindled and the Rockefeller Foundation redirected its relatively modest resources to supporting higher education research and training capacities in less industrialized countries.

Still in need of science-based research for their programs, international development organizations launched a two-pronged strategy. First, the World Bank, primarily involved in the construction components of education projects until the early 1970s, began producing its own research on education in less industrialized countries. By the mid-1980s, the Bank had published over 250 research reports dealing with education in less industrialized countries (Kollodge and Horn, 1986). By 1988, planning documents for a regular meeting of the international donor organizations involved in education show that the World Bank supplied 11 of the 18 substantive background papers.[54]

54. Meeting of the Planning Committee of the International Working Group on Education, Paris, 28–29 August 1986 (IWGE/List of Documents [Rev. 2], 4 August 1986).

Second, new regional groups of international education specialists went into operation in the early 1970s.[55] Through these groups, often donor-funded, educational professionals in donor organizations promoted professional networking and exchange of research among educational researchers in Eastern and Southern Africa, Southeast Asia, an Latin America. The Northern Research Review and Advisory Group (NORRAG, f. 1985) produced a quarterly newsletter that provided information on donor policies and interests in education, as well as reviews of recent research and publications, to the Southern RRAGs. These efforts are related to donor efforts to bring less industrialized countries into "partnership" by providing them with much of the same data and research that donors use and by later giving southern researchers an audience for their data and research. This exchange was promoted as a way to establish an objective/scientific basis for evaluating prospective and ongoing education projects.[56]

The RRAGs were just one of the outcomes of a series of meetings in Bellagio, Italy, beginning in 1972, for the heads of international donor organizations and hosted by the Ford and Rockefeller foundations on the topic *Education and Development Reconsidered* (Ward, 1974). The purpose of the meeting was to "improve their understanding of the role of education in the general advance of Third World nations." The subtext of this conference was that appropriate international development aid had not been forthcoming from donors because they lacked proven sound "investment" opportunities and/or they needed better, more scientific research on the link between development and education.

The first two Bellagio meetings included 14 heads of organizations, nine specialists from less industrialized countries, and 43 foundation and organization staff and specialists. These two meetings were followed by two more at the heads of organizations level and two at the staff level, as well as a host of working group meetings. A few scholars from less industrialized countries were asked to prepare background papers. Other than to present case studies relevant to their countries, no government officials represented less industrialized countries at these meetings.

The products of these meetings include:

1. an International Educational Reporting Service (f. 1974) within the International Bureau of Education to collect and disseminate information about improvements and innovations in education;

---

55. REDUC (Latin America, f. 1972) predated the Bellagio Conference; the Southeast Asian Research Review and Advisory Group (SEARRAG, f. 1982); and the Educational Research Network for Eastern and Southern Africa (ERNESA, f. 1985).
56. For more details about the RRAGs and other research and policy networks for educational development, see McGinn (1996).

2. a series of papers on the state of the art of education research and an Educational Research Review and Advisory Group, to identify shifts in priorities and gaps in knowledge, to disseminate information to the interested public;[57]
3. a higher education for development study;[58] and
4. on-site case studies of various donor-funded basic education programs.

The first product recalls the 1960s interest in disseminating existing technologies, which inspired the creation of various clearinghouses for information about innovations, such as UNESCO's Functional Education Clearinghouse. The remaining three products set the tone for the following two decades. Both reports on the state of the art of education research and on higher education established a rationale for shifting the focus of higher education and research from the industrialized countries to universities and research centers in less industrialized countries. Finally, the basic education focus carried over into the International Working Group on Education (IWGE, f. 1984), described below.

In 1982, a planning committee drawn from the staff of organizations that had participated in the Bellagio meetings convened to discuss their future. The committee reconfigured the Bellagio meetings into a new entity, the IWGE, composed of governmental and nongovernmental donor organization staff, rather than leaders, who would meet every 18 months beginning in October 1984. From the first meeting, "basic education" was adopted as their substantive focus.

The establishment of the IWGE marked several important turning points for educational development professionals. First, after decades of leadership in both the international development field and comparative education discipline, the Ford Foundation, in the midst of a major reorganization, effectively withdrew and left the World Bank as the largest funder of research and operational activities for educational development. Second, the IWGE laid the groundwork for donor education policy coordination previously lacking at the global level (Spaulding, 1981). More than 80 international development professionals, many of them specialists in education, met during the three IWGE sessions between 1984 and the 1990 WCEFA. Third, the IWGE started the process of solidifying the educational development community around a common theme, thus reducing the preparation time necessary to gain the community's support for EFA.

---

57. Organized around following problems/areas: (a) learning, (b) education for employment, (c) imbalances in educational opportunities, (d) educational planning, management, and administration, (e) education costs and finance, and (f) evaluation (Lyons, 1984).
58. ICED given lead. Provisional reports published in 1975.

The reason for choosing "basic education" as the IWGE's focus is not entirely clear. The term was anathema to UNESCO for much of the 1970s and 1980s as it came to be associated with inferior, short-term education programs unable to address mass demand for formal education in countries with very low literacy rates. Lyons (1984), nonetheless suggests that UNESCO's Universal Program to Eradicate Illiteracy made the organization more open to the term. The term was more acceptable to other donor organizations still trying to operationalize holistic basic human needs strategies. For example, in 1988, the U.S. Congress began setting annual earmarks for initiating new basic education projects USAID. As one USAID staffer explained, "Congress is convinced there's no future for individuals without education."

Basic education was also an attractive term in that it encompassed both the World Bank's increasing focus on primary education and UNESCO's long-term commitment to literacy. By the early 1980s, the World Bank had a decade-long history of promoting a method of calculating internal rates of return (IRRs) for investments in different types of education (Psacharopoulos, 1973; Psacharopoulos & Woodhall, 1985). Although strongly challenged in international and comparative education circles for its heroic assumptions, this method consistently demonstrated much higher returns to investments in primary education than in other levels of education in less industrialized countries. Despite many objections, IRR and cost-benefit analyses were the closest the international development field had come to a scientific, empirically based argument for education and for differentiating the relative returns to different types of education.

Many of the professionals who attended the IWGE had been working in educational development for more than a decade. More than any other group, these professionals were aware of chronic funding problems for education in less industrialized countries and of the likelihood that donor funding would not be adequate to ensure education for everyone within the foreseeable future. They had witnessed many quick fix campaigns to expand primary enrollments or to achieve universal literacy that produced neither quality education nor lasting literacy. Moreover, they were conscious of the threat of "donor fatigue" in a long-term activity such as building primary education systems. Finally, they were skeptical about the quality and sustainability of alternative, low-cost models of schooling, particularly those sponsored by NGOs in hard to reach areas of less industrialized countries.[59] Governments could use such programs to claim dramatic increases in enrollment rates, without having to spend any additional government funds for education and

59. These included IMPACT schools in Asia, Escuelas Nuevas in Colombia, Fe y Alegria schools throughout Latin America, and the Bangladesh Rural Advancement Committee's Non-Formal Primary Education program.

without subjecting the program to the scrutiny of foreign or domestic professional educators.

A UNESCO staffer suggested that perhaps the basic education theme was attractive to the IWGE because the members wanted to discourage participation by organizations or individuals anxious to pursue organizationally or nationally self-interested agenda: "Basic education is harder to turn into something that ends up being spent back in donor countries. So political types in the donor organizations are just not interested." Finally, one participant declared that the basic education emphasis was proposed by two UNICEF delegates to the IWGE, Nyi Nyi and Manzoor Ahmed, who eventually presented the case for a world conference on basic education for all to the IWGE in November 1988.

The establishment of the IWGE provided a reference group for individual donors looking for expert feedback on educational initiatives. Later it would provide a model for the Donors to African Education (DAE, f. 1989) and the European Donors to Education to replicate or react against. However, in 1988 if the EFA sponsors to take their proposed world conference were looking for a stamp of approval from the educational development professionals, the IWGE was the group most qualified to give it. This process and the process by which the professionals recruited to the WCEFA staff subsequently shaped the structure and substance of the conference is the subject of the following section.

The Role of Educational Development Professionals in EFA

In February 1988, a group of 31 educational professionals representing 10 international organizations[60] gathered at UNICEF headquarters in New York to review a paper on basic education.[61] In the course of the meeting UNICEF Executive Director James P. Grant demanded, "How many illiterates are there in the world? And how much does it cost to make one illiterate literate?" Grant explained if he could demonstrate to the world how inexpensive it could be to educate one human being, the world could be shamed into supporting a global effort to educate all. One participant explained that he and colleagues were scandalized when they realized Grant was talking about education as if it were immunization, and that Grant proposed to promote education in a manner similar to the way he had promoted child survival.

---

60. UNICEF, UNESCO, IIEP, World Bank, USAID, the Swedish International Development Authority, the Canadian International Development Agency, Queen Noor Foundation (Amman, Jordan), the Institute of Education (London), and the International Council for Education Development.
61. Prepared as an outcome of UNESCO Secretary General Mayor's discussions with UNICEF's Executive Director Grant in 1987 and 1988 (see Chapter 3).

Present at the meeting was someone who might have been the first educational development professional, now nearing the end of his career. Philip Coombs had joined the Ford Foundation–financed Fund for the Advancement of Education in the early 1950s to work with educational Television in Africa. From 1961 to 1965, he was the assistant secretary of state for educational and cultural affairs, in which capacity he served as the chairman to the Washington Conferences on Education and Economic Development. He was commissioned to prepare the background report for the Williamsburg Conference on the World Educational Crisis in 1967. Coombs was the founding director of the International Institute for Educational Planning in 1968. In the 1970s, he founded, with Ford Foundation support, the International Council for Educational Development (ICED) and prepared a new education strategy for Unicef focusing on basic education. Coombs' colleague in preparing that report, Manzoor Ahmed, was one of the authors of the basic education paper prepared as background for the February 1988 meeting.

The formal concept of a World Conference on Education for All was first presented to a larger audience of educational development professionals at the plenary meeting of the IWGE in November 1988. This presentation included distribution of a revised version of the background paper prepared for the February meeting at UNICEF, *Moving towards Basic Education for All* (United Nations Children's Fund, 1988). The presentation emphasized that the conference would not contain a set of proposals to be implemented, but that a charter and a world plan of action would be drafted in advance through a series of regional consultations and then presented for adoption by acclamation at the conference. The conference was promoted as a forum for creating good will and for mobilizing additional resources. Thus, both ministers of planning and finance and ministers of education would be encouraged to attend, and both governments and donor organizations would be encouraged to pledge increased funding for basic education. The need for objective, quantitative indicators to measure progress was also emphasized. The November 1988 IWGE plenary registered qualified approval for the conference proposal.

Between August 1988 and April 1989, staff at UNICEF, UNESCO, and the World Bank outlined the working documents, the EFA Charter (later the EFA Declaration), and the framework for action. The initial drafting of these documents highlighted differences in sponsoring organizations' education policies and operational approaches. The World Bank staff brought to the table econometric research on positive economic returns to formal primary education and a strong preference for working with existing governmental structures. UNICEF staff brought hands-on experience with nonformal approaches, a keen appreciation for the potential value of mass media for mass mobilization, and no hesitation about working outside existing government structures, with or without NGOs. UNESCO staff brought substantial expertise in adult literacy.

The initial compromise reportedly worked out among these staff focused on formal and nonformal primary schooling. This compromise would have satisfied UNICEF's pragmatism—educating all children and adults was probably not possible within a decade but universal primary education perhaps was—and its emphasis on children. The compromise also reflected the World Bank's determination to support only those aspects of education for which the Bank's research had shown significant positive economic rates of returns. The compromise, however, does not appear to incorporate UNESCO's historic concerns with literacy and adult education.

The reason for the lack of representation of UNESCO's long-term interests is not altogether clear. Far in advance of the EFA initiative, UNESCO had designated 1990 as International Literacy Year, making it all the more unusual not to highlight literacy at the WCEFA. In 1988 and early 1989, many education professionals at UNESCO unsuccessfully resisted their director general's enthusiasm for the World Conference on Education for All. Many of the EFA discussions took place in Washington or New York, far from UNESCO's Paris headquarters. Some have suggested that the UNESCO staff did not fully engage in strategic planning in the early months while waiting to see if the EFA effort would die of its own weight. But it may also have been that the EFA staff sensed that in the global culture, international development programs backed up by "solid" economic research focusing on children simply "sell" better than literacy programs for undifferentiated adults.

Ironically, what UNESCO lost in the professional drafting stage was regained at the regional consultation stage. The concerns raised and amendments proposed at regional preparatory meetings, by delegates representing less industrialized nation-states, mirrored UNESCO's concerns with teachers, with learners and classroom-level interactions and with the needs of illiterate adults.[62] Probably not incidentally, these topics had been the subject of scores of UNESCO-sponsored regional conferences throughout the 1960s, 1970s, and 1980s (see Chapter 6).

The EFA staff had less success in resolving an issue introduced repeatedly by Grant and his colleagues at UNICEF: specifically, targets. Targets fit into an American model of management and UNICEF was convinced that setting targets had been critical to the success of the Health for All campaign and the Child Survival revolution. Targets were anathema to educationists for

---

62. See King and McNab (1990) for some verbatim reactions from the regional consultations.

precisely that reason; they would argue that education is not a "service delivery system" to be simply "managed," and parallels between education and health were unwelcome. As discussed in the following chapter, targets do not appear in the final version of the declaration, but the framework for action does encourage countries

> ... to set their own targets for the 1990s in terms of the following dimensions: early childhood care and developmental activities ... universal access to and completion of primary education ... improvement of learning achievement ... reduction of the adult illiteracy rate ... expansion of provision of basic education and training in other essential skills required by youth and adult ... [expanding use of] mass media and other forms of modern and traditional communication. (paragraph 8)

The sponsors each contributed US$ 500,000 and, in March 1989, set up an Inter-Agency Commission (IAC) at UNICEF headquarters in New York to plan the conference, together with a secretariat to execute the plans. EFA's image as an American initiative was reinforced when four of the six positions under the executive secretary were filled with Americans. Even further, both UNESCO's and UNICEF's assigned "point men" on site in Jomtien were also American. Significantly, none of the staff had any previous experience with global or regional education conferences, though the executive secretary had recently been involved in regional consultations in connection with the World Bank's 1988 policy paper *Education in Sub-Saharan Africa*. Of the three deputy executive secretaries, all were career international development professionals but only one held a postgraduate degree in education.

Indeed several of the senior members of the Interagency Commission's Executive Secretariat appear to have been chosen more for their professional dedication and operational ability in development than for their substantive background in education. All of them knew their own organizations' idiosyncrasies, yet most had changed organizations several times in their careers and expressed more allegiance to international development than to their present organizations.

The schedule of proposed international preparatory meetings (see Table 6.2 in the next chapter) was very compressed, as were the logistics required to accommodate thousands of participants for five days in Thailand. The extremely short preparation period—just nine months from the creation of the IAC to the start of the conference—placed the entire staff under severe strain, complicated by their close quarters in temporary offices at UNICEF. Nonetheless, some were prepared to work 16 or more hours per day to meet impossible deadlines. Others used frequent flyer miles to attend meetings when travel vouchers did not get processed on time and one described breaking into the apartment of a vacationing colleague in order to access the right type of computer to finish an important document.

In the summer of 1989, the Secretariat set about recruiting cosponsors. USAID, the first to sign on for US$ 250,000, is illustrative of the role of educational development professionals in international development organizations in this process. Education specialists from UNICEF, the Secretariat, and USAID met in May 1989 in Washington, D.C. The USAID specialists were enthusiastic about the conference for several reasons, the foremost being the close match between the basic education focus of the draft EFA documents and the existing USAID strategy in education. (Lindblom, 1990) The USAID educationists, however, faced a number of hurdles in assuring U.S. participation in the conference. Principally, they needed clearance from the US Department of State's Office of International Organizations. However, just three years after engineering the U.S. withdrawal from UNESCO, the U.S. Department of State was determined to boycott any event or activity in which UNESCO played a leading role. To secure that approval, the USAID staff adopted a complex strategy.

First, the staff assembled USAID's contribution to the conference from discretionary funds and contributions from U.S.-based education NGOs, thereby circumventing the need for formal approval from the Department of State or the Foreign Affairs Committee of the U.S. Senate. USAID, rather than the United States, is listed as a cosponsor in all the conference literature. Second, USAID staff drafted a "new" basic education policy paper, which rephrased their existing programs, incorporating more references to the World Bank and to empirical research, in an effort to stress the "scientific" immediacy of the conference to USAID. Third, they highlighted the prestige of the World Bank and downplayed the role of UNESCO in the World Conference. Fourth, the educationists attempted to co-opt EFA's potential constituency in the U.S. federal government by creating an EFA Coordinating Committee composed of representatives from other US federal organizations involved in education.

Though they did not provide the initiative for the WCEFA, educational development professionals guided its format and substance throughout the preparatory stage consistent with conventional wisdom and professional standards already existing in the international development field.

Conclusion

The international development profession has been shaped by over 40 years of international development organization and discourse. International development professionals gain legitimacy in the international community by associating themselves with scientific communities in various sectors that have what Haas calls "recognized expertise and competence . . . and an authoritative claim to policy-relevant knowledge." International development professionals working on educational development activities turn to the comparative and international education community to provide this type of recognized expertise. As noted in the previous chapter, organizations and individuals who could help create apparently scientific rationales for education—what kind is the most important, what are the best delivery mechanisms, how is it best financed—such as the World Bank, become relatively central to the field.

Relative to the scientific community in some other sectors such as agriculture or health, the international and comparative education community is less authoritatively established and provides the international development community with comparatively less universal, policy-relevant science and technology. Since such science and technology is difficult to evaluate, it is possible for different ideas in educational development to accrete over time, as discussed in Chapter 3. Placed in the environment of international development, expert knowledge about education tends to mutate into something consistent with world cultural concepts of justice and progress, of education as a human right, and education as a vital input to economic growth. Knowing that educational development depends on funding from international development donors, professionals work to translate expert knowledge on education into international development scripts. The debate over "basic education" in the late 1970s and early 1980s was, in part, a debate about tactics: what was the best way to coax more funds out of donor organizations.

One tactic was to pool the funds at hand and use them to fund demonstrably "successful" activities. Several World Bank reports had already devised a way to demonstrate that the economic rates of return were higher for primary schooling than for any other type of schooling. In addition, the World Bank was in a position to increase funding to the education sector more quickly than any other donor. There was a strong case, therefore, for narrowing the focus of EFA, either before or after the conference, to primary education for children.

Any debate on WCEFA among professionals was in part about whether the conference would indeed succeed in securing more funds for education from governments in industrialized and less industrialized countries, or whether it would simply contribute to "donor fatigue." In this sense, by Haas's criteria, the development professionals were acting more as bureaucrats than as an epistemic community. The educational development professionals were fully aware that available funding was more than likely to fall short of the needs implied by the EFA framework. However, they were also cautious about the usefulness of low-cost, alternative, nongovernmental schooling, since such schooling could raise enrollments while permitting governments to sidestep their international commitments to fund and ensure quality basic education.

Educational development professionals did not initiate the WCEFA, but in 1988 one of their principal forums, the IWGE, did provide a site for international development professionals to receive token approval for the conference from educational experts. Throughout the early preparatory stages for the WCEFA, the staff was a mix of international development and educational development professionals. No teachers' or administrators' organizations participated in these early discussions. Nation-state sponsorship was engineered, in at least one case, by educational development professionals and driven by professional and organizational considerations rather than by nation-state interest.

De jure, international and educational development organizations and professionals are supposed to work at the behest of nation-states. The following chapter describes the conferences that provided the sites where international development organizations and professionals could orchestrate the expression of nation-state concerns and priorities into forms consistent with the professionals' concerns about educating everyone.

6

Conferences to Universalize Education, 1945–1990

Conferences the world over have a bad reputation. Whether small professional meetings or global extravaganzas, conferences are often characterized as a waste of time and money, a poor substitute for action, or "nothing but talk." In contrast, this chapter argues that international conferences play an important role in the smooth functioning of world society. They consolidate standards within the international development field; raise public awareness and support for specific sectors, such as education; promote networking and expanding linkages between the global and the local level; and, most importantly, provide some global governance. Conferences have become the sites and opportunities for reaffirming and consolidating common "education for development" talk, and common talk has its share of intended and unintended consequences.

The role of conferences in global governance is not immediately obvious. In recent decades, the lack of a world government has led to the search for some actor or actors to fill an apparent political void at the center of the post–World War II global order. The contenders, willing or otherwise, include multinational corporations, the World Bank, and the UN, among others. World conferences provide a stage where some potential ways to govern world society are rehearsed and premier. Although the issues presented on this stage are among the most compelling for world society—hunger, human rights, saving the environment—many of the resolutions proposed do not become institutionalized in the sort of binding international agreements that might provide more governance in world polity. A global summit featuring heads of state, and even smaller, local productions, such as NGO forums, however, can have their inspired moments.

Between 1945 and 1990, the period covered by this study, international organizations sponsored dozens of global conferences on broad sectoral issues such as education, human rights, the environment, and food. These conferences produced hundreds of widely distributed reports, declarations, and targets, many of which incorporated highly idealized, causal assertions about the relationship between activities/events in these sectors and economic and social development. Over time, professionals played an increasingly pivotal role in preparing background papers and draft statements before the conferences convened and the nation-state representatives arrived to play their parts. These documents contributed to an ever-widening construction of the scope of development, in this case education for all, and they extend and deepen the rationalizing discourse.

The international conferences examined in this chapter each share some common characteristics. First, the conferences all assume that the proper unit of planning is the nation-state and that every nation-state should have equal representation at each international conference, regardless of size or wealth. This means that the majority of representatives at these conferences will be from less industrialized countries and will focus on issues relevant to them, that is, on development. Second, the national and international development imperatives enter into the discourse of the conferences soon after World War II. Third, different sectors become the center of attention in different eras; education, for example, doesn't comes into its own until the 1960s, as human capital becomes the presumed key to national economic growth.

Absent a world-state, despite calls at each conference for funds to finance a wider definition of educational development, the required financial support simply cannot be coerced from nation-states. Instead, professionals have developed a multipronged strategy to increase the profile of their sector on the world development agenda. This strategy includes recruiting INGOs and NGOs to raise funds and to emphasize the grassroots character of new educational development programs. In the 1990s, the strategy also includes incorporating goals promulgated at one conference into the declarations and strategies promulgated at other sectoral conferences and summits. Another strategy has involved shifting the public emphasis from adults to a more appealing category of persons: children. Children, as discussed in the last chapter, are appealing to the extent they appear both innocent and vulnerable at the same time they embody the future of the nation. This creates inevitable tensions with the tacit prohibition against leaving any category of person out of the education system as too young, too old, too costly. All of these ideas and practices, improvised and improved upon throughout the last half of the twentieth century, made possible the 1990 World Conference on Education for All.

This chapter is divided into three sections. The first section describes the growth in the number of international conferences on education. The second, much shorter, section describes the chronology of international conferences on other broad sectoral issues and, again, their implications for the WCEFA.

The third section describes the way in which the WCEFA planners drew on models and scripts from earlier conferences to structure the consultative and follow-up process for the World Conference on Education for All.

Please note that this chapter suffers from a surfeit of acronyms, in large part because such acronyms are part of the specialized language typical of professionals in the international development field.

International Education Conferences

A complete list of the major intergovernmental conferences that addressed education in universalizing terms is provided in Appendix B and is summarized in Table 6.1. Ad hoc, usually non-governmental, international conferences for teachers and school administrators took place in the last half of the nineteenth century, but it was not until the second half of the twentieth century that intergovernmental conferences began to prescribe education policies for nation-states. Over time, these policies increasingly contained common elements designed to attain many common goals as delegates came to perceive education systems other than their own not as mere curiosities, but as similar entities subject to universal laws.

The following subsections describe different types of education conferences roughly in the order in which they were held. The first conference series began in 1934 with formal meetings of diplomats and pedagogues who exchanged descriptions of their national education systems and were reticent to issue general prescriptions for improving other countries' education systems. Since that time, several conference series were started and continue up to the present time, including regional ministers of education meetings, adult literacy conferences, and international development donor meetings. The delegates to many of these more recent conferences were no longer diplomats but rather professionals, both bureaucrats and experts, who expect to derive something universal—or at least generalizable to a significant subset of the world's educational systems—from systematic comparisons of international educational development activities.

The early international conferences produced reports, yearbooks, recommendations, and increased contact among a small, highly specialized group of psychologists, practicing educationists, and a revolving group of diplomats. In addition, later conferences also produced global and national declarations and national action plans, as well as research networks and databases (described in Chapter 5) to disseminate educational innovations and research. The early conferences were dominated by psychologists and others interested in the New Education, in "child-centered" rather than direct, whole-group pedagogies. Later conferences emphasized economics and systems analysis, and were oriented towards planning and evaluating the expansion of education systems to meet the needs of national development.

Table 6.1. Major Conferences on Educational Development, Illustrative List, 1934–1990

International Conferences on Public Education Sponsored by International Bureau of Education

Year(s)	Number and Frequency of Conferences	Outcome:
1934–39, 1946	7 annual conferences (IBE only)	20 recommendations
1947–63, 1965–68	21 annual conferences (IBE and UNESCO)	45 recommendations
1970–90	10 biannual conferences (IBE and UNESCO)	12 recommendations

Regional Conferences of Ministers of Education Sponsored by UNESCO, OAS, others

1936–87	12 meetings in Latin America	Lima Declaration (1956), Mexico Declaration (1979)
1952–85	11 meetings in Asia and the Pacific	Karachi Plan (1959)
1960–85	14 meetings in Africa	Addis Ababa Plan (1961), Harare Declaration (1982)
1960–87	8 meetings in the Arab States	

International Literacy Conferences, Symposia, and Consultations Sponsored by UNESCO

Year	Number and Frequency of Conferences	Outcome
1965–82	5[+] conferences	Persepolis Declaration (1975)
1984–90	7 collective consultations of NGOs on literacy and adult education	

Meetings Sponsored by Various Donor Organizations

1961–63	3 seminars in Washington, D.C., on the Role of Education in Economic Growth, sponsored by USAID
1967	International Conference on the World Crisis in Education in Williamsburg, sponsored by U.S. Department of State
1972–79	3 meetings at Bellagio and 2 meetings in Geneva, under the auspices of the Rockefeller and Ford foundations
1982–90	3 meetings of the International Working Group on Education, sponsored by the International Institute for Educational Planning
1988–90	4 meetings of the Donors to African Education in Paris, London, and Vienna, sponsored World Bank and UNIDO
1990s	Various meetings of the European Donors to Education

Concerns about the learner and classroom environment, submerged for a decade or two, reemerged in the 1980s.

This analysis does not include conference series sponsored by the international teachers or administrators, such as the nongovernmental World Confederation of Organizations of the Teaching Profession (f. 1952), now World Education. The analysis includes only partial data on teachers' conferences organized by nongovernmental teachers' organizations; these tend to address narrower classroom and learner issues rather than the universalization themes common to this chapter. The dichotomization of these two types of educational issues—pedagogy versus access—is interesting in and of itself but is not treated here.

The International Conferences on Education

The longest running, extant intergovernmental conference on education began in 1934. The International Bureau of Education (IBE, Geneva, f. 1925) sponsored the International Conference on Public Education[63] annually until 1939, suspending meetings during World War II and resuming in 1946.

These conferences brought together representatives of both IBE member and non-member countries. Though targeted at educationists, many delegations, for lack of travel funds, consisted of diplomats assigned to Geneva with no particular expertise or interest in education. Each delegation was encouraged to present to the conference a report describing his or her national educational system, including both narrative and statistical sections. From 1933 on, these reports formed the core of the *International Yearbook of Education*. Rossello notes the standardizing value of these yearbooks, even at this early stage of the development of comparative education:

> Although these national reports have been criticized as being overoptimistic, it is not certain that some exaggerations [were not useful] in that they gave rise to emulation among the various countries. (1979, p. xiii)

In addition to the national reports, IBE staff also prepared a report for each conference with recommendations on one or more specific educational issues. Between 1934 and 1990, the conference issued 77 recommendations, of which 28 addressed the organization of schooling, 27 addressed the content of education, 16 addressed teachers, and six addressed the functioning of school systems (Courtney and Kutsch, 1980, Annex III). Rossello (1979, pp. xv–xvi) emphasizes that these recommendations were considered relatively bold for their time:

---

63. Renamed the International Conference on Education (ICE) in 1968.

Educationists were suspicious of government interference in this field and governments themselves were wary of any international action in this connection. A member of the International Commission for Intellectual Cooperation [an intergovernmental forerunner of UNESCO] had even gone so far as to write that the League of Nations would never concern itself with education!

In 1947, IBE and the newly formed UNESCO reached a provisional agreement on the joint convening of the International Conferences and the publication of the *International Yearbook of Education*; this agreement was confirmed and enlarged in 1952 and amended in 1968.

The usefulness of this particular conference series to the emergence of either comparative education or educational development is not clear. During the 1950s and 1960s, the international conferences, like many other UN functions, deteriorated into Cold War battlegrounds, joined in the 1970s and 1980s by strident exchanges over the New International Economic Order; as recently as 1992, Bosnia and Serbia used the conference for mudslinging. At the same time, by the late 1970s the conference was so underfunded one commentator described it as "a formidable editing machine, in which there is no place for profound dialogue" (Sucholdolski, Avanzini et al., 1979, p. 113).

As a result, few international development professionals mention the IBE/UNESCO conference recommendations as a reference point for educational development discourse and activity. Presumably in cooperation with the launching of UNESCO's Major Program of Education for All in the mid-1980s, the 1984 International Conference on Education promoted "education for all in the new scientific and technological environment and taking into account disadvantaged groups"—a telling composite of international development themes in the 1980s. Neither program nor conference, however, in terms of staff, documents, or networks, appears to be an important precursor to the World Conference on Education for All.

Nonetheless, the *International Yearbook of Education* is still widely distributed throughout the world, and three editions of summaries of these recommendations had appeared by 1979. Yearbooks and summaries were and are generally available to newly independent countries and to the international consultants who helped them to design new educational systems, serving as widely accepted models of what national educational policies should look like.[64]

---

64. McNeely (1995) cites Aggarwal and Aggarwal (1982) as confirming the importance of the IBE/UNESCO conference recommendations as "a body of educational doctrine of very wide scope and importance," having served as a "valuable source of inspiration and guidance" at the national level. Aggarwal's basis for this assertion, however, is not clear.

Regional Education Conferences

Several regional education conferences in the first half of the twentieth century supplemented efforts to organize global educational discourse. In Latin America, for example, the Organization of American States convened the 1936 Inter-American Conference for the Consolidation of Peace, which produced the "Convention on the Pacifist Orientation of Education," and the 1943 Inter-American Ministers of Education produced a "Convention on the American University." In Africa, the U.S.-funded Phelps-Stokes Commissions (1920s) covered 14 Anglophone, five Francophone, and two Lusophone countries; the Brazzaville Conference (1944) covered French-speaking African countries; a British Colonial Office Advisory Committee produced the report *Mass Education in Africa* (1944); and the Cambridge Conference of 1952 included all Commonwealth African countries.

The origins of UNESCO itself lie in a regional education conference. Beginning in 1942, the Conferences of the Allied Ministers of Education (CAME) met bimonthly in London to discuss postwar reconstruction of educational systems. By 1944, these meetings included representatives of more than 18 countries and territories.[65] The Allied Ministers eventually produced one of the two proposals presented at the UNESCO Establishment Conference (London, November 1945). The second proposal was prepared by the League of Nation's International Institute of Intellectual Cooperation (IIIC, f. 1926) based in Paris, the city promoted by the French as the secretariat for any future educational organization. According to Jones (1988), the Allied Ministers' proposal emphasized the importance of an intergovernmental organization to provide assistance to governments in creating and improving broad-based educational systems. In contrast, the IIIC proposal emphasized UNESCO as a locale for "high level exchanges between leading world intellectuals" (Jones, 1988), that is, a continuation of the IIIC's own work. The Allied Ministers' emphasis prevailed, and, as a compromise, UNESCO headquarters were established in Paris, rather than in Geneva or New York.

UNESCO continues to receive its direction from biannual general conferences to which all ministers of education are invited. Since 1946, the general conference has issued hundreds of resolutions dealing with various aspects of education. There are, for example, four resolutions dealing with "education for all:" the first in 1949 and one each in 1983, 1985, and 1987. UNESCO conferences also generated an international convention against

---

65. The original 10 participating countries included Belgium, Britain, Czechoslovakia, Greece, Luxembourg, the Netherlands, Norway, Poland, Yugoslavia, and the French National Commission on Liberation. By 1944, Australia, Canada, China, India, New Zealand, South Africa, the Soviet Union, the United States were official participants (Jones, 1988) and Spain, though technically neutral, also participated.

discrimination in education (1960) which reinforces UNESCO's mandate to promote education for all.[66]

Formally, the general conference provides a venue for ministers of education and their staffs to meet, develop coalitions, and promote various agendas. In fact, high turnover rates of ministers of education[67] ensure that this rarely occurs for the ministers, although the conferences may be more useful for their staffs. At the same time, some educational professionals complain that the high level of protocol associated with these conferences and the political nature of the speeches delivered by the ministers render these occasions useless for "substantive" work.

Within 10 years of its founding, UNESCO organized several regional conferences on "Free and Compulsory Education" (see Appendix B). The titles of these early regional meetings suggest that they were not focused as exclusively on ministers of education as were later conferences; they also incorporated international and national nongovernmental organizations and universities as observers. The titles also suggest that UNESCO brought an agenda to these conferences—free and compulsory education—and that the conferences represented an attempt to integrate the regions into a worldwide plan of action to implement this agenda. These early conferences produced no declarations.

Both the Lima and Karachi conferences, however, produced ambitious, precedent setting statements. The Lima Declaration (1956), in particular, appears closely related to later declarations emanating from UNESCO's World Conference on Literacy (Tehran, 1965), the International Symposium on Literacy (Persepolis, 1975), the Persepolis Declaration (1975), and a continuing series of meetings on adult education and literacy, leading up to and following the WCEFA (see "Meetings on Adult Education and Literacy," below).

The Karachi Plan (1960) emerged just two months before the start of several conference series explicitly targeted at ministers of education: the Meeting of Ministers and Directors of Education of Tropical African Countries (Addis Ababa, 1960) and the Conference of Representatives of Ministries of Arab Member States of UNESCO on the Needs for Educational Development (Beirut, 1960). Of these three conferences, the Addis meeting is usually cited as the most important and references to the Addis Plan

---

66. With or without funding.
67. In many countries, ministers are political appointees and, in political terms, the ministry of education is not as attractive a posting as the ministries of finance, planning, or foreign affairs. Regionally organized annual and biannual ministers of education meetings, such as the Southeast Asian Ministers of Education Meetings (f. 1976), the Conference of Commonwealth Ministers of Education, and the Conference of Ministers of Education of Francophone Countries (f. 1960), may help offset this problem.

abound in the educational development literature. Nonetheless, the logistics
of the conference, like that of many others, ensured that

> ... the understandably ambitious call by a busy conference for a synthesis
> of its wide-ranging deliberations was followed by the work of a committee
> who, in the time outside conference and commission hours, could do no
> more than produce an "outline of a plan." But the world "plan" slipped
> firmly into their presentation of aspects of objectives, which could be short-
> handed in figures under the captions, Long-Term Plan (1961–1980) and
> Short-Term Plan (1961–1966).
>
>   By the end of the conference, however, the outline had become the
> substance of the whole exercise. . . . It sought to provide for ministers of
> education of newly independent states of Africa a regulative instrument
> which would help them, in a situation of competing claims on limited
> resources, to establish an internationally authenticated demand for the
> means with which to do the work of education. (Bartels, 1983, pp. 5–6)

Although the Addis Plan is now considered wildly optimistic, particularly in its goal for universal primary education throughout Africa by 1980,
it, in effect, put the brakes on some newly independent countries' aspirations
to offer immediate free and universal primary education (Bartels, 1983).
These aspirations were not new or without respected international promoters.
The pre-UNESCO education conferences and commissions in Africa, as well
as the Cambridge Conference of 1952 for Commonwealth African countries,
and even the meeting of Ministers and Directors of Education of Tropical
African countries in 1960, all affirmed the critical role of mass and primary
education in educational development. Given W. Arthur Lewis's warnings
about the drawbacks of mass primary education programs (see Chapter 3),
and Ralph Harbison's estimates of the vast number of technical and higher
education graduates needed in Nigeria in the short term, these early conferences focused attention on secondary and higher education and downplayed
primary education.

The Addis Plan, therefore, proposed strategic, rather than universal,
manpower development at the secondary and tertiary levels of education as
the key to economic and social development, while still guaranteeing universal primary education. The plan envisioned a "master plan" for all of Africa,
coordinated and monitored by a commission meeting annually to review
national educational plans and budgets on a country-by-country basis, to
identify shortfalls, and to increase access to international educational aid. In
addition, the ministers of education would meet every two years to review the
work of and provide guidance to the commission. The commission, however,
met only once, in Paris in March 1962, and played a major role in only one
ministers of education conference, in Abidjan in 1964, before turf battles
between UNESCO and the Organization of African Unity (f. 1963) effectively crippled it (Bartels, 1983).

Southeast Asian ministers of education had more success in establishing both permanent and temporary organizations to follow-up their deliberations. Formed after the Asian Ministers of Education Meeting in November 1965, the Southeast Asian Ministers of Education Organization (SEAMEO) eventually spun off seven organizations, partly funded by Southeast Asian governments and partly funded by donors, some of which are over 30 years old.[68]

By the time of the 1962 Inter-American Conference of Ministers of Education in Santiago, the financial implications of earlier plans had emerged as the most critical components and additional invitations to the conference were extended to "those responsible for economic planning and social development." One contemporary study (Cerych, 1965, p. 26f) estimated the cost of meeting the goals of the Karachi, Addis, and Santiago Plans for the entire less industrialized world between 3.6 percent and 5.4 percent of all less developed countries' combined GNP between 1963 and 1970.

In the UNESCO-sponsored ministers of education conferences convened after 1962, explicit efforts were made to attract ministers of economic planning, though by the 1980s, the target group had dropped to "those responsible for economic planning." A 1967 conference on "The Progress Realized since the Addis Conference" came to fairly dismal conclusions and in the early 1970s UNESCO, the Organization for African Unity (OAU), and the Economic Commission for Africa held intersecretariat meetings to revise the Addis targets. Throughout the remainder of the 1970s and 1980s, chronic shortfalls between the goals of educational development and the domestic funds available to meet those goals led to a series of international conferences that attempted to bring together both less industrialized countries and potential donor countries. The next section describes these conferences.

In summary, regional conferences may be differentiated from the early IBE conferences on several levels. First, in terms of delegates, the regional conferences moved away from random diplomats to focus on ministers of education and later ministers of finance, assuming that all governments in the late twentieth century would have such clearly identifiable posts (Kim, 1996). Second, the regional conferences recruited experts, generally economists from industrialized countries, to offer advice to the ministers. Third, over time, the conferences in fact did not slight any group, though they were interpreted later to focus attention on secondary and higher education. The Addis Plan, for example, included targets for universal primary and adult education, as well as secondary and higher education. The ministers, experts,

---

68. These include the SEAMO Regional Centres for Education in Science and Math (RECSAM, Penang, f. 1967); for Graduate Study and Research in Agriculture (SEAMEO-SEARCA, Laguna, f. 1967); for Tropical Biology (SEAMEO-BIOTROP, Bogor, f. 1968); for Language (RELC, Singapore, f. 1968); for Educational Innovation and Technology (INNOTECH, Manila, f. 1970); for Archaeology and the Fine Arts (SPAFA, Bangkok, f. 1985); and for Vocational and Technical Education (VOCTECH, Brunei, f. 1990).

and donor organizations derived the emphasis on secondary and higher education after the fact.

Fourth, the conference planners assumed that all nation-states could benefit from learning about other educational systems, that there was something common about them, and that all aspects of education were not necessarily unique to each national context. Because of these shared assumptions, the delegates were able to make declarations on a regional, if not a global level. Fifth, the regional meetings, in their explicit plans and calls for major assistance from international donors, made plain that education was indeed an international issue. Finally, and paradoxically, the delegates to these conferences became adept at making the appropriate references to the link between education and development, at least in part to attract donor funding. At the same time they refused to limit education to just an input to economic development. In all the regional ministers of education declarations, education is predominantly couched as a human right in terms of the Universal Declaration of Human Rights. Thus education is characterized as important for economic development, but more important as a human right, a theme which became an established feature of later conference plans and resolutions.

International Donor Conferences

In the 1950s, accelerated industrialization was expected to produce both a demand and an adequate local tax base for mass education. UNESCO's fundamental education activities in this decade focussed on disseminating innovations in mass education and establishing teacher training centers, rather than on funding primary education systems.

In June 1960, the Rockefeller Foundation, the Ford Foundation, and the International Association of Universities brought together economists, educators, and educational administrators at Rockefeller Foundation's conference center in Bellagio to discuss "the economics of education in Europe" (Lyons, 1984). The conclusions that Lyons suggests may have influenced thinking about educational development in the less industrialized countries included:

> There is little or no *real* economic problem in finding the resources for the
> use of education. An abundantly provided society can pay for education in
> all senses—as well as providing finance, it can release able people as pupils
> and teachers. (p. 2)

This faith was reiterated in a series of conferences in Washington, D.C., between 1961 and 1963 sponsored by the U.S. Department of State and USAID. The 1961 Washington Conference primarily focussed on OECD countries, especially those that were growing relatively slowly in economic terms, such as Italy and Greece. At the same time, the conference took stock of the Karachi and Addis plans and concluded that, consistent with the emphasis on comprehensive economic planning in development discourse in the 1950s and 1960s,[69] ministries of education in many newly independent countries needed to undertake more comprehensive planning exercises in order to optimize the use of their limited resources in education. The Washington conferences helped to create the impetus for the establishment of the International Institute for Educational Planning (IIEP, Paris, f. 1963).

In the mid-1960s, U.S. President Lyndon B. Johnson's staff approached the president of Cornell University, James Perkins, to organize, with U.S. funding, a world conference on education in Williamsburg, Virginia. In preparing for the conference, Perkins turned to Phillip Coombs, then director at IIEP, for a background paper. The resulting document, *The World Crisis in Education: A Systems Analysis* (Coombs, 1968), set a more sober tone for educational planning in less industrialized countries for the last half of the decade. It pointed out that much of the failure of educational development might be attributed to a piecemeal approach and to attempts to transfer inappropriate models to the newly independent countries. The solution suggested included greater attention to systems analysis and to innovations, in order of priority, in management, in preparing teachers, in the learning process, and in greater emphasis on nonformal methods of education. Coombs, at the same time, warned the industrialized countries that such a solution required sustained, higher levels of development assistance to less industrialized countries.

Many educational development professionals point to the Williamsburg Conference as a turning point in international development assistance to education. It gave educational professionals inside international development organizations internationally legitimated evidence to argue for greater investments in education. In 1972, the Ford and Rockefeller foundations together hosted a meeting of the heads of international donor organizations at the Rockefeller's Conference Center in Bellagio, Italy, on the topic *Education and Development Reconsidered* (Ward, 1974), discussed in Chapter 5.

The last half of the 1980s was a period of intense interaction for education staff in the donor organizations. Sub-Saharan Africa, with persistently low and falling rates of literacy and enrollment, was the focus of much concern. In 1984, the European Donors to Education, a relatively informal group without the benefit of a secretariat, met at Windsor Castle for a conference on

---

69. But somewhat oblivious to the pattern of development of educational systems in European countries. See, for example, Boli, (1989, passim); Sutton (1989 pp. 35–58); and Soysal and Strang (1989 pp. 277–288).

education priorities in sub-Saharan Africa.[70] In 1988, the World Bank sponsored several regional meetings in Africa to discuss the findings and implications of its special report, *Education in Sub-Saharan Africa: Policies for Adjustment, Revitalization, and Expansion* (World Bank, 1988). The Bank also held follow-up meetings with other donor organizations that later evolved into a group called the Donors to African Education (DAE,[71] f. 1984). The DAE, in turn, created working groups around special topics, with various donors providing support to the working groups in keeping with their individual interests. As with the Bellagio meetings, such support allows the DAE working groups to hold preparatory meetings and plan follow-up activities.[72] Though usually modest, these supporting funds gave the working groups an opportunity to make progress in the interim between meetings that some larger conference series, such as the Regional Ministers of Education Conferences, lacked.

The frequency of donor meetings in the late 1980s had the potential to give educational development professionals in donor organizations more opportunity to formulate and articulate coherent agendas on educational development than any other group, including ministers of education. Standards within the international development field, however, emphasize that action within the field must be driven by needs articulated by the intended beneficiaries of international development assistance. Thus, in the early 1990s the DAE began inviting African government officials, including ministers of education, to participate in the DAE meetings.[73] Furthermore, in an apparent effort to promote meaningful participation on the part of Africans and in recognition of the high rate of turnover among ministers of education, the DAE also provided the African invitees time to meet together privately as a group to identify common interests and agendas.

In summary, an expanded vision of international educational development in the 1960s and 1970s defined a larger role for international assistance in less industrialized countries, which, in turn, called for coordination among international development donors. This coordination led to a series of donor conferences. These donor conferences performed many of the same functions for educational development professionals as regional conferences per-

---

70. Since that meeting, the European Donors to Education have had several ad hoc meetings and, as of 1995, were still active; however, I have no further information on their activities.
71. When the DAE expanded its membership beyond donors, its name changed to the Association for the Development of Education in Africa (ADEA).
72. The topics include: capacity building in educational research and policy analysis (f. 1989, IDRC), early childhood education, education sector analysis (f. 1989, UNESCO), education statistics (f. 1989, SIDA/UNESCO), female participation (f. 1990), finance and education (f. 1993, CIDA), higher education (f. 1989, WB), school examinations (f. 1989–93, HEDCO), the teaching profession (f. 1989, CS), textbooks and libraries (UK), vocational education and training (ILO).
73. With the understanding there would be no formal speeches.

formed for ministers of education. In the face of "competing claims on limited resources," the conferences helped the professionals "establish an internationally authenticated demand for the means with which to do the work of education" (Bartels, 1983, pp. 5–6).

The extent to which international financial support for educational development in less industrialized countries did or did not expand as a result of these conferences remains unclear. First, comparable baseline data is not available for many donor organizations.[74] Second, until the early 1990s, education sections in different donor organizations used noncomparable budget categories. For example, how does one estimate changes in contributions to girls' primary education when most development organizations did not begin routinely disaggregating project data by gender until the late 1980s? Even more difficult is recalculating from earlier data how much funding was provided for an activity that didn't exist in 1964, such as basic education (King, 1991).

What is certain is that the frequency of these working group meetings among a fairly small group of professionals created the conditions for more consensus on educational development than had previously been possible. The various conference series and meetings they organized and the background papers they commissioned helped to produce more of a common scientific base for planning education either directly—through reports to working groups—or indirectly—through spurring individual organizations to undertake more research. Nonetheless, the conclusions reached at all these meetings remained essentially decoupled from the budgeting authorities in the donor nation-states.

Meetings on Adult Education and Literacy

As part of the optimism of the First Development Decade, the UN General Assembly in 1961 invited UNESCO to explore possibilities for the mass eradication of illiteracy. In response UNESCO proposed a ten-year, US$ 1.9 billion, World Campaign for Universal Literacy (Jones, 1988). Insufficient funding eventually caused the campaign to be scaled back to an Experimental World Literacy Program (EWLP), undertaken in cooperation with UNDP. The World Conference of Ministers of Education on the Eradication of Illiteracy, held in Tehran in 1965 and planned while there was still hope the

---

74. Various types of development assistance are supervised by several different government agencies, which may or may not supply information to their own bilateral aid organization. For example, donor assistance to education includes: scholarships to foreign students often managed by the ministry of foreign affairs or the domestic ministry of education; short term training and scholarships provided as part of a project in another sector such as agriculture or health; schools built with proceeds from sale of surplus agricultural commodities handled by the Ministry of Agriculture.

World Campaign might materialize, in fact became a kick-off for the Experimental Program.

In part because of its limited resources, the EWLP shifted the focus from universally oriented "fundamental" education to "functional" education of a type that was supposed to contribute to short-run economic development and production. The EWLP converted the focus of two preexisting regional UNESCO training centers[75] from fundamental (basic, universal) to functional (work-related) education, and a new International Institute for Adult Literacy Methods (Tehran, f. 1968) focused on research and development work (Jones, 1988, pp. 164–65). The EWLP was not a great success and UNESCO planned no celebration for the tenth anniversary of the Tehran conference in 1975. Instead, the government of Iran took the initiative to sponsor the follow-up International Symposium for Literacy, in Persepolis in 1975. This symposium produced a declaration and a series of national conferences, and some regional plans of action for Latin America and the Caribbean; Africa, the Arab States; and Asia and the Pacific.[76]

In 1982 UNESCO and UNICEF together launched a working group on the Universalization of Primary Education and Literacy (UPEL). In 1983, in the wake of the failure of the world literacy campaign and in keeping with growing respect and interest in the larger international development field for NGOs, UNESCO's NGO Standing Committee organized a meeting for NGOs interested in UPEL on "Literacy—Education—Safeguarding of Cultures" (Thomas-Fontaine, 1993). One of the outcomes of that meeting was an annual Collective Consultation on Literacy and Adult Education,[77] alternating between the field and UNESCO headquarters. More than 70 NGOs attended one or more of these meetings between 1984 and 1990. UNESCO, unable to secure funding from other donors for its own projects, used these consultations to encourage the NGOs to prepare project proposals for submission to other donors. For example, the 1990 consultation included a workshop with handouts titled "Minimum requirements for a project proposal to an international donor."

---

75. What was presumably the Arab States' Fundamental Education Center (ASFEC, f. 1952), became the Arab States' Regional Center for Functional Literacy in Rural Areas (ASFEC), and the Latin American Regional Center for Fundamental Education (CREFAL) became the Latin American Regional Center for Cooperation for Adult Education (CREFAL).

76. These regional programs include the Regional Program for the Universalization and Renewal of Primary Education and the Eradication of Illiteracy in the Arab States by the Year 2000 (ARABUPEAL); Regional Program for the Universalization and Renewal of Primary Education and the Eradication of Illiteracy in Asia and the Pacific (APPEAL); Regional Program for the Eradication of Illiteracy in Africa; and Major Project in the Field of Education in Latin America and the Caribbean.

77. The consultation changed its focus to "Literacy and Education for All" at its eighth session in 1992.

This series of conferences serves to reinforce UNESCO's enormous mandate with respect to adult literacy. UNESCO's inability to secure funding for adults suggests the degree to which children as a category of persons increased their claim on limited educational development funds throughout this period. Insufficient funding, nonetheless, did not lead UNESCO to cut back its mandate; instead UNESCO continued to look for ways to package its programs and its training centers in ways that will better fit current development models, and, alternatively, to combine its resources with those of UNICEF and NGOs.

World Development Conferences

The most frequently cited precedent for the World Conference on Education for All is not an education conference but rather one dealing with health: the Health for All Conference in Alma Ata in 1978. The Alma Ata conference itself benefited from models derived from more than a dozen world conferences organized under UN auspices around broad sectoral themes between 1945 and 1977. Table 6.2 lists some of the better known of these world conferences.

The very first conference on this list, the one that created the UN, is instructive. The United Nations Conference on International Organization produced the Charter of the United Nations and a nonbinding Declaration of Universal Human Rights, the latter running the gamut from the rights of children to love and education, to the rights of political refugees to asylum. The declaration was not formalized into covenants until 1966, and those covenants remain to this day unratified by several members of the UN. Nonetheless, parts of the substance of the declaration have been discussed in dozens of world conference since 1945, and some of those parts have been incorporated in freestanding, more sectorally specific, nonbinding declarations and binding conventions. Examples include the 1954 Declaration of Population and the 1993 Convention on the Rights of the Child.

Since the first UN Conference on International Organization, other ingredients have been added to the world conference recipe. Of special importance are the procedures for a series of preconference regional consultations to discuss draft texts of proposed declarations, frameworks, and/or recommendations that the conference is expected to issue; a series of follow-up meetings; and procedures for preparing, submitting, and monitoring national plans of action. Finally, each world conference has seen greater and greater participation on the part of NGOs, for many of the reasons described in Chapter 4.

Unlike the education conferences described above, some of these world conferences were very successful at mobilizing world attention around a particular issue; others created new regulatory organizations or dramatically

Table 6.2. World Development Conferences, Illustrative List, 1945–1995

Year	Conference	City	Outcome
1945	UN Conference on International Organization	San Francisco	Universal Declaration of Human Rights (1948A)
1954	First World Population Conference		
1963	UN Conference on the Application of Science and Technology for the Benefit of Less Developed Areas		
1965	World Conference on the Eradication of Illiteracy	Teheran	Declaration of Population (1966)
1965	Second World Population Conference	Belgrade	Convention on Economic, Social and Cultural Rights (1966A/1976EF)
1966	First International Conference on Human Rights		Convention on Civil and Political Rights (1966/1976EF)
1966	World Land Reform Conference	Rome	
1972	UN Conference on the Human Environment	Stockholm	
1972	International Symposium for Literacy	Persepolis	Persepolis Declaration
1974	World Food Conference		
1975	World Conference on the UN Decade for Women	Mar del Plata	
1976	UN Water Conference	Vancouver	
1977	UN Conference on Human Settlements	Alma Ata	Declaration of Health for All
1978	International Conference on Primary Health Care		
	Equality, Development, and Peace		

A = adopted
EF = entered into force

152

Table 6.2. (cont.)

1979	UN Conference on Science and Technology for Development	Vienna	
1980	World Conference on the UN Decade for Women	Copenhagen	
1981	UN Conference on the Least Developed Countries	Paris	
1981	International Conference on Family Planning in the 1980s	Jakarta	
1983	World Conference on Oral Rehydration Therapy	Washington	
1985	World Conference to Review and Appraise UN Decade for Women	Nairobi	
1989	World Summit for Children	New York	Convention on the Rights of the Child (1989A/1990EF)
1990	World Conference on Education for All	Jomtien	Declaration of Education for All (1990)
1992	International Conference on Nutrition	Rome	Declaration and Plan of Action for Nutrition
1992	UN Conference on Environment and Development	Rio de Janeiro	
1993	World Conference on Human Rights	Vienna	
1994	International Conference on Population and Development	Cairo	
1995	World Summit for Social Development	Copenhagen	
1995	Third World Conference on Women	Beijing	

A = adopted
EF = entered into force

increased the amount of donor funding provided for an issue. James P. Grant, executive director of UNICEF during the first 15 years of the Health for All Conference follow-up (1980–1995), related much of that initiative's success to three factors (Personal communication, July 1994). These included an intellectual/professional consensus around (1) the effectiveness and priority of one or more technologies; (2) one or more rapid, low-cost grassroots dissemination strategies; and (3) ways of building sustainable linkages into the existing system.

In the case of the Health for All initiative, there was broad agreement in the public health community that universal promotion of oral rehydration therapy, childhood immunization, and breast-feeding could radically increase the child survival rate in most countries.[78] Furthermore, inexpensive and rapid delivery methods were feasible in even the lowest-income countries. A package of oral rehydration salts that could save a child from dehydration costs less than five cents (US) and anyone can be trained to prepare and administer it. After many years of controversy, the medical community was ready to allow minimally trained paramedics to transport and dispense essential immunizations. Finally, the international health community endorsed breast-feeding over bottle-feeding infants and had developed a variety of means to get the message out. In many countries, delivery systems for these innovations drew heavily on NGOs and the articulation between these organizations and government systems became a key part of their success.

Beyond this professional level, however, James P. Grant, the UNICEF executive director who oversaw the Child Survival Initiative, emphasized the importance of political will on the part of national leaders and the importance of encouraging those leaders to make public commitments to take specific actions. Along these lines, in September 1990, the leaders of Canada, Egypt, Mali, Mexico, Pakistan, and Sweden, with substantial help from UNICEF, hosted 71 heads of state and 88 senior delegations at the World Summit for Children in New York. The Summit created the momentum for ratifying the Convention on the Rights of the Child (1989) in record time (less than two years) and it also issued a declaration and a 10-point plan of action that set "attainable" goals for children by the year 2000 (United Nations Children's Fund, 1990).

The importance that the international development community attributes to world conferences and summits is illustrated in the major multimedia exhibition mounted by UNICEF for the World Summit for Social Development in Copenhagen in 1995. The exhibition, titled "Summitry Works: Words into Actions," describes the usefulness of the world conferences convened in the first half of the 1990s in focusing the world's attention on important development issues:

---

78. UNICEF itself often added "growth monitoring," but there was less general acceptance of this as an essential intervention by the public health community.

Summitry has been the engine and the catalyst towards obtaining more
equitable and sustainable human development through the personal commitment of heads of state and the commitment of governments; by building
global awareness and consensus; by spurring the collaborative efforts of the
UN secretariat and agencies, NGOs, and individuals; and by motivating the
media to cover and report on global issues which concern all people.
(Exhibit publicity materials, UNICEF, June 1996)

The Structure of the WCEFA

The various conference series described above provided the WCEFA planners with many of the key ingredients for a successful world conference
recipe. The first subsection below points out parallels between WCEFA and
earlier education conferences. The second subsection highlights the same for
earlier international development conferences.

Parallels from Earlier Education Conferences

Based on more than 40 years of experience with the IBE/UNESCO's international conferences, WCEFA planners took for granted they would need background documents that could be circulated, both before and after the
conference, to provide common data and to promulgate a common rationale
for action. In the case of the WCEFA, one background report prepared in
advance by WCEFA staff[79] and three reports synthesizing 24 thematic roundtables held as part of the meeting prepared subsequently filled this require-
ment (Windham, 1988; Fordham, 1992; Haggis, 1992).

Since the declarations issued in connection with regional and literacy
conferences had produced few results, both planners and participants in
regional WCEFA consultations debated whether the conference should issue
a charter or a declaration. Those who wanted to make the outcome of the
conference as binding as possible leaned toward a charter. Binding international agreements, however, require more formal, diplomatic conference
structures, raising the specter of formal speeches deteriorating into polemics
as sometimes occurred at the IBE/UNESCO meetings. Moreover, a formal,
diplomatically correct meeting would exclude full participation by NGOs.
The WCEFA, by taking the non-binding declaration option, was able to
include both NGOs and government officials responsible for economic planning, in an effort to match budgets to plans.

Drawing in part on the World Bank's recent experience with vetting its
Education in Sub-Saharan Africa (1988) report, WCEFA planners met the
international development field's standards for adequate nation-state "participation" by scheduling nine regional consultations prior to March 1990

---

79. *Meeting Basic Learning Needs: A Vision for the 1990s* World Conference on Education for
All Inter-Agency Commission, (1990b).

(a complete list of the WCEFA meetings is provided in Table 6.3). Rapporteurs from these regional consultations then assembled in Nice in December 1989 to consolidate their work. Finally, the conference planners allocated to each region one hour on the conference program to make a collective statement, effectively precluding individual ministers of education from unduly long speeches and/or nation-states from forming blocks across regional lines.

To ensure adequate NGO participation, those with a previous history of working with UNESCO or UNICEF were provided with terms of reference for the WCEFA and the regional consultations and were invited to submit applications to attend. Many NGOs participated actively in regional consultations and 125 were eventually invited to send delegations to the World Conference. In an effort to provide both geographic and substantive diversity, some prominent INGOs were not invited while other national and local NGOs, many of them virtual newcomers to the international conference scene, were. Of the 70 NGOs that had participated in the annual UNESCO/UNICEF/NGO Collective Consultations on Literacy from 1984 to 1989, only 23 were invited to the WCEFA. In attempting to be inclusive, the secretariat inadvertently ensured that the NGO contingent at EFA would not, unlike many of the governmental donor organizations, form a preexisting, coherent group. The secretariat hosted a meeting for the NGOs the day before the start of the conference precisely to help the NGO delegates to caucus, formulate their agenda, and select one of the ten vice presidents to preside at the conference.

The establishment of targets was among the more controversial issues at the preparatory regional consultations. The Africans, in particular, protested that efforts to include targets in the declaration and framework would drag Africa back to the 1970s and 1980s, when the articulation of ambitious and, ultimately, unachievable goals from the 1961 Addis Plan proved an embarrassment. Yet the more recent, sectorally based world conferences, described below, placed heavy emphasis on targets. Eventually targets—to achieve the equivalent of universal primary school for all children by the year 2000, for example—were included in the Framework for Action, but not in the Declaration.

The distinction here between what the conference planners would call "lessons learned" from earlier regional and global education conferences and what an institutionalist would call "recipes" or "frameworks" is somewhat subtle but important. The idea of "lessons learned" implies that certain ways of doing things, derived from experience, produce more efficacious results. The "lessons learned" from these international education conferences, however, did not produce more funding for education programs or faster rates of growth for literacy or improve any other educational outcome. Rather, they produced a more smoothly operating organizational field, more consistent with world cultural standards. First, from a professional standpoint, these

Table 6.3. Preparatory and Follow-up Meetings to the World Conference on Education for All

Organizational Meetings

Date	City	Meeting
February 1988	New York	Educational Consultation Meeting
November 1988	Paris	International Working Group on Education Consultation
December 1988	Washington, D.C.	First Meeting of EFA Sponsors
March 1989	New York	Establishment of Interagency Advisory Council and Executive Secretariat
October 1989	Paris	First International Steering Group Meeting
		First Consultation of Major Funding Agencies
December 1989	Nice	Second International Steering Group Meeting
March 1990	Jomtien	Third International Steering Group Meeting
		Fourth (Final) International Steering Group Meeting

Regional Consultations

Date	City	Region	Date	City	Region
October 1989	Strasbourg	Europe	November 1989	Nairobi	Eastern and Southern Africa
November 1989	Boston	North America	November 1989	Quito	Latin America
November 1989	Amman	Arab States	November 1989	Dhaka	South Asia
November 1989	Kingston	Caribbean	January 1990	Bamako	Sahelian countries
November 1989	Dakar	West and Central Africa	January 1990	Jakarta	East Asia and Pacific

Follow-up Meetings

Date	City	Meeting
December 1991	Paris	First Education for All Forum
June 1992	Paris	Basic Education: Donor Roles and Responsibilities (sponsored by OECD/DAC)
September 1993	New Delhi	Second Education for All Forum
December 1993	New Delhi	Education for All Summit
June 1996	Amman	Mid-Decade Meeting

ingredients produced more smoothly functioning conferences, that is, more "substantive" and "scientific," and less "political." Second, they created a common, noncontroversial language, so that donor organizations and recipient countries could talk about and come to a consensus on written statements about educational development in a relatively short time. The importance of this common, noncontroversial language is discussed more thoroughly in the following section.

Parallels from International Development Conferences

The educational development professionals, working in the context of the international development field, were familiar with world conferences. Although this analysis cannot determine the degree to which the WCEFA planners consciously borrowed ingredients from these broader world conference models, it can highlight certain striking parallels, particularly in follow-up strategies. Many of the principles underlying the Declaration on Education for All came directly from documents generated by these earlier world conferences: the Declaration of Universal Human Rights; the International Covenant on Economic, Social, and Cultural Rights (Article 13, 1966); and the Declaration (1959) and Convention on the Rights of the Child (Articles 28 and 29, 1989).

The core EFA documents include not only a declaration but also a framework for action. In order to make both of these "nonbinding" documents as binding as possible, the WCEFA follow-up invoked a recipe already established by earlier world conference. The nation-states whose delegates acclaimed the EFA Declaration agreed to take several follow-up steps, including drafting a national EFA strategy and a national plan of action (NPA) for implementing that strategy and increasing budgetary support to education commensurate with the plan of action. In addition, less industrialized countries agreed to establish a donor coordination mechanism and find additional support to achieve their national strategies. Each country then was to submit its national strategy and plan of action to a monitoring cell set up by a Forum for Education for All. The forum periodically published a progress report showing which countries have completed which steps of their plans (UNESCO, 1994). Furthermore, follow-up forums with hundreds of delegates, both governmental and nongovernmental, started to meet biannually, beginning in 1991.

Should EFA ever become a formal international convention, these EFA national plans of action would become binding. Each country that ratified EFA would be required to demonstrate acceptable progress toward goals elaborated in the EFA Framework and Plan of Action in order to maintain an acceptable human rights record. In the meantime, much of the EFA Framework and Plan of Action that relates to basic education for children is already incorporated into Articles 28 and 29 in the Convention on the Rights of the

Child. Within two years of ratifying this convention, states must devise a plan of action to meet the goals of the convention—including the EFA goals. For example, India ratified the Convention on the Rights of the Child in 1990; this meant it had to devise a national plan of action by 1992 to ensure that 80 percent of all children would achieve the equivalent of a primary education by the year 2000. A UN commission monitored India's progress towards this goal, and, technically, could have judged India's failure to make adequate progress towards this goal by 2000 as a human rights violation and liable for sanctions.

Similarly, sponsoring organization professionals have succeeded in incorporating EFA language into the declarations and conventions associated with the International Conference on Population and Development in Cairo in 1994; the Summit on Social Development in Copenhagen in 1995; and the Third World Conference on Women in Beijing in 1995. But while EFA could incorporate or piggyback on various winning structural elements of conferences both before and after 1990, its success in educational terms, like many education conferences before it, may be hobbled by the lack of several of the factors professionals referred to as key to the success of the Health for All campaign.

First, EFA lacks an intellectual consensus in each of the three areas described above. Article 5 of the declaration refers to "the means and scope of basic education" as early childhood care and development; primary schooling; training programs for youth and adults that lack the skills to participate fully in their societies; and mass education through electronic and other, more traditional media. Apart from the last area, there were few new, low-cost, noncontroversial technological innovations associated with these four areas in the decade preceding the WCEFA.

Furthermore, in terms of low-cost delivery mechanisms, while many NGOs had been involved in training for youth and adults, few had been involved in the other three key intervention areas mentioned in the declaration. In particular, NGOs running mass primary education systems could be counted on one hand.[80] Finally, articulation between governmental and nongovernmental education systems is particularly difficult given the role of education in legitimating nation-states.[81]

The WCEFA also differed from the Health for All Conference in the lack of an ongoing high level task force charged to follow up the decisions of the conference. The Child Survival Task Force is backed by the resources of the

80. See Ahmed, Chabbott et al. (1993), for a description of the BRAC Nonformal Primary Education Program, the only example as of 1993. UNICEF tried to promote the BRAC model during and after the WCEFA as a potential breakthrough technology but has met with substantial resistance from educational development professionals concerned that the model promotes a two-track approach to basic education.
81. In fact, the last two areas of intellectual consensus—that is, acceptable, low-cost delivery mechanisms and articulation between the public, formal system and the nonformal system—may not have existed in the health sector prior to 1982. Consensus may have built over time.

Center for Disease Control in the United States. In contrast, the executive secretariat of the WCEFA was disbanded immediately after the conference, in March 1990, to be succeeded by a small office at UNESCO to organize follow-up forums and meetings.[82] However, various preexisting coalitions of international development organizations, such as the Consultative Group for Early Childhood Care and Development picked up momentum from EFA and may yet "succeed" in substantive terms.[83]

In summary, the WCEFA incorporated various recipes from other world conferences to ensure its declaration and framework endure and are incorporated into national and international development agenda. Although often associated with the Health for All Conference, the WCEFA does not appear to contain several of the elements that made it possible for the Health for All to turn its agenda into a major movement: intellectual consensus on the definition of the problem and its solution, a technological innovation that created a new way of attacking the problem, and an inexpensive means of delivering the innovation to remote areas. As shown in Table 3, priorities for education had not entirely converged on a priority type—such as primary education—as they had in health around primary health care. Most technological innovations in education—programmed learning, distance learning, the uses of radio and television—are more expensive and/or require more ongoing support in their new environment—electricity, maintenance, parts—than, for example, vaccination. Vaccinated individuals without any other changes in their environment survive at a higher rate than those unvaccinated. But adult graduates of literacy programs today, without any change in or support from their environment, are likely to be illiterate again next year. Finally, the education community has not come to an acceptance of any of the low cost methods presently available for delivering mass primary education.

Despite great hopes, throughout the 1990s no new science or low-cost technology emerged to level the playing field between the education and health sectors. This reinforced institutional isomorphism within the education sector; education conferences became less a means to an end than ritual enactment of a shared worldview regarding educational principles and priorities.

Conclusions

The international education conferences described above produced a common language, a body of research and extensive professional interaction for donor organization personnel and, to a lesser extent, for conference delegates

---

82. First Education for All Forum, Paris (1991); Second Education for All Forum, Delhi (1993), Mid-Decade EFA Meeting, Amman (1996).
83. It is probably not incidental that this apparently successful group is organized around "children."

from less industrialized countries. World conferences organized around specific sectoral issues have provided a widely accepted format in which formal, regionally based, preconference consultations give legitimized broad declarations, and in which NGO participation insures that the conferences are perceived as "participatory" and "grassroots oriented."

By 1990, various UN and other donor organizations had sponsored hundreds of world and regional educational conferences, and had produced more than 77 recommendations to education ministers and about a dozen general declarations on the subject of education. Many of the delegates to the regional consultations that produced the Declaration of Education for All were, therefore, no strangers to each other. They had often met and discussed with each other the same issues. In addition, many of the principles underlying the declaration came directly from documents with which the delegates were already familiar: the Declaration of Universal Human Rights; the International Covenant on Economic, Social, and Cultural Rights (Article 13, 1966); the Declaration (1959) and Convention on the Rights of the Child (Articles 28 and 29, 1989); and a half-dozen other conventions and agreements.

It is then small wonder that the regional consultations produced the draft declaration for the WCEFA in just six months. Indeed, the final wording of the Declaration of Education for All evoked such deeply felt international ideals, that on the last day of the world conference the delegates rose and accepted it by acclamation, according to one staffer, with "more than a few with tears in their eyes." Thus by imitating the format of earlier conferences and invoking ideals that were, by that time, taken for granted in international discourse, the organizers of the WCEFA created institutional pressures to ensure its success, if only in rhetorical terms.

7
Conclusion

In late 1999, I visited Afghanistan for a few weeks as an education consultant to an INGO. At the time, a militant fundamentalist group, the Taliban ("talib" meaning student) had imposed harsh mixture of Islamic law and tribal justice throughout the country. I was told that this group formed to fight Soviet occupation and in the 1970s and 1980s had attracted many young recruits from refugee camps in Quetta, in southern Pakistan. There the Taliban had close connections to fundamentalist religious schools that offered the only education available to many refugee boys. When the Taliban later recruited them to fight the civil war in Afghanistan in the 1990s, these boys relied on a rigid fundamentalism to justify harsh treatment of civilians.

During the visit, I met a professional relief worker responsible for delivering food aid to the widows and orphans whose lives were rendered so difficult by Taliban laws prohibiting women to appear in public. When I explained I was a visiting education "expert," she half-seriously demanded, "Where were you education guys when we needed you?! If you had just established some [modern] schools in the Quetta camps back in the 1980s, maybe this whole Taliban thing would never have happened!"

The hope that education will foster peaceful, rational, compassionate human beings, who will, in turn, create peaceful, rational, compassionate societies, is a tenacious one in the modern world. The power of education to incorporate self-actualized citizens into nation-states and into world society remains central to Western notions of development. The notion that some international development activity, such as a few schools, might change the course of a nation-state's history is a cherished one, perhaps even more so among those professionals who spend long stretches of their working lives in less industrialized countries. As a professional relief worker, the woman in this story assumed some responsibility for the care and feeding of widows with whom she has no ties in terms of family, nationality, language, or race. Likewise, she was only half-joking when she implied that I and expatriate education "experts" more generally were responsible for delivering Western-style education to Afghan refugees in a remote city in Pakistan. She has her role and her script and we have ours; but in our case, we failed to arrive on cue and didn't deliver our lines before the curtain came down.

World culture has institutionalized rules—transcending local culture, politics, and economics at every level of society—that define how society works—or should work—to attain collective purposes. At the same time, these rules define legitimate actors, script those actors' activities, and designate their spheres of influence. As these actors and activities grow, the "iron cage" of Western rationality forces more organization and more bureaucracy into their activities, even as it creates tension with some of the higher forms of both traditional values and Western-oriented world culture.

In the last half of the twentieth century, discourse at the global level legitimated new types of international actors—developed/less developed/least developed nation-states and development organizations/professionals/donors/beneficiaries. These new actors have rationalized new types of international activities, such as world development conferences and global development campaigns, that, in turn, produce more discourse, that, in turn, legitimates more actors and activities. For most of the post–World War II period, this process resulted in a top-down, supply-driven development approach directly in conflict with several core world cultural values. Since the 1970s, these values, expressed in the development discourse in terms of more broad-based participation in development planning and more benefits aimed at the grassroots, call for a more demand-driven process than the structure of Western-rationalized development organizations typically allows. Similarly, more recent efforts to address the "needs" of the poor majority in international development projects have been frustrated at every turn by various aspects of world culture, though they have not been entirely foiled.

For example, over time, less industrialized countries, at the behest and sometimes with the aid of international organizations, have improved their capacity for Western-style planning: expanding the gathering of statistics to more areas of life and, in the process, discovering many new citizens. At the same time, international development organizations have been identifying more and more special categories of traditionally disadvantaged persons—women, the disabled, language minorities—who are entitled to more equitable treatment in the future. Finally, in places where Western science has increased the child survival rate faster than the contraceptive prevalence rate, the absolute number of all types of citizens is growing rapidly. Where progress is measured in per capita terms, increases in the number of citizens from all these sources slows the real rate of growth of all measures of progress and contributes to the proliferation of development "failures." On the other hand, increasing discourse about expanded government responsibilities increases the legitimacy with which future citizens can agitate for expanded rights, even as the minimal ones have not been met.

As another example, Enlightenment logic gravitates toward universal knowledge claims and delegitimates particularistic, beneficiary-driven development plans derived from the idiosyncratic demands of the poor on a village-by-village basis. Ironically, demand-driven, grassroots development projects must include on their staff community "mobilizers" and "promoters," whose job is to help local communities define their needs in rational terms consistent with current development discourse and the narrow range of activities donors' current projects are able to support. This is not to disparage efforts to help communities look for common ground between the long list of things they might like to do and the much shorter list of things that international development organizations are prepared to support. Rather, the tension inherent in this arrangement derives from two clashing values within development organizations, a tension that will cause the organization—or the villagers—to go looking for a better arrangement

The persistence of top-down approaches tempts one to conclude that those at the top—the industrialized countries or the development professionals—must somehow be benefiting from, and therefore be perpetuating existing development structures. However, the evidence does not generally support such a conclusion, either at the national or individual level. The current structures place industrialized countries under constant pressure in international forums to fund more development activities; though they give far less than the tasks at hand require, nonetheless, they give more than national interest alone would justify. Interest in less industrialized countries as hedges against the Communist bloc evaporated more than a decade ago; though the end of the Cold War has not delivered a "peace dividend" in the form of dramatic increases in development aid funding that many hoped for, neither has governmental development funding dried up.

Similarly, national EFA frameworks in many less industrialized countries, though they are often constructed in a top-down manner, are not necessarily products of elite interests or local conditions. Isomorphism among these frameworks is at least in part coercive; countries that hope to receive funding from international donors are often required to have a framework for action consistent with international agendas. The presence of an internationally sanctioned framework for action signals the state's posture as a rational and responsible actor, ready to take on the duties ascribed to it by various international covenants and agreements (Meyer, Boli et al., 1997, p. 153).

Given these tensions, it is no surprise to find loose coupling, and the proliferation of similar specialized organizational forms and procedures, at all levels of both the international development field and the educational development enterprise. Fuller (1991), Meyer (1995), and others have described the contradictions created in applying ritualistic Western bureaucratic management approaches from the classroom through the ministry of education level. This book, however, argues that these contradictions extend to the international level. Down at the grassroots, schools in the least industrialized countries often lack many essentials: roofs, textbooks, teacher salaries. Schoolteachers, nonetheless, often accommodate the district education officer's demand for statistics and produce daily attendance records, in many cases whether or not classes meet or a lesson is taught. The district education officers, fully cognizant of both the questionable quality of the school-level statistics and the unquestionable demand for them from the national level, construct district education statistics from the daily attendance records. Further, the district officials post wall charts showing the projected increase in primary enrollment rates in their district from 50 percent to 80 percent in the coming decade, as prescribed by the national framework. These charts will be displayed for the benefit of visitors, though they raise embarrassing questions, such as how, absent massive, but unlikely, increases in funding, such targets can be met. At the national level, in the ministry of education, many staff, often trained and supplied with computers by foreign donors, will be primed to receive and analyze the district-level monthly data so that the government and international development donors can measure "progress" towards national goals. At the international level, consultants and staff in international development organizations, fully cognizant of five decades of missed targets and questionable statistics, nonetheless regularly meet to revise target levels of world wide education expansion and to contemplate the need for regional or international conferences to rekindle commitment to these targets.

This book stresses that such behavior is not unique to the international development community. In any industry where output is difficult to measure, norms of Western rationality pressure workers to rationalize their work and to standardize their production processes around best practices that they, collectively, socially construct. In a world where education constitutes both an essential input to development and a basic human right, enormous pressure is placed upon development practitioners to rationalize the promotion of educational development. Western notions of individual organization, purposive action, and the universal applicability of Western science, plus chronic crises caused by lack of funds, propel conscientious professionals into action. Fueling this is the moral weight of being associated with organizations so tightly tied into the primary goals of society—progress and justice— (Meyer, Boli et al., 1997). And thus a conference is born.

International development professionals bear the weight of the tension between goals expressed in the high form of the development imperative and attainable progress. To some, their work "packaging" or "spinning" disappointing results of educational development activities such as EFA into "lessons learned" may appear hypocritical. Again, organizational analysis suggests that such hypocrisy is not unique to the development field, nor is it uniformly dysfunctional. In *The Organization of Hypocrisy*, Brunsson (1989) writes:

> If we want to preserve high and inconsistent values we must be prepared to handle them more on procedural lines, rather than linking them to the achievement of action and results; values are better suited to handling in talk than in action, and by reference to the future rather than the present. If we are to be able to maintain high values, we must not adapt them to reflect our action.... Those without sin or hypocrisy are those who pursue or advocate realizable goals, trading in their morality in exchange.... High morality should characterize our intentions, our talk, and our decisions, even if it cannot imbue our actions.

The WCEFA was, of course, a textbook manifestation of what Brunsson calls "high values."

Paradoxically, professionals' commitment to eliminating hypocrisy, to reducing the dissonance between high values and routine action, to tightening the loose coupling between policy and practice, may, at times, be counterproductive. Universal standards and structures for education are formulated at a rarified global level and, if they are to become functional, often must be adapted to local legacies and circumstances. Hence, in some countries, local schools that do not meet many of the global criteria for "good" schools, nonetheless, may be well adapted to the local milieu. Loose coupling may give some schools the space to develop something more appropriate than the global standard. To outsiders, however, particularly visiting educational development professionals, it is difficult to discern the difference between adapting to local conditions and lowering standards.

Recalling Figure 1, the earlier diagram of the mechanisms for carrying blueprints of development, the relatively less institutionalized mechanisms are those closest to the local and grassroots levels: national/local social movements and national/local NGOs. In the 1990s, new information and communication technologies, primarily fax machines and the Internet, have reshaped and strengthened feedback between the grassroots and local NGOs and other levels of the development field. Better coordination may result but caution is called for, given the artificially inflated role science and technologies such as the Internet play in Western cultural accounts of progress. Historically, few new educational technologies—radio, television, film—have lived up to their early promise to facilitate the spread of quality education. More importantly, outsiders, including development professionals, typically find it difficult to discriminate between messages coming from the poor vs. the rich, the downtrodden vs. their oppressors at the grassroots level.

The current world culture incorporates many inconsistencies besides those related to education. Although DiMaggio (1988) proposes that interests and organization play a necessary and important role in both creating and dismantling institutional structures, Meyer and colleagues (1997) envision a world where conflict and change arise in the generative tensions inherent in world culture. In this account of the development field, world cultural norms of equity and norms of economic growth are often in conflict. At the WCEFA, as at all world development conferences since the mid-1970s, tensions simmered between the discourse of equity (justice) and the discourse of economic growth (material progress). Closer to the surface, organizations associated with instrumental or human rights rationales for education jockeyed for wording that would privilege their preferred approach. Changes in the balance between these two justifications implied changes in the balance of resources among the organizations in the international development field, in the legitimacy of approaches recommended by one group of experts rather than another, or in the exemplary nature of one nation-state's policy versus another.

If tension is rampant in the international development field, how much change in the culture of development can be reasonably expected in the foreseeable future? Is the culture of development likely to change now that Japan, a non-Western power, and other countries have surpassed the U.S. as the largest donors to development? Perhaps not, given the nonevangelical nature of Japanese culture, particularly in comparison with the United States, the previous largest donor. Will a Japanese approach to education alter future discourse on educational development? Probably not, but alternatives to approaches advocated by the United States in the past will likely make themselves heard more often.

Since the WCEFA, the status of NGOs in the international development field has continued to grow, as has research on the role of transnational advocacy networks, as well documented by Mundy and Murphy (2001). Oxfam, for example, played a major role at the EFA Plus 10 conference in Dakar, bringing no additional resources to the table, only their network of members to bring pressure to bear on more and less industrialized countries to commit the resources necessary to meet their targets in EFA.

Western development professionals and the public at large too often succumb to treating as ignorant and reactionary fundamentalist groups that reject formal secular schooling as an indoctrination into "decadent" Western culture. But in one sense the fundamentalists see schools much more clearly than those who live in the industrialized world or aspire to join that world. A culture based in Western Enlightenment ideas about the supreme value of rationality and the cult of the individual is at the heart of world culture and of the Western model of schooling. This culture, so focused on individuals, is indeed inconsistent with more traditional values that place the needs of family, tribe, and religion above those of individuals. Some fundamentalists properly recognize world culture as a social construction or, more bluntly, the "religion" of the West and as such, they reject it. However, Western culture is so pervasive that no fundamentalist group has, as yet, managed to completely excise it from their schools or their own efforts.

In the mid-1990s, when most of the data for this book was assembled, it seemed likely that EFA, having won the education sector its decade in the limelight but having failed to produce dramatic progress, would be written out of the development drama in favor of some other brighter star. In the story told here, the international development field is the play, the discourse its script, the organizations the protagonists, the professionals the actors, the experts or epistemic communities the talent agents, and the conferences merely a stage. Following the WCEFA, the environment and population, double-billed as "sustainable development," made an effort to seize the limelight.

The tendency, however, for discourse and development approaches to accrete, rather than replace each other suggests that educational development, as an undertaking, will not be easily eclipsed. The main EFA goals are now embedded in a dozen or more subsequent world-level declarations—on the environment, population, and social development, to name only a few—meaning that the development discourse has now created a cognitive link between progress in these sectors and education for all. Meanwhile, the development imperative continues to demand both individual and societal progress, and progress involving technical, economic, and social dimensions. But such progress is impossible to conceive of in the current world culture without education. And education, as a universal social good, it seems, must be for all.

Appendix A
Protocol for Identifying International Development Organizations

NB: Since 1995, when the lists of international development organizations used for analysis in Chapter 4 were originally compiled, information on international organizations on the WorldWideWeb has increased exponentially. For the purposes of this historical analysis, however, I have chosen to use information that would have been available before or slightly after the time of the World Conference on Education for All in 1990.

1. To be counted as a member of the international development field, an organization must meet one of three conditions:

A) appear in an international development directory or database and work in at least one less industrialized country, other than its country of origin, OR

B) be indexed as a live organization (Types A-D) under the subject heading "development" in the Union of International Association's Yearbook of International Organizations (1993/94).

Because of lags in identifying new organizations and the time needed to publish books, directories published in the mid-1990s may only be complete up to the mid-1980s.[84]

The following development directories were primary sources for development IGOs:

East, R., Smith-Morris, M., et al., Eds. (1990). *World development directory*. Cambridge International Reference on Current Affairs. Essex (UK): Longman.

Gale & Associates (1995). *Encyclopedia of associations: International organizations*. Munich (Germany): KG Saur.

---

84. Boli and Thomas (1999) estimated that the UIA Yearbooks were complete only up to 10 years prior to the yearbook's publication date.

Korsmeyer, P., Ed. (1991). *The development directory 1991: A guide to the international development community in the United States and Canada.* Detroit: Omnigraphics.

Organization for Economic Cooperation and Development. Development Assistance Committee. (2001). Annex Z: Main International Organizations. In DAC Statistical Reporting Directives. Paris: OECD

Organization for Economic Cooperation and Development. Development Center (1991). *Directory of development research and training institutes in Europe.* Paris: OECD.

Organization for Economic Cooperation and Development. Development Center (1992). *Directory of research and training institutes in Africa.* Paris: OECD.

Organization for Economic Cooperation and Development. Development Center (1993). *Directory of research and training institutes in Latin America.* Paris: OECD.

Organization for Economic Cooperation and Development. Development Center (1993). Union of International Associations (1993/1994). *Yearbook of international organizations.* Munich: KG Saur.

Union of International Associations (2001/2002). *Yearbook of international organizations.* Munich: KG Saur.

The following development directories and databases were sources for information on development INGOs:

Organization for Economic Cooperation and Development (1988). *Voluntary aid for development: The role of nongovernmental organizations.* Paris: OECD.

Organization for Economic Cooperation and Development. Development Center (1981). *Directory of nongovernmental organizations in OECD member countries active in development cooperation.* Paris: OECD.

Organization for Economic Cooperation and Development. Development Center (1990). *Directory of nongovernmental development organizations in OECD member countries.* Paris: OECD.

Organization for Economic Cooperation and Development. Development Center (1996) *Directory of NGOs active in sustainable development.* Part I: Europe. Paris: OECD.

Organization for Economic Cooperation and Development. Development Center (1998). *Directory of NGOs active in sustainable development. Part II.* Paris: OECD.

United Nations Educational, Scientific, and Cultural Organization (1991). *African development sourcebook*. Paris: UNESCO.

Organization for Economic Cooperation and Development. Development Center (1995). Database of nongovernmental development organizations in OECD member countries. Paris: OECD.

World Bank. Operations Policy Research and Planning Group. Operations Policy Department. NGO Unit (1996). Development NGO Database. Washington, DC: World Bank.

2. The analysis in this book focuses on formally organized efforts to reach out beyond traditional boundaries of kinship and nationality. As a result, this list of international development organizations does not incorporate the vast number of national non-governmental organizations (NNGOs) and local nongovernmental organizations (LNGOs) that work on social or economic development in just one less developed country, that is, their own[85] As of 1990, the vast majority of international nongovernmental development organizations (development INGOs) were based in OECD countries and only a few were based in Africa, Asia, and Latin America. An OECD database (as of 7/95) provided data on OECD-based development INGOs. A working database at the World Bank provided limited data on non-OECD-based development INGOs.

3. It is difficult to distinguish between (a) a full-fledged specialized organization affiliated with the UN and (b) simple funds. The funds listed under UN organizations have appeared in more than one directory. OECD (2002) was considered decisive.

4. A crude estimate of the number of private, for-profit contractors was derived as follows: In 1995 the international development section of the U.S. Professional Services Council, a membership organization of most of the contractors who work with the U.S. government, consisted of 29 organizations.

Given:

a) The US Agency for International Development was the second largest bilateral donor that year and

b) there were about 30 bilateral donors that year

Then:

the total number of private, for-profit, nongovernmental organizations involved in international development is not likely to be more than 900 firms (that is, 30 donors × 30 firms) + 320 commercial banks involved in loans to projects in less industrialized countries, for a total of 1,220 organizations, and probably far fewer.

---

85. For a good overview of the work of these organizations, see Fisher (1993) and Fisher (1998).

5. A 1966 OECD publication identifies 340 public and private development finance institutions, that is, providing general medium- and long-term financial assistance to a developing economy. In the World Federation of Development Financing Institutions claimed 349 members (East, Smith-Morris et al., 1990). These development banks may be public or private. Central banks, commercial banks, short-term credit institutions, and a number of specialized institutions (such as, marketing boards, mortgage banks, and land reform authorities) are excluded.

6. The non-UN multilateral organizations were the most difficult to identify. When in doubt, they were excluded, therefore they are probably under-counted in the analysis in Chapter 4.

Appendix B

Major Postwar International Conferences on
Mass Education

UNESCO Regional Meetings—Africa

Date	City	Title/Declarations/Plans
yy/mm/dd		
61/05/15	Addis Ababa	Conference of African States on the Development of Education in Africa that formulated the Addis Ababa Plan
62/03/26	Paris	Meeting of Ministers of Education of African Countries participating in the implementation of the Addis Ababa Plan
64/03/17	Abidjan	Conference of Ministers of Education of African Countries participating in the implementation of the Addis Ababa Plan
67/01/NA	Paris?	Progress realized since the Addis Conference
67/01/NA	Lagos	Meeting of Ministers of Education of African Member States
68/07/16	Nairobi	Conference on Education and Scientific and Technical Training in Relation to Development
70/07/22	Addis Ababa	InterSecretariat Meeting UNESCO-OAU-ECA on the Revision of the Addis Targets
72/09/12	Addis Ababa	InterSecretariat Meeting UNESCO-OAU-ECA on the Revision of the Addis Targets
76/01/26	Lagos	Conference of Ministers of Education of African member states
79/09/17	Dakar	Regional Meeting of Heads of Educational Planning and Administrative Services in Africa
82/06/21	Harare	Preparation Meeting of Experts for the Conference of Ministers of Education and those responsible for economic planning in African member states
82/06/28	Harare	Vth Regional Conference of Ministers of Education and those responsible for economic planning in African member states
85/05/06	Dakar	Ist Regional Technical Follow-Up to MinedAf V
91/07/02	Dakar	Preparation Meeting of Experts for MinedAf V
91/07/08	Dakar	VIth Conference of Ministers of Education and of those responsible for economic planning in African member states

UNESCO Regional Meetings—Asia

Date	City	Title/Declarations/Plans
yy/mm/dd		
59/12/31	Karachi	Regional meeting of [17] Asian member states on primary & compulsory education: Karachi Plan
62/04/02	Tokyo	Meeting of Ministers of Education of Asian member states participating in the Karachi Plan
65/11/22	Bangkok	Conference of Ministers of Education and Ministers for economic planning of member states in Asia
69/09/16	Bangkok	Preparation meeting of experts for the IIIrd Regional Conference of Ministers of Education and ministers responsible for economic planning of member states in Asia
71/05/31	Singapore	IIIrd Regional Conference of Ministers of Education and ministers responsible for economic planning in the Asia
74/02/19	Bangkok	Regional experts meeting on the Asian Program of Educational Innovation for Development (APEID), established by IIIrd RCME/Asia
74/02/25	Bangkok	Follow-up meeting on the recommendations of the Singapore Conference
77/07/25	Bangkok	Preparation meeting of experts for IVth Regional Conference of Ministers of Education and ministers responsible for economic planning in Asia and Oceania
78/07/24	Colombo	IVth Conference of Ministers of Education and those responsible for economic planning in Asia and Oceania
85/03/04	Bangkok	Vth Regional Conference of Ministers of Education and those responsible for economic planning in Asia and the Pacific
93/06/21	Kuala Lumpur	VIth Regional Conference of Ministers of Education and those responsible for economic planning in Asia and Oceania

175

UNESCO Regional Meetings—Arab States

Date	City	Title/Declarations/Plans
yy/mm/dd		
94/06/11	Cairo	Conference of Ministers of Education and ministers responsible for economic planning in the Arab States
87/06/22	Amman	Meeting of high level officials in the Ministers of Education in the Arab States
84/03/00	Rabat	Conference of Mined/Arab did not take place
82/03/22	Tunis	Preparation meeting of experts for the Conference of Ministers of Education and ministers responsible for economic planning in the Arab States
77/11/07	Abu Dhabi	Conference of Ministers of Education and ministers responsible for economic planning in the Arab States
76/10/18	Cairo	Meeting on the implementation of the recommendations of the IIrd Regional Conference of Ministers of Education and ministers responsible for economic planning in the Arab States
70/01/12	Marrakesh	IIrd Regional Conference of Ministers of Education and ministers responsible for economic planning in the Arab States
66/04/09	Tripoli	Conference of Ministers of Education and ministers responsible for economic planning in the Arab States
60/02/09	Beirut	Conference of representatives of Ministries of Education of Arab member states of UNESCO on the needs for educational development

UNESCO Regional Meetings—Europe

Date	City	Title/Declarations/Plans
yy/mm/dd		
42/11/16	London	First Conference of Allied Ministers of Education (CAME) (10 countries)
43/07/00		Fifth CAME added Australia, Canada, China, India, New Zealand, South Africa, U.S.S.R., United States

UNESCO Regional Meetings—Latin America and the Caribbean

Date	City	Title/Declarations/Plan
yy/mm/dd		
1936		Inter-American Conference for the Consolidation of Peace: "Convention on the Pacifist Orientation of Education"
1943	Panama	Inter-American Meeting of Ministers of Education: "Convention on the Inter American University" (not yet in force)
56/03/09	Lima	IIIrd Inter-American Meeting of Ministers of Education: Lima Declaration
56/04/23	Lima	Conference on major project on the extension of primary education in Latin America (teacher training)
62/03/05	Santiago	Inter-American Conference of Ministers of Education and those responsible for economic planning and social development in Latin America
1963	Bogota	IIIrd Inter-American Conference of Ministers of Education
66/06/21	Buenos Aires	IIIrd Conference of Ministers of Education and ministers responsible for economic planning in the Countries of Latin America and the Caribbean
71/12/06	Caraballeda	Conference of Ministers and Education and those responsible for the promotion of science and technology in relation to development in Latin America and the Caribbean
76/02/09	Panama	Meeting on the application of recommendations of MINEDLAC/Venezuela
79/04/02	Caracas	Preparation meeting of experts for the Regional Conference of Ministers of Education and those responsible for economic planning of member states in Latin America and the Caribbean
79/12/04	Mexico City	Regional Conference of Ministers of Education and those responsible for economic planning in member states in Latin America and the Caribbean: Mexico Declaration
87/03/30	Bogota	VIth Regional Conference of Ministers of Education and those responsible for economic planning of member states in Latin America and the Caribbean

U.S. Government-Sponsored Conferences

Date	City	Sponsor	Title/Declarations/Plans
yy/mm/dd			
1961	Washington	USAID/DoS	Role of Education in Economic Growth
62/06/18	Washington	USAID/DoS	Seminar on Problems of Manpower Planning: Development, Utilization, Distribution, Administration
63/06/NA	Washington	USAID/DoL	IIIrd Seminar on Human Resources Development in Relation to Social and Economic Planning
67/10/05	Williamsburg	US	International Conference on the World Crisis in Education
Bellagio Conferences			
72/05/03	Bellagio	Rockefeller/Ford	Education and development reconsidered
73/11/07	Bellagio	Rockefeller/Ford	Education and development reconsidered
76/01/27	New York	Rockefeller/Ford	Education and development reconsidered
78/11/19	Geneva	Rockefeller/Ford	Bellagio staff meeting
79/11/11	Geneva	Rockefeller/Ford	Bellagio staff meeting
International Working Group On Education Meetings			
82/11/03	—	IIEP	International Working Group on Education: Planning Committee Meeting
83/12/08	—	IIEP	International Working Group on Education: Planning Committee Meeting
84/10/02	Paris	IIEP	International Working Group on Education
86/08/28	—	IIEP	International Working Group on Education: Planning Committee Meeting
88/11/23	London	IIEP	International Working Group on Education
90/05/30	Paris	IIEP	International Working Group on Education
91/11/06	Nice	IIEP	International Working Group on Education
93/04/14	Nice	IIEP	International Working Group on Education
94/11/16	Nice	IIEP	International Working Group on Education
96/03/NA	—	IIEP	International Working Group on Education

Date yy/mm/dd	City	Sponsor	Title/Declarations/Plans—Sub-Saharan Africa
			Sub-Saharan Africa
84/12/03	Windsor	ODA/LIE	Conference on Education Priorities in Sub-Saharan Africa
88/01/25	Paris	WB	Meeting of representatives of donor agencies to discuss the implications for donors of education in sub-Saharan Africa
88/06/20	London	WB	Education in Sub-Saharan Africa: Policies for Adjustment, Revitaliation, and Expansion
89/10/23	Paris	WB	Donors to African Education
90/07/20	Vienna	UNIDO	Donors to African Education
91/10/28	Manchester	IIEP	Donors to African Education
93/10/21	Angers	IIEP	Donors to African Education
			Universal Literacy
1965	Tehran	UNESCO	World Conference of Ministers of Education on the eradication of illiteracy: established International Institute for Adult Literacy Methods (1968)
72/07/25	Tokyo	UNESCO	IIIrd International Conference of Adult Education
75/09/03	Persepolis	GoIran	International Symposium for Literacy: Persepolis Declaration: followed by many national conferences including: Suriname (1980), Francophone African University, Dakar (1982)
82/01/04	Udaipur	ICAE, DSE, Seva Mandir	International Seminar: Campaign for Literacy
82/12/14	Madras	IIEP/UNESCO	International Literacy Workshop on the Planning and Implementation of Literacy and Postliteracy Strategies
83/07/NA	Paris	UNESCO	NGO Symposium on Literacy, Education, and Safeguarding of Cultures
84/11/08	Paris	UNESCO	Ist Collective Consultation of NGOs on Literacy and Adult Education
85/12/14	Prague	UNESCO	IInd Collective Consultation of NGOs on Literacy and Adult Education
86/10/30	Paris	UNESCO	IIIrd Collective Consultation of NGOs on Literacy and Adult Education
87/12/08	Bangkok	UNESCO	IVth Collective Consultation of NGOs on Literacy and Adult Education
88/09/97	Istanbul	UNESCO	Vth Collective Consultation of NGOs on Literacy and Adult Education

Date	City	Sponsor	Universal Literacy
yy/mm/dd			
89/11/28	Paris	UNESCO/NGO	NGO Conference, seminar on Literacy: Role of the NGOs and their place in the partnership (on the occasion of ILY)
89/12/11	Quito	UNESCO et al	VIth Collective Consultation of NGOs on Literacy and Adult Education
90/12/03	Hamburg	UIE	VIIth Collective Consultation of NGOs on Literacy and Adult Education

References

Abbott, A. (1988). *The System of Professions: An Essay on the Division of Expert Labor.* Chicago: University of Chicago.

Aggarwal, J. C., & Aggarwal, S. P. (1982). *Role of Unesco in Education.* New Delhi: Vikas.

Ahmed, M., Chabbott, C., Joshi, A., & Pande, R. (1993). *Primary Education for All: Learning from the BRAC Experience.* Washington, DC: Academy for Educational Development.

Allen, D. W., & Anzalone, S. (1981). "Basic Needs: New Approach to Development—But New Approach to Education?" *International Review of Education,* 27(3), 209–226.

Alliance for a Global Community. (1996). *Connections.* Various.

Altbach, P. G., & Tan, E. T. J. (1995). *Programs and Centers in Comparative and International Education: A Global Inventory* (1st ed. Vol. 34). Buffalo, NY: Graduate School of Education Publications, SUNY-Buffalo.

Anderson, B. (1991). *Imagined Communities* (2nd ed.). London: Verso.

Arndt, H. W. (1987). *Economic Development: The History of an Idea.* Chicago: University of Chicago.

Arnove, R. F. (Ed.) (1980). *Philanthropy and Cultural Imperialism: The Foundations at Home and Abroad.* Boston, MA: G.K. Hall.

Aronowitz, S. (1988). *Science as Power: Discourse and Ideology in Modern Society.* Minneapolis: Univ. of Minnesota.

Association of Commonwealth Universities (Various). *Commonwealth Universities' Yearbook* (Annual). London: Association of Commonwealth Universities.

Barrett, D. (1995). *Reproducing People as a Public Concern: The Making of an Institution.* Unpublished doctoral dissertation, Stanford University, Stanford, CA.

Barrett, D., & Frank, D. J. (1999). "Population Control for National Development: From World Discourse to National Policies." In J. Boli & G. M. Thomas (Eds.), *Constructing World Culture: International Nongovernmental Organizations Since 1875* (pp. 199–221). Stanford, CA: Stanford University.

Bartels, F. L. (1983). *Regional Conferences and Educational Development in Africa from the Addis Ababa Conference 1961 to the Lagos Conference 1976.* Unpublished manuscript, Paris.

Beeby, C. E. (1962). "Stages in the Growth of a Primary Education System." *Comparative Education Review,* 2–11.

Benveniste, G., & Ilchman, W. F. (Eds.). (1969). *Agents of Change: Professionals in Developing Countries.* New York: Praeger, in cooperation with the Professional Schools Program of the University of California, Berkeley.

Berger, P. (1992). *A Far Glory.* New York: The Free Press (MacMillan).

Berger, P. L., Berger, B., & Kellner, H. (1973). *The Homeless Mind: Modernization and Consciousness.* New York: Vintage (Random House).

Berger, P. L., & Luckmann, T. (1966). *The Social Construction of Reality: A Treatise in the Sociology of Knowledge.* New York: Anchor Books (Doubleday).

Berkovitch, N. (1999). *From Motherhood to Citizenship: Women's Rights and International Organizations.* Baltimore, MD: Johns Hopkins University Press.

Berman, E. H. (1983). *The Influence of the Carnegie, Ford, and Rockefeller Foundations on American Foreign Policy: The Ideology of Philanthropy.* Albany, NY: State University of New York Press.

Bienen, H. (Ed.). (1993). *A Career in Development: A Seminar in Honor of John P. Lewis.* Princeton: Princeton University.

Black, M. (1986). *The Children and the Nations: The Story of Unicef.* New York: Unicef.

Boli, J. (1989). *New Citizens for a New Society: The Institutional Origins of Mass Schooling in Sweden.* New York: Pergamon.

Boli, J., & Meyer, J. W. (1987). "The Ideology of Childhood and the State: Rules Distinguishing Children in National Constitutions, 1870–1970." In G. M. Thomas & J. W. Meyer & F. O. Ramirez & J. Boli (Eds.), *Institutional Structure: Constituting State, Society, and the Individual* (pp. 217–241). Newbury Park, CA: Sage.

Boli, J., & Thomas, G. M. (Eds.). (1999). *Constructing World Culture: International Nongovernmental Organizations Since 1875.* Stanford, CA: Stanford University Press.

Bray, M. (1986). "If UPE is the Answer, What Is the Question? A Comment on the Weaknesses in the Rationale for Universal Primary Education in Less Developed Countries." *International Journal of Educational Development,* 6(3), 147–158.

Brown, D. S. (1966). "Strategies and Tactics of Public Administration Assistance: 1945–1963." In J. D. Montgomery & W. J. Siffin (Eds.), *Approaches to Development: Politics, Administration, & Change.* New York: McGraw-Hill.

Brunsson, N. (1989). *The Organization of Hypocrisy: Talk, Decisions and Action in Organizations.* New York: John Wiley.

Bude, U. (1983). "The Adaptation Concept in British Colonial Education." *Comparative Education,* 19(3), 341–355.

Bundy, M. (1989, Winter). *Comments during Plenary Session.* Paper presented at "A World to Make: Development in Perspective", Harvard University.

Byers, P. K. (1998). "Barber B. Conable, Jr." In P. K. Byers (Ed.), *Encyclopedia of World Biography* (Vol. 4, pp. 369–371). Miami: Gale Research.

Carlson, S. (1964). *Development Economics and Administration.* Uppsala (Sweden): Institute of Business Studies, University of Uppsala.

Carnoy, M. (1974). *Education as Cultural Imperialism.* New York: David McKay.

Carr, W. G. (1928). *Education for World Citizenship.* Stanford, CA: Stanford University Press.

Cerych, L. (1965). *Problems of Aid to Education in Developing Countries.* New York: Praeger (for the Atlantic Institute).

Chabbott, C. (1998). "Constructing Educational Consensus: International Development Professionals and the World Conference on Education for All." *International Journal of Educational Development,* 18(3), 207–218.

Chabbott, C. (1999). "Development INGOs." In J. Boli & G. M. Thomas (Eds.), *Constructing World Culture: International Nongovernmental Organizations Since 1875* (pp. 222–248). Stanford, CA: Stanford University.

Chabbott, C., & Ramirez, F. O. (2000). "Development and Education." In M. Hallinan (Ed.), *Handbook of the Sociology of Education* (pp. 163–187). New York: Klewer/Plenum.

Clark, J. (1991). *Democratizing Development: The Role of Voluntary Organizations.* Hartford, CT: Kumarian.

Cleveland, H., Mangone, G. J., & Adams, J. C. (1960). *The Overseas Americans.* New York: McGraw-Hill.

Coale, A. J. (1963). *The Population Dilemma.* Inglewood Cliffs, NJ: Prentice Hall.

Cohen, M. D., March, J. G., & Olsen, J. P. (1976). "People, Problems, Solutions, and the Ambiguity of Relevance." In J. G. March & J. P. Olsen (Eds.), *Ambiguity and Choice in Organizations* (pp. 24–37). Bergen, Norway: Universitetsforlaget.

Coombs, P. H. (1968). *The World Educational Crisis: A Systems Analysis.* New York: Oxford University.

Courtney, W., & Kutsch, G. (1980). *Major Issues in Educational Policy Since 1946 as Perceived by the Member States of UNESCO* (Manuscript). Paris: Unesco.

Cowen, R. (1990). "The national and international impact of comparative education infrastructures." In W. D. Halls (Ed.), *Comparative education: Contemporary issues and trends* (pp. 321–352). Paris: Jessica Kingsley/Unesco.

Cox, R. W. (1968). Education for Development. In R. N. Gardner & M. F. Millikan (Eds.), *The Global Partnership: International Agencies & Economic Development* (pp. 310–331). New York: Frederick A. Praeger.

DiMaggio, P. (1983). "State Expansion and Organizational Fields." In R. H. Hall & R. E. Quinn (Eds.), *Organizational Theory and Public Policy* (pp. 146–161). Beverly Hills, CA: Sage.

DiMaggio, P. J. (1988). "Interest and Agency in Institutional Theory." In L. Zucker (Ed.), *Institutional Patterns and Organizations* (pp. 3–21). Cambridge, MA: Ballinger.

Dore, R. P. (1976). *The Diploma Disease.* Berkeley, CA: University of California.

East, R., Smith-Morris, M., & Wright, M. (Eds.). (1990). *World Development Directory.* Essex: Longman.

Escobar, A. (1995). *Encountering Development: The Making and Unmaking of the Third World.* Princeton: Princeton University.

Etzioni, A. (1964). *Modern Organizations.* Englewood Cliffs, NJ: Prentice-Hall.

Ferguson, J. (1990). *The Anti-Politics Machine: "Development", Depoliticization, and Bureaucratic Power in Lesotho.* New York: Cambridge University.

Finnemore, M. (1991). *Science, the State, and International Society.* Unpublished doctoral dissertation, Stanford University, Stanford, CA.

Finnemore, M. (1996a). *National Interests in International Society.* Ithaca: Cornell University.

Finnemore, M. (1996b). "Norms and Development: The World Bank and Poverty." In M. Finnemore (Ed.), *National Interests in International Society* (pp. 89–127). Ithaca, NY: Cornell.

Fisher, J. (1993). *The Road from Rio: Sustainable Development and the Nongovernmental Movement in the Third World.* Westport, CT: Praeger.

Fisher, J. (1998). *Non-Governments: NGOs and the Political Development of the Third World.* West Hartford, CT: Kumarian.

Fordham, P. (1992). *Education for All: An Expanded Vision* (World Conference on Education for All Monograph II). Paris: UNESCO.

Frank, D. J., & McEneany, E. (1999). The Individualization of Society and the Liberalization of State Policies on Same-Sex Sexual Relations, 1984–1995. *Social Forces, 77,* 911–944.

Freire, P. (1972). *Pedagogy of the Oppressed.* New York: Herder & Herder.

Fry, G., & Thurber, C. E. (Eds.). (1989). *The International Education of the Development Consultant: Communicating with Peasants and Princes.* New York: Pergamon.

Fuller, B. (1991). *Growing-Up Modern: The Western State Builds Third-World Schools.* New York: Routledge.

Gale & Associates. (1995). *Encyclopedia of Associations: International Organizations* (CD Rom ed.). Munich (Germany): KG Saur.

Goffman, I. (1959). *The Presentation of Self in Everyday Life.* Garden City, NY: Doubleday Anchor.

Goulet, D. (1977). *The Uncertain Promise: Value Conflicts in Technology Transfer.* New York: IDOC/Overseas.

Goulet, D., & Hudson, M. (1971). *The Myth of Aid: The Hidden Agenda of the Development Reports.* Maryknoll, NY: Orbis Books.

Grant, J. P. (1979). Perspectives on Development Aid: World War II to Today and Beyond. *Annals of the American Academy of Political and Social Science,* 442(March), 1–12.

Grant, J. P. (1988). "Hard Choices: Putting Crises to Work for People." *Development Journal of the Society for International Development,* 25–29.

Grant, J. P. (1995). "Oral History of James P. Grant." Unpublished.

Haas, P. M. E. (1992). "Knowledge, Power, and International Policy Coordination." *International Organization (Special Issue),* 46(1, Winter), 1–367.

Haggis, S. M. (1992). *Education for All: Purpose and Context* (World Conference on Education for All Monograph I). Paris: UNESCO.

Hallinan, M. (Ed.). (2000). *Handbook of the Sociology of Education.* New York: Kluwer.

Hancock, G. (1989). *Lords of Poverty: The Power, Prestige and Corruption of the International Aid Business.* New York: Atlantic Monthly.

Hansen, J. S., & Guthrie, J. W. (Eds.). (1995). *Worldwide Education Statistics: Enhancing UNESCO's role.* Washington, DC: National Academy Press.

Harcourt, W. (1994). "Negotiating Positions in the Sustainable Development Debate: Situating the Feminist Perspective." In W. Harcourt (Ed.), *Feminist Perspectives on the Sustainable Development Debate* (pp. 11–25). Atlantic Highlands, NJ: Zed.

Hill, P. (1986). *Development Economics on Trial: The Anthropological Case for a Prosecution*. New York: Cambridge University.

Hirschman, A. O. (1958). *The Strategy of Economic Development*. New Haven, CT: Yale University.

Hirschman, A. O. (1968). "Underdevelopment, Obstacles to the Perception of Change, and Leadership." *Daedalus*, 925–937.

Hossain, M. H. (1994). *Traditional Culture and Modern Systems: Administering Primary Education in Bangladesh*. Lanham, MD: University Press of America.

Illich, I. (1970). *Deschooling Society*. New York: Harper and Row.

Jackson, D. (Ed.). (1980). *Development Studies in the UK: A Guide to Post-Graduate Courses*. Brighton: Institute of Development Studies.

Jang, Y. S. (2000). "The Worldwide Founding of Ministries of Science and Technology, 1950–1990." *Sociological Perspectives*, 43, 247–270.

Jones, P. W. (1988). *International Policies for Third World Education: UNESCO, Literacy, and Development*. New York: Routledge.

Jones, P. W. (1990). "UNESCO and the Politics of Global Literacy." *Comparative Education Review*, 34(1), 41–60.

Jones, P. W. (1992). *World Bank Financing of Education: Lending, Learning and Development*. New York: Routledge.

Kay, D. A., & Skolnikoff, E. B. (Eds.). (1972). *International Institutions and the Environmental Crisis*. Madison: University of Wisconsin.

Keohane, N. O. (1982). "The Enlightenment Idea of Progress Revisited." In G. A. Almond & M. Chodorow & R. H. Pearce (Eds.), *Progress and Its Discontents* (pp. 21–40). Berkeley, CA: University of California.

Kim, Y. S. (1996). *Ministerial Expansion of Modern Nation-States and Its Historical Institutionalization*. Unpublished doctoral dissertation.

King, K. (1991). *Aid and Education in the Developing World: The Role of the Donor Agencies in Educational Analysis*. Essex (UK): Longman.

King, K., & McNab, C. (Eds.). (1990). *Special Issue: World Conference on Education for All and International Literacy Year* (March). Stockholm, Sweden: Swedish International Development Authority (SIDA).

Klitgaard, R. (1990). *Tropical Gangsters: One Man's Experience with Development and Decadence in Deepest Africa*. New York: Basic Books (Harper & Row).

Kollodge, R., & Horn, R. (1986). *Education Research and Policy Studies at the World Bank: A Bibliography* (Discussion Paper, Education & Training Series EDT23). Washington, DC: World Bank.

Korsmeyer, P. (Ed.). (1991). *The Development Directory 1991: A Guide to the International Development Community in the United States and Canada*. (Third ed.). Detroit: Omnigraphics.

Krugman, P. (1994). "The Fall and Rise of Development Economics." In L. Rodwin & D. A. Schon (Eds.), *Rethinking the Development Experience: Essays Provoked by the Work of Albert O. Hirschman* (pp. 39–58). Washington, DC: Brookings Institution and Lincoln Institute of Land Policy.

Lauglo, J. (1995, June). *Banking on Education and Uses of Research: A Critique of Priorities and Strategies for Education* (*World Bank, 1995*). Paper presented at the Nordic Association for the Study of Education in Development Countries, As, Norway.

Levy, M. J. (1972). *Modernization: Latecomers and Survivors.* New York: Basic Books.

Lewis, W. A. (1955). *The Theory of Economic Growth.* Homewood, IL: Richard D. Irwin.

Lindblom, E. N. (1990). *Building on Basics: A Report on the Global Education Crisis and US Foreign Aid to Basic Education.* Washington, DC: RESULTS Educational Fund.

Lumsdaine, D. H. (1993). *Moral Vision in International Politics: The Foreign Aid Regime, 1949–1989.* Princeton, NJ: Princeton University.

Lyons, R. F. (1984 (Unpublished)). *Background Document. The International Working Group on Education: Notes on its History and Its New Topic (Working Draft).* Paper presented at the Meeting of the International Working Group on Education, Paris.

Marshall, G. (Ed.). (1994). *The Concise Dictionary of Sociology.* New York: Oxford University.

McClelland, D. C. (1961). *The Achieving Society.* Princeton, NJ: D. Van Nostrand.

McGinn, N. F. (Ed.). (1996). *Crossing Lines: Research and Policy Networks for Developing Country Education.* Westport, CT: Praeger.

McNeely, C. L. (1995). "Prescribing National Education Policies: The Role of International Education." *Comparative Education Review,* 39(4, November), 483–507.

McNeely, C. L., & Cha, Y.-K. (1994). "Worldwide Educational Convergence Through International Organizations: Avenues for Research." *Educational Policy Analysis Archives,* 2(14).

Mead, G. H. (1934). *Mind, Self, and Society.* Chicago: University of Chicago.

Meier, G. (1995). *Leading Issues in International Development* (6th ed.). New York: Oxford University.

Meyer, J. W. (1994). "Rationalized Environments." In W. R. Scott & J. W. Meyer & Associates (Eds.), *Institutional Environments and Organizations: Structural Complexity and Individualism* (pp. 28–54). Thousand Oaks, CA: Sage.

Meyer, J. W. (1995). *Organizational Integration in Lesotho Primary Education: Loose Coupling as Problem and Solution.* Maseru (Lesotho): USAID/PEP.

Meyer, J. W., Boli, J., Thomas, G. M., & Ramirez, F. O. (1997). "World Society and the Nation State." *American Journal of Sociology,* 103(1), 144–181.

Meyer, J. W., Nagel, J., & Snyder, C. W., Jr. (1993). "The Expansion of Mass Education in Botswana: Local and World Society Perspectives." *Comparative Education Review,* 37(4, November), 454–475.

Meyer, J. W., & Ramirez, F. O. (2000). "The World Institutionalization of Education." In J. Schriewer (Ed.), *Discourse Formation in Comparative Education* (pp. 111–132). Berlin: Peter Lang.

Morris, M. D. (1979). *Measuring the Condition of the World's Poor: The Physical Quality of Life Index* (Pergamon Policy Studies). Washington, DC: Overseas Development Council.

Mudd, S. (1964). *The Population Crisis and the Use of World Resources.* The Hague: W. Junk.

Mundy, K. (1995). *Canadian Educational Policies.* Paper presented at the Comparative and International Education Society, Boston, MA.

Mundy, K., & Murphy, L. (2001). "Transnational Advocacy, Global Civil Society? Emerging Evidence from the Field of Education." *Comparative Education Review*, 45(1), 85–126.

Myrdal, G. (1970). *The Challenge of World Poverty: A World Anti-Poverty Program in Outline*. New York: Vintage.

Nagel, J., & Snyder, C. W. (1989). "International Funding of Educational Development: External Agendas and Internal Adaptations—The Case of Liberia." *Comparative Education Review*, 33(1), 3–20.

Nurkse, R. (1953). *Problems of Capital Formation in Underdeveloped Countries*. Oxford (UK): Basil, Blackwell, and Mott.

Oliver, C. (1991). "Strategic Responses to Institutional Processes." *Academy of Management Review*, 16(1), 145–179.

Organization for Economic Cooperation and Development. (OECD) (1988). *Voluntary Aid for Development: The Role of Non-Governmental Organisations*. Paris: OECD.

Organization for Economic Cooperation and Development. Development Assistance Committee. (1985). *25 Years of Development Coooperation* (Annual). Paris: Organization for Economic Cooperation and Development.

Organization for Economic Cooperation and Development. Development Assistance Committee. (2001). Annex 2: Main International Organizations. In OECD (Ed.), *DAC Statistical Reporting Directives*. Paris: Organization for Economic Cooperation and Development.

Organization for Economic Cooperation and Development. Development Centre. (1981). *Directory of Non-Governmental Organizations in OECD Member Countries Active in Development Cooperation*. Paris: OECD.

Organization for Economic Cooperation and Development. Development Centre. (1990). *Directory of Non-Governmental Development Organizations in OECD Member Countries*. Paris: OECD.

Organization for Economic Cooperation and Development. Development Centre. (1991). *Directory of Development Research and Training Institutes in Europe*. Paris: OECD.

Organization for Economic Cooperation and Development. Development Centre. (1992). *Directory of Research and Training Institutes in Africa*. Paris: OECD.

Organization for Economic Cooperation and Development. Development Centre. (1993). *Directory of Research and Training Institutes in Latin America*. Paris: OECD.

Organization for Economic Cooperation and Development. Development Centre. (1995). *Database of Non-Governmental Development Organizations in OECD Member Countries* (Version: July). Paris: Organization for Economic Cooperation and Development.

Organization for Economic Cooperation and Development. Development Centre. (1996). *Directory of nongovernmental organizations active in sustainable development. Part I: Europe* (Vol. 1). Paris: Organization for Economic Cooperation and Development.

Organization for Economic Cooperation and Development. Development Centre. (1998). *Directory of nongovernmental organizations active in sustainable development. Part II: Australia, Canada, Korea, United States, Japan, New Zealand* (Vol. 2). Paris: Organization for Economic Cooperation and Development.

Pearson, L., Boyle, E., Oliveira Campos, R. D., Dillon, C. D., Guth, W., Lewis, W. A., Marjolin, R. E., & Okita, S. (1969). *Partners in Development: Report of the Commission on International Development* (Special). Washington, DC: World Bank.

Psacharopoulos, G., & Hinchcliffe, K. (1973). *Returns to Education: An International Comparison*. San Francisco, CA: Jossey-Bass.

Psacharopoulos, G., & Woodhall, M. (1985). *Education for Development: An Analysis of Investment Choices*. New York: Oxford University Press.

Ramirez, F., & Lee, M. (1995). "Education, Science, and Development." In G. A. Postiglione & L. W. On (Eds.), *Social Change and Educational Development* (pp. 15–39). Hong Kong: University of Hong Kong.

Ramirez, F. O. (1997). The Nation-State, Citizenship, and Educational Change: Institutionalization and Globalization. In W. K. Cummings & N. F. McGinn (Eds.), *International Handbook of Education and Development: Preparing Schools, Students, and Nations for the Twenty-First Century* (First ed., pp. 47–62). New York: Pergamon.

Ramirez, F. O., & Ventresca, M. J. (1991). "Building the Institution of Mass Schooling: Isomorphism in the Modern World." In B. Fuller & R. Rubinson (Eds.), *The Political Construction of Education* (pp. 47–59). New York: Praeger.

Rice, A. E. (1982). *The First Quarter-Century of the Society for International Development: A Personal Reflection* (Society for International Development 25th Anniversary World Conference: The Emerging Global Village). Washington, D.C.: Society for International Development, Washington Chapter.

Riddell, R. C. (1987). *Foreign Aid Reconsidered*. Baltimore, MD: Johns Hopkins University.

Riddell, R. C., Bebbington, A., & Peck, L. (1995). *Promoting Development by Proxy: An Evaluation of the Development Impact of Government Support to Swedish NGOs* (SIDA Evaluation 1995/2): Swedish International Development Authority.

Rohde, J. E. (1995). "Oral History of James P. Grant" (pp. 1–9).

Roosevelt, F. D. (1932). "Commencement Address, May 23, 1932, at Oglethorpe University, Atlanta, Georgia." In S. I. Rosenman (Ed.), *The Public Papers and Addresses of Franklin Roosevelt*. New York.

Rosenstein-Rodan, P. N. (1944). "The International Development of Economically Backward Areas." *International Affairs*.

Rossello, P. (1979). "Historical Note." In International Bureau of Education (Ed.), *International Conference on Education Recommendations, 1934–77* (3rd ed., pp. xi–xxvi). Paris: UNESCO.

Rostow, W. W. (1960). *The Stages of Economic Growth: A Non-Communist Manifesto*. New York: Cambridge University.

Rueschemeyer, D., & Evans, P. B. (1985). "The State and Economic Transformation: Toward an Analysis of the Conditions Underlying Effective Intervention." In P. Evans & D. Rueschemeyer & T. Skocpol (Eds.), *Bringing the State Back In* (pp. 44–77). New York: Cambridge.

Sachs, W. (1991). *The Development Dictionary*. London: Zed.

Salda, A. C. M. (1997). *Historical Dictionary of the World Bank*. Lanham, MD: Scarecrow Press.

Sanyal, B. (1991). "Antagonistic Cooperation: A Case Study of Nongovernmental Organizations, Government and Donors Relationships in Income-Generating Projects in Bangladesh." *World Development*, 19(10), 1367–1379.

Schultz, T. W. (1961). "Investment in Human Capital." *American Economic Review*, 51, 1–16.

Schumacher, E. F. (1973). *Small is Beautful: Economics as if People Mattered.* New York: Perennial Library (Harper & Row).

Schumpeter, J. (1934). *The Theory of Economic Development.* Cambridge, MA: Harvard University.

Scott, W. R. (1992). *Organizations: Rational, Natural, and Open Systems* (3rd ed.). Englewood Cliffs, NJ: Prentice-Hall.

Scott, W. R. (1993). "Conceptualizing Organizational Fields: Linking Organizations and Societal Systems." In U. Gerhardt & H.-U. Derlien & F. W. Scharpf (Eds.), *Systems Rationality and Partial Interests* (pp. 1–45). Unpublished manuscript.

Scott, W. R., & Meyer, J. W. (1983). "The Organization of Societal Sectors." In J. W. Meyer & W. R. Scott (Eds.), *Organizational Environments: Ritual and Rationality* (pp. 129–153). Beverly Hills: Sage.

Shapiro, R. (1996). *Foreign Aid Decision-Making: The Case of USAID and JICA.* Unpublished doctoral dissertation.

Skilbeck, M. (2000). *Education for All: Global Synthesis.* Paris: UNESCO. Education for All Forum Secretariat.

Smillie, I., & Helmich, H. (1993). *Nongovernmental Organizations: Stakeholders for Development.* Paris: OECD Development Centre.

Smith, B. (1990). *More than Altruism: The Politics of Private Foreign Aid.* Princeton, NJ: Princeton University.

Social Watch. (1998). *Social Watch* (Annual report 2). Montevideo (Uruguay): Instituto del Tercer Mundo.

Society for International Development. (1959). "The SID story: Constitution and by-laws." *International Development Review*, 1(1), 42–43.

Sommer, J. G. (1977). *Beyond Charity: U.S. Voluntary Aid for a Changing Third World.* Washington, D.C.: Overseas Development Council.

Soysal, Y. N., & Strang, D. (1989). "Construction of the First Mass Education Systems in Nineteenth Century Europe." *Sociology of Education*, 62(October), 277–288.

Spaulding, S. (1981). "The Impact of International Assistance Organizations on the Development of Education." *Prospects*, XI(4), 421–433.

Streeten, P., Burki, S. J., Haq, M. U., Hicks, N., & Stewart, F. (1981). *First Things First: Meeting Basic Human Needs in the Developing Countries.* New York: Oxford Univeristy (for the World Bank).

Sucholdolski, B., Avanzini, G., Roller, S., Egger, E., & Stock, R. (1979). *The International Bureau of Education in the service of educational development.* Paris: Unesco.

Sufrin, S. C. (1966). *Technical Assistance—Theory and Guidelines.* Syracuse, NY: Syracuse University.

Sutton, F. X. (1987). "The Ford Foundation: The Early Years." *Daedalus: Journal of the Academy of Arts and Sciences*, 116, 41–91.

Sutton, F. X. (1989). "Development Ideology: Its Emergence and Decline." *Daedalus*, 118(1, Winter), 35–58.

Sutton, M. (1993, November). *Research Notes: International Content of Graduate Courses in Education*. Paper presented at the Western Regional Comparative International Education Society, Los Angeles, CA.

Tendler, J. (1975). *Inside Foreign Aid*. Baltimore, MD: Johns Hopkins University.

Therien, J.-P. (1991). "Nongovernmental Organizations and International Development Assistance." *Canadian Journal of Development Studies*, XII(2), 263–280.

Thomas, G. M., Meyer, J. W., Ramirez, F. O., & Boli, J. (1987). *Institutional Structure: Constituting State, Society, and the Individual*. Newbury Park, CA: Sage.

Thomas-Fontaine, J. (1993). *Collective Consultation on Literacy and Education for All: Appraisal and Prospects*. Paris: UNESCO.

Toynbee, A. (1947). The Present Point in History. In A. Toynbee (Ed.), *Civilization on Trial* (pp. 16–28). Oxford (UK): Oxford University.

Union of International Associations. (1993/94). *Yearbook of International Organizations* (11th ed. Vol. III). Munich: KG Saur.

United Nations Children's Fund. (1990). *First Call for Children: World Declaration and Plan of Action from the World Summit for Chilren and Convention on the Rights of the Child*. (Occasional). New York: UNICEF.

United Nations Economic Commission for Latin America. (1949). *Economic Survey of Latin America*. New York: United Nations.

United Nations Educational Scientific & Cultural Organization. (1992). *Directory of Early Childhood Care and Education Organizations in Sub-Saharan Africa*. Paris: UNESCO.

United Nations Educational Scientific and Cultural Organization. (1991). *African Development Sourcebook* (First ed.). Paris: UNESCO.

United Nations Educational Scientific and Cultural Organization. (1994). *Monitoring Education-for-All goals: Focussing on Learning Achievement*. (Joint UNESCO-Unicef Project). Paris: UNESCO.

United Nations Educational Scientific and Cultural Organization. World Education Forum Drafting Committee. (2000). *Expanded Commentary on the Dakar Framework for Action*. Paris: UNESCO.

United Nations. Advisory Committee for the Co-ordination of Information Systems (ACCIS). (1992). *Register of Development Activities of the United Nations Systems* (Annual ACC/ACCIS SER.Z/1/1992). New York: United Nations.

United Nations. Institute for Training and Research. (1984). *The Principle of Participatory Equality of Developing Countries in International Economic Relations: Analytical Paper and Supplementary Notations and Amendments to Analytical Compilation of Texts of Relevant Instruments (Progressive Development of the Principles and Norms of International Law Relating to the New International Economic Order UNITAR/DS/6/Add. 1)*. New York: United Nations.

United Nations. Secretary General. (1949). *Technical Assistance for Economic Development: Plan for an Extended Cooperative Programme through the United Niations and the Specialized Agencies. Report prepared in Consultation with the Executive Heads of the Interested Specialized Agencies through the Administrative Committee on Coordination pursuant to Resolution 180 (VIII) of the Economic and Social Council*. Lake Success, NY: United Nations.

van Ufford, P. Q., Kruijt, D., & Downing, T. (1988). *The Hidden Crisis in Develop-ment: Development Bureaucracies*. Amsterdam: Free University.

Ward, F. C. (Ed.). (1974). *Education and Development Reconsidered: The Bellagio Conference Papers*. New York: Praeger.

Weick, K. E. (1976). "Educational Organizations as Loosely Coupled Systems." *Administrative Science Quarterly*, 21(March), 1–19.

Wieland, G. F., & Ullrich, R. A. (1976). *Organizations: Behavior, Design, and Change*. Honeywood, IL: Richard D. Irwin.

Willinsky, J. (1998). *Learning to Divide the World: Education at Empire's End*. Min-neapolis, MN: University of Minnesota.

Wilson, D. N. (1994). "Comparative and International Education: Fraternal or Siamese Twins? A Preliminary Genealogy of Our Twin Fields." *Comparative Education Review*, 38(4), 449–486.

Windham, D. M. (1988). *Indicators of Educational Effectiveness and Efficiency* (Occasional). Washington, DC: Improving the Efficiency of Educational Sys-tems Project. USAID Contract No. DPE-5283-C-00-4013-00.

Winks, R. W. (Ed.). (1969). *The Age of Imperialism*. Englewood Cliffs, NJ: Prentice-Hall.

World Bank. (1988). *Education in Sub-Saharan Africa*. Washington, DC: World Bank.

World Bank. (1993). *Implementing the World Bank's Strategy to Reduce Poverty: Progress and Challenges*. Washington, DC: The World Bank.

World Bank. Operations Policy Research and Planning Group. Operations Policy Department. NGO Unit. (1996). Development NGO Database (Version January) [Database]. Washington, DC: World Bank.

World Conference on Education for All Inter-Agency Commission. Executive Secre-tariat. (1990a). *Final Report*. New York: UNICEF.

World Conference on Education for All Inter-Agency Commission. Executive Secre-tariat. (1990b). *Meeting Basic Learning Needs: A Vision for the 1990s. Back-ground Document*. New York: UNICEF.

World Food Conference. (1974). *Things to Come: The World Food Crisis*. Paper pre-sented at the World Food Conference, Rome, Italy.

Wuthnow, R. (1980). "The World Economy and the Institutionalization of Science in Seventeenth Century Europe." In A. Bergesen (Ed.), *Studies of the Modern World System* (pp. 25–55). New York: Academic Press.

Young, C. (1982). "Ideas of Progress in the Third World." In G. A. Almond & M. Chodorow & R. H. Pearce (Eds.), *Progress and Its Discontents* (pp. 83–105). Berkeley, CA: University of California.

Index

Lightning Source UK Ltd.
Milton Keynes UK
24 August 2010

158675UK00008BA/3/P